GERMANY'S
EASTERN
FRONTIERS

The Problem of the Oder-Neisse Line

GERMANY'S EASTERN FRONTIERS

The Problem of the Oder-Neisse Line

by

ZOLTAN MICHAEL SZAZ

with a Foreword by

HAROLD ZINK

Published in cooperation with
Foundation for Foreign Affairs, Inc.

HENRY REGNERY COMPANY

CHICAGO: 1960

FOUNDATION FOR FOREIGN AFFAIRS SERIES, NUMBER 4

The Foundation for Foreign Affairs, 64 East Jackson Boulevard, Chicago 4, Illinois, is a non-profit corporation devoted to the promotion of a wider understanding of international relations—political, economic, and cultural. Books in the Foundation for Foreign Affairs Series are published in the interest of public information and debate. They represent the free expression of their authors and do not necessarily indicate the judgment and opinions of the Foundation.

TO MY WIFE

A REALISTIC policy for Central as well as East-Central Europe, that is, concerning Czechoslovakia and the Sudeten Germans, as well as concerning Poland, the Germans of East Prussia, and the other provinces east of the Oder-Neisse rivers can only be a policy that is both just and moral. It must be firmly based upon historical truth and the rule of international law. To assume that any government can ever develop a successful policy on the shaky structure of a wrong, and on perpetuating that wrong is an illusion and, let me emphasize it with all solemnity, a dangerous illusion.

—*The Honorable B. Carroll Reece on the floor of the United States House of Representatives, April 25, 1958*

Foreword

STRICTLY speaking, the problem of Germany's eastern frontiers, especially since it involves the Oder-Neisse Line, was born of World War II, but in a larger sense it extends over a period of many decades and relates to Poland's long struggle for a national existence, the deep-seated desire on the part of many Germans for *Lebensraum*, the urge of the Russians to expand, or at least to set up a buffer against the West, and various other significant factors. Few areas present such a tangled skein of past developments, so many current complications, and such far-reaching possible consequences for the future as the area involving the eastern frontiers of Germany. It is conceivable that a peace treaty in the foreseeable future may stipulate formal eastern frontiers for the Germans, but it will be only slightly less than miraculous if any such international agreement achieves a genuine and lasting solution to the problem. Indeed, one may wonder whether the larger question presented here is not one of those persistent problems confronting the modern world which defy anything like a full solution.

Many scholars in both Europe and the United States have given their attention to various aspects of this ramified and often burning overall issue. Books have been written about the German pressures, about the aspirations and tragedies of Poland, about Russian nationalism, about Danzig and Silesia, and about other aspects of this knotty problem. But it is perhaps surprising that so little attention has been given by English-speaking scholars during the post–World War II years to the immediate situation, considering the deep interest of the United States and Britain in Germany and the frequent use of the term "Oder-Neisse" in the press and in the debates of international bodies. It is true that central and eastern European matters as a whole, except, possibly, the occupation of Germany, have not fared well in this respect recently, but this particular aspect seems to have received even less attention from scholars than other less important elements.

It is, therefore, of more than ordinary moment that a young American scholar with the advantage of a European background has essayed to analyze the many difficult questions which are integral parts of or closely related to the basic issue of the eastern German frontiers. Dr. Szaz, making use of a considerably large body of source material, including newspaper files and other references not readily available in the United States, begins his analysis with an account of the territory and people of the Oder-Neisse provinces. He then passes to a fairly detailed discussion of the historical background of German-Polish relations prior to World War I. A third chapter covers the heated controversies and spectacular developments during the period of the Second Reich. Chapter IV deals with German and Russian designs on Poland during World War II, and Chapter V proceeds to a consideration of the events leading to the drawing of an Oder-Neisse Line by the Russians. In Chapter VI, a severe indictment of the appeasement policy of the Western Allies at Yalta and Potsdam is drawn up. Chapter VII, a discussion of the administration of the Oder-Neisse provinces by Poland during the post–World War II years, presents much new material and is of special interest to political scientists and others interested in current problems. The final chapter—which deals with the official and unofficial attitudes of the Germans, particularly the people of the West German Federal Republic; the attitudes of the expellees, who were forced to leave their old homes in the Oder-Neisse provinces and take up residence in West Germany; and related matters—constitutes a fitting climax to the entire study, and although it is perhaps more subjective in character than other parts, it is more than ordinarily interesting to serious students. And the extensive bibliography will be useful to those desiring to pursue further study of the Oder-Neisse area.

HAROLD ZINK

OHIO STATE UNIVERSITY

Contents

> The Potsdam solution is not a German, not a
> Polish, not even a Russian solution; it is a Bolshevik
> solution. What we need is a European solution.
>
> —Jakob Kaiser at the Deutsche Heimat in Osten
> Exposition in November, 1950.

Introduction

BETWEEN the Polish plains ending in the infinite steppes of
Russia and the central German plains extending to the English Chan-
nel lies an area which, until recently, formed the eastern provinces of
Prussia. Its precise boundaries changed according to the prevailing
political and military balance between Prussia-Germany and Russia.
After the Treaty of Versailles and Marshal Pilsudski's victory over the
Communists at Warsaw (1920), Poland seemed to recover her control
over the Polish plains, and it was hoped that oustanding problems
could be negotiated without outside interference between the Germans and the Poles living in this frontier zone.

The sadistic rule of the Red Army in the region in 1944-45 and the
shrewd Russian maneuvering over Poland from the Teheran Conference to the Polish-Russian "troop rights treaty" of 1956 demonstrated,
however, that the present ultimate control of the region is in the
hands of the U.S.S.R. Thus the change between 1913 and 1959 was
a turn for the worse because Russian power now extends from central
Poland to the German-Polish frontier zone and to a considerable part
of central Germany, facetiously called the German Democratic Republic (GDR). Under such military auspices, the expectation of
major changes in Polish foreign policy, despite the pro-Western sympathies of the population, would be without foundation. Halfhearted
efforts of the Gomulka regime in its early days were neutralized by
Russian countermoves and by the ideological contradiction produced
by the regime's reliance on both nationalism and Marxist-Leninist
dogma.

The years from 1913 to 1959 are marked by tragic events and mis-
understandings on the part of Germany, Poland, and the West. The
discarded opportunity for the Central Powers to sponsor Polish inde-

pendence on acceptable terms, the arbitrariness of the Versailles frontiers, the Polish revolts during the plebiscite in Upper Silesia, and the continuous dispute over Danzig and the minorities in the interwar period—all were phases in the deterioration of Polish-German relations leading to the mutual catastrophe of World War II. The downfall of the two nations was the consequence of both the imperialism of the fanatically anti-democratic Führer and Western complacency toward Russian expansion after the invasion of central Europe by the Red Army on the heels of the retreating Wehrmacht.

Then *divide et impera,* the effective method of the Roman emperors of antiquity, was successfully applied by their modern followers in efforts to achieve hegemony. The regime of Joseph Stalin was aware that co-operation between the non-Russian peoples of the region might constitute a formidable barrier to Russian expansion into the German and Polish lowlands. These peoples, Germans, Poles, Ukrainians, Byelorussians, and Balts, separate the Great Russians from the western edge of the central European Iron Curtain at Magdeburg. To foment antagonisms among these peoples as they filed competing claims to certain territories in the region has been a time-honored practice of the Kremlin. Polish and Ukrainian patriots were to be hopelessly divided over Galicia, which, although one of the cradles of Polish culture, possessed a Ukrainian majority, and the Polish-Lithuanian dispute over Vilna was not abated by the incorporation of Lithuania into the U.S.S.R. The greatest obstacles remaining in the path of Russian expansionism were, however, the fanatic nationalism of the Poles, who were willing to fight insuperable odds in 1830 and 1863, and the strong geopolitical position held and influence exerted in the region by Germany.

It must be recognized that the unjustifiable severity of the German occupation of Poland, resulting in injustice and suffering of the population, had created an excellent point of departure for Soviet Russian intrigues. The ruthless and insane policy aimed at the decimation of a highly developed nation which for the past millennium had belonged to the West was both criminal and stupid. It rendered Russian propaganda effective and aroused that feeling of revenge without which the Oder-Neisse frontier would never have been accepted by the people of Poland. This line was conceived in the Kremlin and was designed to eliminate the possibility of any Polish-German entente, regardless of the future political ideology of the two governments.

The "Pax Stalinica" of the last decade is coming to an end in the region, despite the present efforts of Nikita Khrushchev to turn back the clock and to consolidate the partition of Germany. Tremendous forces have shaken some of its bases, which consisted of tight political control and military preponderance. The October events in Poland and Hungary in 1956, in addition to the unexpected industrial and military recovery of the German Federal Republic, continue to exert influence on the Soviet Union for a settlement in central Europe in order to forestall violent outbreaks. The two peoples, the Poles and the Germans, seem to be gradually escaping foreign tutelage and will have to take their seats at the conference table and discuss the heritage of the past era: the German-Polish frontiers. The first negotiation will undoubtedly consist of an exchange of opinions only, for the existence of the German Democratic Republic renders any present settlement illusory.But as the problem of German reunification grows in both intensity and urgency, Moscow will have to concede it within the next few years or face revolt by a people who, unlike the Hungarians, possess well-armed blood relatives in the West. Should German unity and German-Polish negotiations be realized, Moscow's sabotaging influence will still remain to be neutralized, for the Kremlin knows that the only guarantee of permanent Polish-Russian co-operation consists of the maintenance of a western Polish frontier unacceptable to Germany.

Thus the problem of the Oder-Neisse provinces is not exclusively a German-Polish problem, nor should it be left to Soviet Russian arbitration, as it was in 1944-45. The outbreak of the Second World War over Danzig and the Polish Corridor should have demonstrated the potential explosiveness of such disputes, while the advance of the Russian glacis from Minsk-Zhitomir to the heart of Europe demonstrates the dangers inherent in Russian arbitration. In 1944-45, while exercising restraining influence, the United States allowed the creation of a *fait accompli* which she reluctantly accepted as a *provisorium*. The next time, however, the United States would not have the excuse of conducting a global war on several fronts, nor could she plead the ignorance that often characterizes American policy toward new and unfamiliar disputes.

An equitable decision which will not deny the historic and legal rights of Germany and will not thereby provide a new impetus for extreme nationalism in that country and which, at the same time will consider Polish claims and the present *status quo* remains the demand of the hour. The United States has a great stake in such a solution, which might be hastened if she acts in consideration of her national interests and obligations while working for fair play on the international scene. American interest in the question is manifest, for the United States has concluded an alliance with the German Federal Republic in which she has pledged to defend the common beliefs in democracy, individual freedom, and social justice, and she has raised Germany to the position of her main Continental ally. Furthermore, American-Polish friendship has withstood the vicissitudes of centuries, and, to the degree to which Poland recovers some quasi-independence, improvement of relations are mandatory in order to reduce Polish dependence on Russia.

The first requirement of an equitable solution is the exposition of facts and events leading to the present situation. This requires research *sine ira et studio,* an almost impossible task on a problem distorted by parties embittered by torture, starvation, and expulsion. Furthermore, short-range interpretation of "state interests" in both Germany and Poland seems to resist an acceptable compromise. Bias enters almost every publication on the question.

In order to set forth the facts and describe the power-political motivations behind the events and trends, the author felt a categoric need to publish the present volume, which he has sought to make a reference work on the current history of the problem—within necessarily imposed space limitations. He has attempted to evaluate past events and present trends and their impact upon the policies of the United States while establishing a relationship between them and the various German and Polish claims. If in the course of his undertaking he seems to favor one claim over another, this is not due to personal prejudice but to his concern for the strengthening of the forces of the free world against those of world Communism led by the U.S.S.R.

The author expresses his sincere appreciation to his wife, without whose careful co-operation and reading services this work would have been impossible. The helpful suggestions of Dr. Edward M. O'Connor were also greatly appreciated, as was the co-operation of Joachim Freiherr von Braun of the Göttinger Arbeitskreis in providing books and newspaper material. Special thanks go to the Pressedienst Osteuropa at Bonn for providing Polish newspaper material.

ZOLTAN MICHAEL SZAZ
ST. JOHN'S UNIVERSITY

GERMANY'S
EASTERN
FRONTIERS

The Problem of the Oder-Neisse Line

CHAPTER I

The Land and the People in the Oder-Neisse Provinces

1. AREA AND POPULATION IN 1939

THE territories detached from Germany as a result of the provisional ruling of the Potsdam Conference of 1945 form the present Polish voivodships of Opole, Wrocław, Zielona Góra, Szczecin, Koszalin, and Olsztyn and parts of the voivodship of Gdańsk. In 1939, they comprised the German administrative districts (*Regierungsbezirke*) of Allenstein, Marienwerder, Köslin, and Stettin; the German provinces of Niederschlesien (Lower Silesia) and Oberschlesien (Upper Silesia) ; and parts of the administrative district of Frankfurt Oder. The Free City of Danzig, under the supervision of the League of Nations, also formed part of the territory now administered by Poland. The districts of Allenstein and Marienwerder were part of the German province of Ostpreussen (East Prussia), and Köslin and Stettin were part of Pommern (Pomerania). Northern East Prussia, which was occupied by the U.S.S.R., will not be dealt with in this context. The territories now under Polish administration comprise 39,400 square miles and are approximately the size of the state of Virginia, or 24 per cent of the territory of the German Reich as of 1937.[1]

These territories are often referred to as "the Oder-Neisse provinces" because they comprise that part of the German Reich, as of 1937, east of the Oder and Neisse rivers. This terminology connotes less partisanship than the German authors' use of the term "Eastern Germany" and the Polish authors' use of the term "Western Poland." An even more inappropriate terminology is found in the works of certain Polish authors who describe these areas—which have not been part of the Polish state since the Middle Ages—as "recovered" or "regained" Polish territories. Therefore, in this book, the term for

1

the territories will be "Oder-Neisse provinces," a geographic concept that is void of politics.

The Oder-Neisse provinces form part of the European lowlands stretching from the Ural Mountains to the North Sea. The territories are located between the Bohemian Forest and the Stettin Lagoon, a sheltered incision of the Baltic Sea. In the west, they border on the Oder and Neisse rivers, and in the east and the south, they are surrounded by the Polish voivodships of Warszawa, Pomorze, Poznań, and Katowice. The provinces occupy the southern and northern limits of the lowlands and a narrow waist of land connecting the two salients in the area of Liegnitz and Schneidemühl. In the south, the Giant (Riesen Gebirge) and Sudeten Mountains close the entrance to Bohemia and Moravia. The hill country has many scenic valleys and resort places, rich pastures, and mines, the latter providing the greatest wealth of the two Silesias in the form of coal and metallic deposits. The hills extend from the mountains to eastern Lower Silesia, to Grünberg, and to some parts of Pomerania, while the central and northern salients are lowlands crossed by a number of rivers (including the Oder, the Netze, and the Warthe) and, to a lesser degree, marshes. In Pomerania and East Prussia, there are many small and middle-sized lakes.

The climate of the Oder-Neisse provinces is cool. While winter is relatively mild in Upper Silesia and in the valleys, both Pomerania and East Prussia have severe Continental winters, with many blizzards. Precipitation amounts to approximately twenty-two to twenty-four inches a year, mostly in the form of spring rain and winter snows.[2]

The Oder river dominates the economic life of the southern and western provinces. It is navigable for 474 of its 538 miles, but its water level fluctuates greatly. As a result, 23 dams, with a composite volume of 404.3 million cubic meters, have been built by Prussia to regulate the stream. The Oder is ice free most of the year and provides the least expensive transportation route for exported Silesian coal and imported Swedish iron ore.[3] The other major stream of the region, the Vistula (Weichsel, Visla), is economically less significant because most of its length is located in prewar Poland; its delta forms part of the Free City of Danzig and the former German province of East Prussia. Among the other rivers, the Netze and Warthe are important because of their utilization for irrigation purposes, while in East Prussia, the Pregel provides an outlet to the Baltic Sea (the harbor at Königsberg-Pillau) for that province.

The two most important canals are the Gleiwitzer, which connects the Upper Silesian mines with the Oder, and the Masurischer, connecting the lake country of southern East Prussia with the Baltic.[4]

The soil of the Oder-Neisse provinces is moderately fertile. Again, it is the Silesian soil which excels in acreage yield and land values, both of which were, in 1939, above the Reich average.[5] The Pomeranian *Kartoffelland* and East Prussia yield only modest crops of wheat and other grains. The ratio of cultivated arable land is very high because the provinces have preserved their basically agricultural character, even in the economy of the Third Reich. In prewar years, 48.3 per cent of the land was cultivated, and wasteland amounted to 0.8 per cent. A total of 26.3 per cent of the area was covered with forests (beech and oak in the south, pine in the north), providing the basis for a well-developed lumber and construction industry.[6]

Among mining resources, Silesian hard coal is of the greatest economic importance. Hard coal has been mined in Upper Silesia for centuries, both in the parts remaining with Germany after the plebiscite of 1921 and in the part allotted to Poland. Although the majority of the mines were awarded to Poland in 1921, the production of German Upper Silesia (Oberschlesien) has continuously expanded, while Polish production increased only during the war years, under German exploitation,[7] despite successful Polish efforts during the depression years to invade the Scandinavian market. Reserves in the Upper Silesian coal basin are estimated at close to sixty-six billion metric tons, lying at a depth of three thousand feet.[8] A secondary coal basin especially suited for coke production is located at Waldenburg in Lower Silesia; its reserves have been depleted to about one billion metric tons.

There is a sizable number of lignite mines in Lower Silesia and eastern Brandenburg and copper and nickel mines in the Giant and Sudeten Mountains of Lower Silesia. In 1938, a total of 75 per cent of the zinc production and 40 per cent of the lead production of the Reich was mined in Silesia (170,000 and 28,000 metric tons, respectively).[9] Arsenic deposits and rich limestone quarries enrich Silesia's mining resources and have given rise to construction industries, making it one of the most valuable provinces of the Reich.

The largest and best-administered cities and industries of the Oder-Neisse provinces are located in Silesia. Lower Silesia's capital is the East German metropolis of Breslau (now renamed Wrocław), which houses the Polish University of Lwów and which had a prewar population of 625,198. In the industrial region of Upper Silesia are the cities of Hindenburg (133,433), Gleiwitz (111,062), and Beuthen (100,-584). On the west bank of the Neisse lies the city of Görlitz (94,-182).[10] In the eastern part of the *Regierungsbezirk* Frankfurt/Oder, there is only one city of importance: Landsberg/Warthe (45,928). Some towns located on the rivers Oder and Neisse are partitioned, and their major part has been allotted to Poland, as in the case of Guben and Forst. In Pomerania, Stettin (270,747), located at the mouth of the Oder, Stolp (45,299), and Schneidemühl (37,500) are centers of municipal administration and local industry. East Prussia has two larger cities; one, Königsberg, the birthplace of Immanuel Kant (316,072), is north of the Polish-Russian demarcation line, and the other, Elbing (72,409), is in the part administered by Poland.[11]

In 1939, some 9,559,514 persons were living in the Oder-Neisse provinces.[12] By 1943, more than 525,000 evacuees had moved to the region from the major cities in the western and northern parts of the Reich which were exposed to Allied air raids. The figures of 1939 and 1943 do not include the Free City of Danzig, which had a population of 410,000 in 1941.[13] The distribution of the population in 1939 was as follows:

Upper Silesia	1,529,258
Lower Silesia	3,029,137
District Zittau (Saxony)	22,941
East Brandenburg	594,041
East Pomerania	1,895,015
Southern East Prussia	1,338,517
Free City of Danzig	410,000
TOTAL	8,819,909
Northern East Prussia	1,149,605
GRAND TOTAL	9,969,514

In 1937, the population of the Oder-Neisse provinces amounted to 13.85 per cent of that of the Reich. The discrepancy between the area and the population percentages is easily explained by the agricultural character of the provinces and by the unusually high population density of the Ruhr area in western Germany.

Not even in Polish literature can arguments be found to refute the

overwhelmingly German character of the provinces as of 1939. In
Lower Silesia, eastern Brandenburg, Pomerania, and East Prussia,
Germans constituted 98 to 100 per cent of the population.[14] The only
province with a sizable Polish-speaking minority was Upper Silesia.
In 1925, German statistics reported 822,277 Germans, 394,891 speaking both the German and Polish languages, and 162,110 Poles in
Upper Silesia.[15] The results of the plebiscite of March 20, 1921, conducted under the auspices of the League of Nations, showed only
194,768 persons voting for Poland in that part of Upper Silesia which
was retained by Germany, so that German claims regarding the pro-
German leanings of the 392,891 bilingual Upper Silesians seem to be
closer to the truth than the Polish claim to these voters as "autochthons."[16]

The same argument is even more valid when applied to the Lutheran Masurians, who have lived in Prussia since the sixteenth century. Of the 41,375 Masurians and Poles who lived in the *Regierungsbezirk* Allenstein, only 7,980 voted for Poland in the 1920 League of
Nations plebiscite. In a similar plebiscite in the district of Marienwerder, only 7,947 people out of a population of 105,004 voted for
Poland.[17]

Thus a fair estimate of nationally conscious Poles in Germany during the interwar period (excluding the minorities in the Ruhr and
Berlin) was about 225–230 thousand. To these could be added 400–
430 thousand persons of Slavic descent who were bilingual but who
preferred to live in Germany under German administration. This
figure seems to be reinforced by post–October, 1956 Polish statistics
(which were, however, denied a few months later) reporting 350,000
Germans and 650–750 thousand "autochthons" in the Oder-Neisse
provinces.

Some Lithuanians were living in the northeastern part of East Prussia when it fell under Russian rule in 1945. Their number hardly
exceeded four to five thousand.[18]

2. MIGRATORY TRENDS IN THE ODER-NEISSE PROVINCES

Contemporary Polish writers place much emphasis on the flight of
the German population from the Oder-Neisse provinces to Berlin,
Saxony, and the Ruhr before 1939. They consider this migration to
be a justification of the Polish[19] claim to the provinces, and they regard the 1945 seizure of them as a demographic-geopolitical necessity.

They want to turn the *Volk ohne Raum* theory against the Germans. What, however, was the extent of this migration? Was it nearing a climax when the end of the Second World War caused a massive dislocation of the German population from the provinces through flight and expulsion? Was it due to local conditions and/or to general migratory trends in Europe? Was the remaining German population inadequate to utilize the area economically? Only after answering these questions can the alleged justification be considered as admissible.

For the past century there has been a steady stream of migration to the west in Germany, Poland, and Austria-Hungary. The progress of industrialization in the Ruhr and in Saxony, the growth of the cities, and the ever expanding birth rate in agricultural areas resulted in an east to west movement as early as 1850. As public health continued to improve and when the family farm no longer offered an adequate livelihood, many of the more adventurous or less favored elements of the peasantry in Lithuania, Poland, and other east central European countries, as well as in the Oder-Neisse areas, moved into towns and to mining camps or emigrated to the United States and other overseas territories. In Lithuania and Poland, the rural population moved into the towns, absorbing the German-speaking, city-dwelling element. Some of the Germans in Congress Poland and Russia resisted the denationalization process and moved to Prussian territories. Even some Poles entered the Prussian provinces in the latter part of the nineteenth century. Yet despite the gains, the flight of the native population of East Prussia to the west assumed major proportions. Between 1870 and 1910, some 717,700 and between 1910 and 1933, some 206,400 persons left East Prussia for other more westerly territories of the German Reich. Emigration figures have been smallest in the two Silesias, where native industry (coal and textiles) and the lesser prevalence of large estates counteracted the desire of the rural youth to seek employment outside his province.[20]

These pre–World War I movements were therefore of great importance. They dealt a blow to the German minority in Congress Poland, necessarily weakening the position of the German population of the Oder-Neisse provinces, without, however, interfering with the economic utilization of the territories by native German residents.

The second wave of westward movement occurred after 1919 when large parts of the German population of the formerly German provinces of Posen and West Prussia moved into the Oder-Neisse provinces and other parts of Germany. In West Prussia, for example, the German minority was reduced from 551,000 to 134,000 between 1919 and 1931, and Nazi authorities counted only 198,000 Germans after reconquering the provinces in 1939.[21] Thus from West Prussia alone, about 280–300 thousand Germans moved west between 1919 and 1931. Therefore, a large number of repatriates from prewar Poland (825,-000)[22] more than compensated for the population losses of the Oder-Neisse provinces through emigration, this amounting to only 392,000 people in the years between 1910 and 1933. Subsidies to German agriculture and stabilization of political conditions after the chaos of 1918 contributed to the drastic decrease of emigration. Only East Prussia, the origin of almost 54 per cent of all the emigrants, remained a sore spot. Thus in the interwar period, the climax of the emigration crisis was overcome in all provinces except East Prussia, which was greatly handicapped by the loss of its land communications with the rest of the Reich.

The slowdown in the exodus from the provinces on the one hand and increasing immigration from prewar Poland on the other helped the population of the Oder-Neisse provinces to stabilize at about 13.5 to 14 per cent in the period between 1933 and 1939, a level below that of 1871 (16.5 per cent).[23]

One of the consequences of the flight from the provinces before the First World War was the importation of seasonal agricultural workers from Poland. Their number, as high as four to five hundred thousand at harvest time in 1913, was reduced considerably during the interwar period, mainly because of deteriorating relations between Germany and the new Poland.

Emigration can be cited as a cause for the lower density of population in the Oder-Neisse province in 1939. With the exception of Upper Silesia, the population density was under the Reich average, in Pomerania and East Prussia by as much as 45 to 50 per cent. This low density is explained in part by the high Reich average, which was greatly conditioned by the enormous overpopulation of the Ruhr, and by the agricultural pursuits of the eastern German population. The fact remains, however, that, as a result of the high Polish birth rate, the voivodships of prewar Poland showed a higher density than the eastern German provinces, thereby exerting a mild population pressure from east to west. However, this relationship was reversed by the war losses of the Polish population, and thus in 1945, there existed little, if any, pressure on which any drastic relocations of populations could have been based.[24]

3. MINING AND INDUSTRIAL RESOURCES

The substantially agricultural structure of the Oder-Neisse provinces is immediately obvious to the economist. The absence of any significant coal and water resources in East Prussia, Pomerania, and eastern Brandenburg and the unfavorable position of the region in relation to the markets of western Europe and overseas, with the exception of Danzig and Stettin, have crippled the development of heavy industry in the northern and central parts of the region. Yet the richness of Silesian soil and the many productive mines in the two southern provinces have promoted the emergence of an industrial nucleus which has equaled most of its western European competitors and which, until 1945, formed the industrial backbone of the regions between the Ruhr and the Ukraine. The Silesian provinces, then, have played the role of the economic-strategic pivot of east central Europe and have influenced the power position of their possessors, as well as the fate of the neighboring countries. The power controlling the entire complex of Upper Silesian industry—after 1921 partitioned between Germany and Poland—possesses, by virtue of its control of the rich coal mines and steel mills, the geopolitical strength needed to achieve regional supremacy.

For both Germany and Poland, the greatest economic asset of the Oder-Neisse provinces consists of the Silesian coal basin and the complementary iron, steel, and other metal industries in Upper and Lower Silesia. The importance of coal mining in the area is so predominant that some German publications[25] have regarded it as a monopoly in Silesian industry. In 1939, at least 8.6 per cent of the population of Upper Silesia[26] was earning its livelihood by working in the mines. Subsequent Polish expansion has increased the role of coal production in the region through large-scale investments and the reuniting of the western Upper Silesian coal basin with the eastern Upper Silesian mines, which have been under Polish control since 1921.

The coal basin of Upper Silesia is not restricted to German Silesia alone. Eastern Upper Silesia and the Dombrau district also have rich coal mines. However, the most profitable mines are located in Germany and Polish Upper Silesia. In 1938, geological surveys indicated sixty-six billion metric tons of coal lying at depths above three thousand feet and forty-seven billion metric tons at depths from six to nine thousand feet beneath the earth's surface. The magnitude of the Silesian coal reserve becomes even more significant if it is realized that certified reserves in the Ruhr amount to only twenty-one billion metric tons at all levels. In Silesian mines, the average shaft is from twenty-one to twenty-four hundred feet deep; the coal veins are about seven feet thick, and a vein less than a foot thick is considered uneconomical.[27]

As a result of such favorable conditions, the productivity of individual miners has been very high.[28] The German part of the basin produced 25,983,000 metric tons of coal in 1939 in only sixteen shafts, reaching a record production figure per shaft in western and central Europe.[29] In 1938, Silesian coal production amounted to from 15 to 16 per cent of the Reich's production, and despite larger reserves, the Polish Upper Silesian mines and the Dombrauan mines in Poland exceeded west Upper Silesian production by only twenty-three million tons.[30]

The iron and steel industry, with its subsidiaries, has played the next important role in the Silesian economy. Although unfavorable transportation conditions prevented the factories from successfully competing with the foundries and arsenals of the Ruhr, their production was far from negligible because of the importation of large quantities of Swedish iron ore, which was worked into machine tools and armaments. In 1936, the net production of these industries amounted to 183,000,000 RM and provided work for 97,200 workers in Silesia and 175,000 workers in all of the Oder-Neisse provinces.[31]

The cheap import route for Swedish ore (via the Oder River and the Gleiwitzer Canal) and the presence of inexpensive coal and power furnished the requirements for the creation of a second "Ruhr basin" in Germany during the interwar period. The Third Reich strongly pressed the expansion of Silesian iron ore production, yet it was only after the consolidation of the Silesian industrial areas in German hands after 1939 that pig-iron production could be raised to 2.2 million metric tons and crude-steel production to 3.2 million metric tons a year.[32] The products of the subsidiary industries were usually pipes, fittings, machines, cast iron, plates, sheets, wheels, and wires suitable for both capital goods and armament production. Among engineering companies, the great locomotive and railroad-car factories of Görlitz and Breslau were outstanding, Silesian firms also produced large numbers of Diesel engines, machine tools, and equipment for the lumber industry. Precision industry had only recently been introduced.[33]

Thermal power and gas are the most common by-products of coal mining. Their net production value in 1939 amounted to 168,000,000 RM in the Oder-Neisse provinces, with the two Silesias responsible for more than 60 per cent of the production. The Waldenburg coal, especially suitable for coke production, balanced the flame coal of Upper Silesia in the generation of thermal electricity. Silesia produced large quantities of surplus power, which was exported through one thousand–kilowatt lines to central Germany, where chronic power shortages were common.[34]

Prior to 1939, there were three other industries of importance in the Oder-Neisse provinces: (1) the construction industry and its subsidiaries, which produced 675,000,000 RM worth of goods in 1936 (12 per cent of German production of 1936) and employed 368,100 persons;[35] (2) the Silesian textile industry, an industrial tradition in the province, with 232,000 workers and 241,000,000 RM yearly production; and (3) the lumber and paper industries, with 164,000 workers and a 204,000,000 RM annual net production.[36]

The role of agriculture in the economic life of the Oder-Neisse provinces was emphasized by the food and liquor industries, which, in contrast to the heavy industries, were scattered throughout the different provinces. The 1936 production amounted to 260,000,000 RM, and the number of gainfully employed in these industries reached 175,300 persons.

It is evident that the Silesian industries contributed greatly to the welfare and the production of the population of the Reich. Not only were the provinces able to satisfy most of their needs without relying on the other parts of Germany, they also increased German potential in the fields of exports and electric power. Without Silesian industry, German economic power would have been fundamentally restricted.

At present, West Germany and the Russian Zone are compelled to maintain the expelled East German population at a reasonably high living standard. This burden renders both parts of Germany extremely vulnerable to the fluctuations of supply and demand on the world market, introducing a new factor of instability into German politics, a situation which is hardly in the best interests of the United States. These facts argue strongly in favor of German demands for a return of the provinces or for the internationalization of the Silesian basin. Poland's prewar western frontiers endowed her with sufficient coal for maintaining her industries,[37] but the same cannot be said for

Germany in 1959, despite the Ruhr production and the relatively high standards prevailing because of the extraordinarily favorable export balance of the past few years.

Despite the October, 1956, events at Warsaw, the production of the two Silesias is still controlled by Moscow, enabling the latter to retain a firm hold on the main artery of central European industry and thus prevent the creation of any economic and military counterweight in the region. Russian control over the industrial basin, expressed economically in the partial replacement of Swedish iron ore by Ukrainian iron ore from Krivoi Rog, and the military occupation of Silesia by Russian troops enable the Warsaw Pact nations to augment their arsenal against the West, regardless of the undeniable sympathies of the majority of the Polish people for the West. The present unilateral control of the basin cannot serve the welfare of the Poles and Germans, for it deprives at least one or (as now) both of them of the profits of the coal and metals production in the region. Neither could partition satisfy the competitors, as the history of the Polish-German Upper Silesian Convention of 1922, establishing the mixed international tribunal, proved.[38] The economic development of one of the most important coal centers of Europe goes far beyond the local horizon and represents one of the most acute problems of Europe, especially central Europe. The economic problem should, therefore, be solved by considering the necessity of the free and unhindered economic and cultural development of Poles and Germans living in or expelled from the area.

4. THE BREADBASKET OF GERMANY

Various publications on the Oder-Neisse provinces describe their agricultural production in detail. German authors usually conclude that the provinces formed the "breadbasket of Germany," without which no permanently balanced German economy could have been created and maintained. Polish writers, in turn, emphasize that the provinces represented a heavy ballast on the German economy by requiring state subsidies and that the products of the Oder-Neisse provinces were either consumed by the population of the provinces and the surplus withered away or was sold at a loss because of existing transportation difficulties.[39] In the following paragraphs, these contentions will be analyzed and an attempt made to assess their validity in view of the economic realities of 1938-39.

None of the authors disagree with the statement that to a nation with modest food-producing areas, every loss of farm land must cause severe hardship. Germany, ever since the coming of industrialization around 1850, was an importer rather than an exporter of food products. Although her birth rate declined in the pre–World War II period, there were still only 101.33 acres per hundred persons.[40] Pre-war Poland, in turn, had 192.75 acres per hundred people, almost twice the amount of farm land per capita.[41] German self-sufficiency of food products was 75 per cent in 1925 and, despite Hitler's campaign of autarchy, 83 per cent in 1938-39. At present, if the Federal Republic of Germany and the Russian Zone are considered as a whole, only 61 per cent of the population is fed from domestic agricultural production, while 39 per cent (twenty-seven million people) is dependent on foreign imports.[42]

These facts certainly militate for the regaining or acquisition of additional farm land by Germany in order to reduce her extraordinary dependence on imports, which could be counterbalanced temporarily only by overindustrialization.

Today's dispute is centered on the rentability, yield, and use of the surplus production of the Oder-Neisse provinces in the years just before World War II. The agricultural acreage of the provinces at that time was 17,643,960 acres. Of this, 13,610,000 acres were arable land; 2,365,000 acres meadows; 1,511,640 acres pastures; and 303,810 acres miscellaneous.[43] The quality of the soil differed from province to province, but the soil was, in general, only moderately fertile. The methods of cultivation, however, surpassed those practiced in Poland and the Baltic States and therefore enabled the provinces to establish a much higher acreage yield. The soil was exceptionally fertile in Lower Silesia only, and the other provinces had to struggle with the problems of rentability and marketing, a result of unfavorable transportation conditions in relation to the central and western German markets. Eastern German agriculture therefore demanded a fairly heavy capital and labor outlay. However, the high acreage yields, which were only a few per cent under the Reich's average, compensated for the additional outlay.[44] If compared with the acreage yield of Poland, the discrepancy in the figures demonstrates the more advanced character of German agricultural methods. The same quantity of soil in Poland (it was even better than that of some of the Oder-Neisse provinces) produced 0.50 metric tons of grain per acre and in the areas ceded to the U.S.S.R. by Poland only 0.41 metric tons per acre, as contrasted to 0.67 metric tons per acre in the Oder-Neisse provinces (1935-1939 figures).[45]

Not only has the acreage yield been high in the provinces, but so also has the entire grain-crop harvest, which amounted to 5.87 million metric tons in 1936, a figure equal to the 1948-49 harvest of Australia or the grain exports of Canada in the same year.[46] Its value in money also equaled the price of 9.2 million metric tons of crude steel in 1949.

The most effective impression can be gained, however, if the harvest figures of the Oder-Neisse provinces are compared with those of the Reich in the years from 1934 to 1939. Such a comparison shows that in bread and fodder grains alike,[47] the percentage of the eastern German harvest was 25.6 per cent of the Reich's harvest, while in potatoes, sugar beets, and other crops, the percentage amounted to 26.2 per cent. It can be safely concluded that in cereals and other crops, the harvest of the Oder-Neisse provinces fed about seven or eight million more people than the population of the provinces. This figure is arrived at after due consideration of unfavorable transportation conditions.

With regard to livestock, 30.4 per cent of the cattle, 22.4 per cent of the pigs, and 20.2 per cent of the poultry of Germany came from the Oder-Neisse provinces. Thus not less than 151.6 pounds of meat per capita were produced in the provinces, more than one-fifth of the German production.[48] Here again, the surplus was sufficient to feed five million people in addition to the resident population.

Several Polish or pro-Polish authors contend,[49] on the basis of a book by Professor Wilhelm Volz,[50] that despite the high harvest figures, the remainder of the Reich used very little of this surplus. In quoting the 1927-28 figures, it is maintained that only 28,000 metric tons of the wheat and 343,000 metric tons of the rye produced in the provinces were sold to western and central Germany, while the remainder merely contributed to the richness of the diet of the native population.[51] Professor Volz's figures are beyond reasonable doubt, but those who quote him fail to take into account two factors which contradict his reasoning that Germany does not need the Oder-Neisse provinces on the basis of agricultural considerations:

(1) In 1927-28, Germany had a favorable export-import balance because of the boom in the world market. Since overseas prices were below domestic costs, *she had imported more grain than at any other time between the two World Wars.* This vantage point is therefore an arbitrary one, selected in order to reinforce arguments rather than to

give a clear picture of the relationship between imports and eastern German surplus in the Reich's grain-crop economy. In the 1930's, imports were greatly reduced, while consumption remained at a fairly constant level, and the difference can only be explained by *the East German surplus' supplying food for at least three to four million more people than the residents of the Oder-Neisse provinces.*[52]

(2) The agricultural production of the German provinces west of the Oder and Neisse was not called upon by the Reich to supply food to the population of the eastern provinces. Since 1946-47, however, *both the economies of the Federal Republic and the Soviet Russian Zone have had to provide food for approximately eight to eight and one-half million East Germans, including natural increase, while the Oder-Neisse provinces are feeding only about one million of the original inhabitants.* Since the Soviet Russian Zone is largely self-sufficient in agricultural products and houses only about three million people from the East, the largest share of the burden rests on the Federal Republic. *West Germany now imports 37 to 39 per cent of her agricultural needs from abroad in order to feed her population,* which has been increased by expellees from the eastern provinces and the Sudetenland.

With regard to dairy production, too, the Oder-Neisse provinces were primary producers during the Third Reich. Twenty-one per cent of the German milk production originated here, together with 26 per cent of the output of lard and bacon, both basic staples in Germany.[53] The progress and achievements of German dairy methods could also be seen in the yearly milk-per-cow production figures, which amounted to 685 gallons in East Prussia in 1938, while the overall average of the Oder-Neisse provinces was 572 gallons. This compares with 396 gallons in Czechoslovakia and 330 gallons in prewar Poland.[54] Only Holland and Denmark surpassed the provinces with regard to milk-production rates.[55]

Two other accomplishments of the people in the provinces were livestock breeding and seed research. In the internationally renowned stables of Trakhenen in East Prussia (they were established in 1732) were bred some of the world's best hackney and tournament horses. The East Prussian–bred cattle, with their high milk-production rates and champion bulls, were well known to agricultural experts all over the world. The successes of the potato "sanitarium" of the Pommersche Saatzuchtgesellschaft at Dramburg, Pomerania, provided the eastern German farmer with superior seed plants and made this area the "natural home of the German potato."[56]

Another great resource of the provinces was lumber. The rate of deforestation was above the Reich average, and the vast lumber and construction industry of the region worked the felled wood into half-processed lumber products for construction and carpentry purposes (60 per cent of the lumber output) or into furniture and other consumer goods (40 per cent).[57]

Thus in 1939, the Oder-Neisse provinces, as a result of their high agricultural standards and first-class livestock, allowed not only a rich, high calorie diet for the resident population, but also the transportation of large surpluses to western and central Germany. Therefore, the allegations that Germany does not need these provinces because her food deficit has always been covered by imports lose their validity. One may argue whether the eastern German surplus actually fed five and one-half million people[58] or only three to four million, but the tremendous importance of the agricultural production of the Oder-Neisse provinces to the maintenance of a balanced and economical German diet cannot be denied. No permanently balanced German economy can be created without the return of at least a larger part of the Oder-Neisse provinces to Germany, despite the present prosperity in West Germany, which is, of course, based on exceptionally high exports and superindustrialization. Any economy which has to import more than one-fourth of its agricultural products is completely at the mercy of the changing law of supply and demand in the world market and is exposed to misery and malnutrition if larger recessions and depressions occur. Such conditions, in turn, might become fertile breeding places for extreme ideologies.

CHAPTER II

Historical Background of the German-Polish Dispute

1. MISINTERPRETATIONS IN HISTORICAL LITERATURE

DURING the past millenium, the course of events in the Oder-Neisse provinces has followed a very diversified pattern. All of the provinces were deeply influenced by fluctuations in German-Polish relations. Both nationalities have been in authority in the area for varying periods of time, while the power-political designs of third parties were of a different character in East Prussia, Pomerania, and the two Silesias. In analyzing the increasing pressures and counter-pressures, it is impossible to disregard trends and developments in West Prussia and Poznań, which form the geographic link between Silesia and East Prussia, for the problems inherent in the geopolitical position of the Polish Corridor and Poznań contributed directly to the outbreak of World War II and indirectly to the creation of the Oder-Neisse Line, the thorniest heritage of that war.

History declines to judge mankind on the basis of power-political interests of one or the other protagonist. This axiom should be kept in mind by present observers, who would like to forget about century-long evolutions in order to promote schemes born of their own understanding of the prevailing political and economic constellation, for history declines to use the present as a permanent yardstick. The motivating forces—social, economic and political—of our era differ essentially from those of the past, including even the nineteenth century, with its rampant industrialization, progressivism, and thirst for freedom and constitutionalism.

In the field of ethnographic disputes, perhaps more than in that of political history, the protagonists are apt to forget this precept because the humanism of the old European society of scholars and diplomats, the religious fervor of the Middle Ages and the era of the Reformation and the Counter Reformation, and the great liberal traditions of the last century are alien to them. They are spellbound by the new demigod, nationalism. The magnetic forces inherent in this concept are undeniable: the common pride; the dissolution of the imperfect individual ego in the perfect national community; the love and predeliction for national culture and customs; the powerful drive to realize this essentially cultural community through a political organism capable of destroying the shackles of restriction and oppression and rendering victorious the national principle within "ethnical" frontiers. This principle enshrines all truth and eternal existence to the extreme nationalist. And nationalism, the new gospel of masses emancipated from the paternalistic regime of kings and emperors in the name of self-determination and individual freedom, has become increasingly widespread and imperialistic since the technological and transportation revolutions made the creation of the powerful, economically united, and mobile nation-state possible.

It was probably fitting that outside the Balkans, where it was the force of survival of the oppressed nations, nationalism has been most all exclusive and fanatic among the peoples of central Europe, who in past centuries were invaded, suppressed, and prevented by outside powers from expressing their national ego.

The Germans, suffering from French invasions since the seventeenth century as the Holy Roman Empire disintegrated and with their political nucleus split into Hohenzollern-Prussia, a Protestant state, in the north and the Habsburg empire in the south, were foremost among the nations experiencing the intoxicating character of extreme nationalism. From Herder through Fichte and Treitschke to Hitler's racism based on the Austro-German *Grossdeutsch* ideology, the concept of nationalism was carried to extremes which would have evoked a shrill protest from its founders in the nineteenth century. The concept of the nation-state was developed into an organic—nay, into an *organistic*—concept denying the proper place of justice (*Recht ist was dem Volke nützt*) and individual freedom (the nation has priority over the individual) while equating nationalism with the nebulous concept of the Nordic race, by whom other races were to be treated with contempt (Alfred Rosenberg). In such an environment, culture was destined to become the gravedigger of creative, independent thinking instead of the work of the best minds of the nation. The results have been only too familiar and sad. Concentration camps, economic exploitation, political imperialism, and utter disregard for moral law by Hitler's Germany in eastern Europe could not be denied, even by a National Socialist, in view of the overwhelming factual evidence.

Condemnation of extreme nationalism, which results in complete disregard of the rights of other nationalities and subsequently in political imperialism, should not be restricted to the Third Reich alone. Arising out of the same milieu of denationalizing cosmopolitanism and foreign oppression as did Fichte's theory of the nation, Polish chauvinism was also a product of the sufferance and vegetating existence of the Polish people under foreign rule (Russian, Prussian, and Austrian). The visionary aspect of nationalism here became united with social-reform ideas, since the Poles represented, for the most part, the peasants and laborers in their own country and the sons of farmers and workers who had received higher education and had become the intelligentsia of the country. As cities and industry progressed under foreign rule, these elements increasingly supplied the most vociferous Polish nationalists. Deprived of national existence for more than a century, the messianic aspect of their nationalism has been surpassed only by Hitler's insistence on the "New Order" and by Israeli nationalism.

Reminiscent of the glory of the Jagellonian empire of the fifteenth and sixteenth centuries, when Poland was the master of east central and eastern Europe, Polish nationalism has assumed many of the characteristics of political imperialism. Its demands embrace a strange mixture of ethnographic (Upper Silesia, Galicia), historical (Vilna, Byelorussia, East Prussia), and strategic-economic (Danzig, Stettin) arguments, to the confusion of the foreign observer, for the arguments often contradict the demands based on the other premises. Polish nationalism has sought the restoration of Jagellonian Poland in the east and Piast Poland in the west, yet the political and ethnic realities of the twentieth century have been and are unfavorable to the realization of the Oder-Dnieper empire. In their zest, Polish nationalists tend, as in the past, to forget the force inherent in the aroused national consciousness of the people inhabiting the areas to which they continue to file claims. They do, however, realize their awkward and exposed geopolitical position in relation to Germany and Russia. Unwilling to accept foreign imperialism, the Poles tend to create an imperialism of their own at the expense of the great powers of the region, but they lack the resources to accomplish their aims.

Although Communist Russia has given a free hand to Polish imperialism in the west and has enabled Poland to occupy more provinces than even her most extreme chauvinists have ever demanded, the Poles have acquired Russian "protection" at an exorbitant price, namely, the ceding of 52 per cent of their prewar territories to the U.S.S.R. The Poles' acquisition of areas which for the past six centuries have not been part of the Polish state while ceding such Polish cities as Lwów and Vilna has produced an almost schizophrenic tendency in interpreting their nationalist doctrine, both in terms of Wladyslaw Gomulka's nationally Communist (*contradictio in adjecto*) Poland and in terms of the Polish exiles in the West. The Polish Communists express their views in vicious tirades against the alleged German "spirit of *revanche*"; they prefer, for reasons of well-understood *Realpolitik*, not to notice the grave injustices committed by the U.S.S.R. against Poland.

Thus scholars must use the works of Polish historians of post–World War II vintage with great caution, regardless of the ideological credo of the author. Researchers have to apply the same yardstick which they have applied to their reading of National Socialist literature on Poland. Needless to say, National Socialist works mocked *die polnische Wirtschaft* (a notorious German description of alleged Polish inefficiency, equivalent to the American colloquialism "big mess") and spoke of an age-old struggle on the frontier between Germans and Slavs.

True nationalism, however, does not consist of the emotional utterances of fanatics, just as the cynical credo of anti-national "world citizens" does not describe the tenets of the believers in an international community of nations. Instead, true nationalism includes a healthy regard for the accomplishments of culture, justice, economics, and state organization by the individual's nation, for which he is willing to lay down his life and wealth should occasion demand such action. It neither excludes the adherence of the individual to other regional loyalties or to religious communities nor eliminates the guarantees of individual liberty within the national group, as is demanded by the extreme nationalists in Germany and Poland. Guided by such an understanding, I will present an analysis of the three provinces of the Oder-Neisse region in the pages which follow.

2. THE BRIDGE FROM WEST TO EAST—SILESIA

No eastern German province has changed foreign masters while peacefully maintaining an almost exclusively German character as often as the economically prosperous but often devastated land of the Oder River and the Giant and Sudeten Mountains. Populated by Slavonic tribes after the Goths and Gepidae left the area during the Völkerwanderung, the land was rarely mentioned in chronicles until the tenth century. At that time the newly established Bohemian kingdom, under the loose suzerainty of the Holy Roman Empire, secured a hold on the Silesias that was not relinquished until the dawn of the eleventh century, when the famous Polish king, Boleslav I (called Chobry), conquered the provinces. His conquest led to the immediate, indirect control of the provinces by the Poles under the Piast dynasty until the Treaty of Trentschin in 1335. The land was thinly populated, with the Slavonic settlements restricted mostly to the Oder and other river valleys. The province had only a few castles and almost no towns besides Breslau.

After the partition of the Piast kingdom of Poland in 1138, conflicts arising out of the division facilitated an increasingly independent position of the Silesian Piasts from Kraków.[1] The first German settlers appeared toward the middle of the twelfth century, a result of the pro-German attitude of Ladislas II of the Piasts and his sons, Boleslav and Mieszko, who had spent seventeen years in exile in the Holy Roman Empire. The German town of Neisse was founded; German monks appeared at Leubus, and by 1252, six other monasteries had been established by the Germans. A rising stream of German clergy, merchants, craftsmen, and peasants poured into the land. The majority of the settlers resided on the slopes of the mountains in the south; they cleared many acres of arable land and opened up mines in the mountainous countryside. By 1350, the Iser and Giant Mountains were settled fifteen hundred feet up the slopes and the Altvater and Glatzer Mountains to about eighteen hundred feet.[2] With the introduction of mining and municipal life, the Germans brought completely new features into the prevailing simple social structure. The division into a noble upper class and a peasant lower class was replaced by a complex social order; co-ordination of law, economics, and defense in the newly established towns and villages became the rule; and the precinct (*Weichen*) system of land planning, a characteristic of German colonization, was adopted.[3] German knights, too, were soon called into Silesia in order to replenish the thinning ranks of native fighters, many of whom had been slain in the decisive Battle of Wahlstatt (1241), a bitter and bloody struggle with the Tartars. It was here that the most talented Silesian Piast, Henry II, fell.

Silesia experienced a golden era in the fourteenth century. By 1350, German colonization there was no longer restricted to the wilderness and the forests on the east side of the Oder but had encroached upon the Slavonic settlements, reforming the legal order in the castles and establishing new villages. The Slavonic *zaude*, the court of law, was suspended in 1337, and the new castles and towns, including rebuilt Breslau, were also inhabited by Germans. In 1332, there was only one town which used a Slavonic language for its annals, and the majority of the burghers in every town were Germans.[4] Altogether, there were 120 new towns and 1,200 new villages by the year 1400.

Politically, the fourteenth century resulted in the return of Bohemian rule, which was not, however, unmitigated Czech rule because the German Luxemburgers were in possession of the Bohemian Crown and German colonization in Bohemia was well advanced. Partitions of the realm of Henry II among his children and grandchildren had effects similar to those of the Carolingian partitions and finally induced the Silesian princes to seek refuge under the protection of Emperor Charles IV. In the twice-ratified Treaty of Trentschin, Casimir III of Poland also recognized the cession of Silesia, and the Silesian frontier, with the exception of the Upper Silesian mining area, was not changed between 1335 and 1945.

In the fifteenth century, chaos and disintegration followed the path of the many Hussite raids on Silesia, with corresponding losses among the German city-dwelling population.[5] The result was a reversion of nationality distribution in the province, especially in Upper Silesia, where the Lassitite Slavonic Code had succeeded in eliminating the German Magdeburg and other codes. The substitution of Slavonic law also resulted in the deterioration of the position of the farmers into serfdom. The process converted many German farmers into Slavonized agricultural serfs, just as, a century before, Slavonic farmers had been Germanized in a peaceful manner.[6] It was only under the rule of Hungarian King Matthias Corvinus that the first moves for organizing a provincial administration were made; he appointed a permanent royal representative and institutionalized the Silesian ducal assemblies.

In 1526, as a result of the Jagellonian-Habsburg family compact of 1515, the Habsburg dynasty acquired both the Bohemian Crown and Silesia. Its rule, which lasted until 1741, brought about many religious and ethnical changes in the provinces. Taking over a land that was largely Germanized in the western and central portions (Lower Silesia),[7] the Upper Silesian part reverting to Polish nationality, the Habsburgs produced varied results with their counterreformatory tendencies. They reintroduced the German language in administration, promoted the *ius Teutonicum,* and ended the intrusion of the Moravian dialect into southern Silesia. But the conversion of the Silesians to Lutheranism and their participation in the Bohemian revolt in 1618, along with their subsequent defeat at White Mountain, led to the decimation of the German Protestant communities of the provinces. The expulsion of Lutheran preachers and artisans, who went to southern Posen from Upper Silesia, weakened the German element as the *émigrés* became Polonized in the eighteenth and nineteenth centuries. After 1650, however, a new wave of settlers came to devastated Silesia. They were induced by the estate-holders, who, as they began to realize the importance of the rich coal resources and iron foundries in the eastern part of Silesia, wanted to repopulate the pillaged and burned villages after the Thirty Years' War.

After the Treaty of Westphalia, the question of Silesian Protestantism became an international issue, with Brandenburg and Sweden playing the part of the champion of the Silesian Protestants, while among the Silesian Catholics, the Polish element became increasingly prominent through the introduction of Polish monks into Silesia by the Habsburgs. This outside intervention, dramatized in 1706 by the appearance of Charles XII of Sweden in the Imperial camp at Saxony, saved the Protestant character of Lower Silesia and restored the status of 1648. The absence of the Habsburgs from the provinces, plus the fact that the ruling house would abstain from a vigorous counterreformation only under external pressure, had inwardly estranged its Protestant subjects. They welcomed the Prussian attack of 1740, which put an explicit end to the Habsburg period.[8]

Demographically, significant changes occurred in Silesia during the sixteenth and seventeenth centuries. They were due to the development of mining (zinc, gold, copper, silver) and the homecraft-textile industries in the mountains, together with glass manufacturing in both the Moravian and Silesian parts of the Sudeten Mountains. The lumber and leather industries also provided a livelihood for the residents of the mountain villages, so that the Sudeten Mountains became the most densely populated part of the Silesias. The situation was to change in the nineteenth century when the textile industry collapsed and the new "Industrial Triangle" was built.

The consequence of the Prussian conquest was geographically unfortunate for Silesia. It converted an administrative delineation into an international frontier in the direction of Bohemia and introduced a new partition as Maria Theresa succeeded in retaining the duchies of Teschen and Troppau south of the Oppa River. The population of Austrian Silesia was now placed between Bohemia with a Czech, Poland with a Polish, and Prussia with a German, but hostile, population.[9]

The position of Catholicism in Silesia was also disturbed. Under the Habsburg, the originally German Catholic church had begun to fall into Polish hands, but the process was now accelerated as the leveling influence of the Austrian Catholic church was removed. The first century of Prussian rule in Silesia was also characterized by the establishment of a smoothly functioning administration which ended the rule of the *Stände* and by the creation of three *Regierungsbezirke* (Liegnitz, Breslau, Oppeln) and the appointment of provincial authorities by the royal government.[10] The assimilation of the province into the Prussian state as a social and political community was achieved to a lesser degree only. Although the Silesian nobles had become loyal subjects of the Crown, the Silesian intellectuals favored Prussia, and Silesian industries produced the howitzers and small armaments employed by the Prussian army at Leipzig, social and economic inequalities, crises, and the coming of nationalism had prevented the assimilation of the Polish-speaking subjects in Upper Silesia *in toto*.

The great event of the nineteenth century in Silesia was the coming of the machine age. The creation of heavy industry, encouraged by the invention of the steam engine and the blast furnace, was promoted by Prussian Minister of Mines Freiherr von Heinitz and his nephew, William Freiherr von Reden.[11] By 1840, a number of private companies, founded by the land barons, such as Count Henckel von Donnersmarck and the Prince of Pless, or by successful commoners, such as Francis Winckler (Kattowitz) and Karl Godula, were prospering alongside state mines and factories. The establishment of the German Customs Union facilitated the expansion of coal, iron, and zinc production and converted the region into one of the most important industrial areas in Europe. Skilled workers, engineers, and miners were originally imported from Lower Silesia and Prussian Saxony, but by the middle of the century, most of the unskilled laborers were Upper Silesians of Polish origin, and large numbers had to be imported from central Poland and Galicia. Thus Sarah Wambaugh's statement that "to the Germans the industries of Upper Silesia have been built by German brains and capital, while to the Poles they are the fruits of Polish labor" is at least partially correct.[12]

The coming of industry gave rise to a spectacular expansion of population in Upper Silesia, but only a lesser extent in Lower Silesia, where the collapse of the textile industry was partially replaced by mining and industrial activities at Waldenburg, Liegnitz, and Breslau. The population increases in Upper Silesia are reflected in the following table,[13] which lists the population of Upper Silesia in the years indicated:

1785	380,000	1871	1,309,563
1819	561,172	1890	1,578,000
1830	730,000	1910	2,207,028
1849	965,912		

The coming of industry also meant, at first, an increase in the Polish-speaking element of Silesia, which was due to a very much higher birth rate (40 to 47 per thousand), with a net increase of 20 per thousand.[14] Thus while the population of Silesia (Lower and Upper) increased 157 per cent between 1817 and 1910, the Upper Silesian district increased from 529,000 to 2,207,000 within the same period, a gain of 232 per cent.

The unexpectedly rapid increase in the population of Upper Silesia and migration from the land to huts inside the teeming industrial settlements brought misery to workers and miners. Furthermore, the situation of the peasants was essentially worse than in other provinces. Although Frederick II passed decrees easing the services of the serfs and the Stein-Hardenberg reforms of 1807 resulted in their liberation, all of the laws were sabotaged by land-owning nobles, who formed the military and financial backbone of the Prussian state and administration. Furthermore, little credit or capital was given to the liberated serfs, and they willingly went to the industrial settlements, looking for a job which, in the nineteenth century, was not equivalent to any kind of personal or social security. While the land question hit Germans and Poles equally hard, the final decay of the homecraft-based textile industry in the Sudeten Mountains and the underpaid, mistreated workers of the Industrial Triangle were causes for an explosive social situation which erupted into riots subdued by the military.[15] Both German and Polish farmers and workers were starving in Silesia at the time of bad harvests in the 1840's, while Silesian magnates were able to gain enormous profits by controlling the newly established industries around Beuthen and Kattowitz. Such conditions prevailed when Prussia's "Iron Chancellor" succeeded in establishing the Second Reich.

3. THE CHANGING FORTUNES OF EASTERN POMERANIA

The historical developments in eastern Pomerania and Stettin differed in character from those in Silesia. First, the differentiation between the Poles and the original inhabitants of the land, the *pomorjane*, or seaside dwellers, was more obvious, even in the centuries before German colonization, and second, the third-power influence here was Danish and less consequential than the Bohemian influence in Silesia. During the tenth, eleventh, and twelfth centuries, Pomeranian princes fought the Poles and the Danes with fluctuating success, and not until the Polish king, Boleslav III, had asked the German bishop, Otto of Bamberg, to convert the Pomeranians did Christianization of the land make any progress.[16]

The sea power of the Pomeranians was significant at times. Based on the Isle of Rügen, it was finally broken in the twelfth century by the many Danish and Polish attacks and the Wendish crusade of 1147. Christianization was the work of both the German monks, who came at the request of Princes Wratislaw and Ratibor, and of the Teutonic Order and the other orders of knights (Johannites and Templars) residing in the eastern and southeastern districts of Hinterpommern. German colonization failed to follow immediately upon the adoption of Christianity by the Pomeranians. Danish power under Canute VI proved to be the strongest of the three contenders in the late twelfth century. It was not until 1227 that Emperor Frederick II of Hohenstaufen wrested control of the duchies from Denmark. In the fourteenth century, the land was divided into the duchies of Wollgast and Stettin, the latter including all of eastern Pomerania except certain small districts held by Brandenburg and the Teutonic Order. The position of Pomerania became that of a principality in the Holy Roman Empire, though its princes sought to retain their domestic sovereignty.[17]

German colonization occurred a century later than in Silesia. By the end of the thirteenth century, however, there were already thirty-four German towns in Pomerania, seventeen of them in eastern Pomerania.[18] The path of colonization followed the coast from Stettin to Stolp and spread to the southern part of the province in the fourteenth century. First towns and then villages were founded, mostly in the neighborhood of Slavonic settlements. The market place, together with the town hall, usually formed the center of the town and was surrounded by a rectangular pattern of streets in which a parish church was located. The Slavonic residents lived in the "suburbs" and earned their livelihood by farming and fishing. The peaceful nature of the colonization was shown by the fact that no German town, except those founded by the Teutonic Order, possessed any castles for defense.[19] Some Slavonic influence was preserved in eastern Pomerania until the seventeenth century because of the survival of Slavonic nobles, who were expelled from western Pomerania, but in the course of the fourteenth and fifteenth centuries, German nobles were also given large tracts of land in eastern Pomerania. The importation of their own peasants caused many of the districts to become overwhelmingly German by the year 1500. The same procedure—that of importing German farmers and merchants, followed by the Church, the monasteries, and the Order—also caused Magdeburg and Kulm law to become prevalent in eastern Pomerania.[20] At first the immigration of German peasants improved the economic and legal position of the Slavonic farmers as the legal protection enjoyed by the Germans filtered down to the Slavs, but by the end of the Middle Ages, the position of the German farmer had deteriorated because of the increased power of the now intermarried German-Slavonic nobility and the subsequent equalization of the German-Slavonic legal principles applicable to peasants.[21]

The fifteenth century saw a further partition of western Pomerania and the gradual involvement of eastern Pomerania in the wars between the Teutonic Order and Poland. The Prince of eastern Pomerania fought on the side of the Order at Tannenberg, but the territorial demands of the new princes of Brandenburg, the Hohenzollerns, induced these princes to seek, temporarily, the friendship of Poland. The ties with the Empire seemed to have been loosened as Frederick II, the "Iron," of Brandenburg, had to withdraw in view of the coalition of Mecklenburg, Pomerania, and Poland, but his successor effected the submission of Boleslav X at Stettin, and under the rule of the latter,[22] the ties with the Reich, though not under the protection of Brandenburg, were reforged. Boleslav reunited his lands and attained an independent position within the Empire. He promoted the arts and sciences, and during his peaceful regime, Pomerania became an intellectual center of northern Germany. Boleslav reformed the laws and fiscal administration, eliminated lawlessness, and promoted commerce with Poland and the Empire as the Hansa's power decline caused a drastic reduction in the Nordic trade.[23]

Dissensions and turbulence marked the last century of the Greifen princes in Pomerania. Reformation was effected, after some hesitation, in the wake of the Treptow Land diet of 1534 at the request of the cities persuaded by Martin Luther's collaborator, Johann Bugenhagen.[24] The bishoprics of Wollin and Kammin were subordinated to the princely power, but efforts to regain the districts of Lauenburg-Bütow, which the Jagellos had acquired in 1466, proved to be unsuccessful. The final decline of the principalities occurred during the Thirty Years' War. Lacking the resources to maintain armed neutrality, Pomerania had to accept Imperial troops under Wallenstein in 1628, but the municipality of Stralsund, in western Pomerania, refused to allow the troops to enter the town. The subsequent siege brought first the Danes and then the Swedes, under Gustavus Adolphus, to Pomerania, turning the tide of the Thirty Years' War. At the Peace of Osnabrück (1648), Pomerania was not restored; the last Greifen prince, Boleslav XIV, had died in 1637. The great Margrave of Brandenburg was allotted the largest slice of eastern Pomerania, while Stettin and western Pomerania became Swedish.

Prussian rule in eastern Pomerania was expanded by the temporary acquisition of Lauenburg-Bütow and through the cession of Stettin by the Swedes in the Peace of Stockholm (1719). During the eighteenth century, eastern Pomerania slowly acquired the characteristics of a Prussian province, partly because of the colonization of the Prussian kings, for hunger and pestilence during the Thirty Years' War had decimated the population to an extent hitherto unknown.[25] Besides Germans from other Prussian provinces—western Germans—some Poles and French Huguenots also settled in eastern Pomerania after the raising of the Edict of Nantes (1696). Frederick II undertook *Peuplierung*, as contemporary Germans called colonization, and his official, Breckendorff, was instrumental in the large-scale land reclamation project which turned the Oderbruch[26] and the southern marshes into fruitful acreage. Frederick's efforts to ease the burden of the serfs, strongly resisted by the local nobility, were only partially implemented.

During the Napoleonic Wars, the provinces abundantly proved their loyalty to Prussia. The legendary defense of Kolberg by Lucadou and Gneisenau and the diplomatic refusal of the nobility and the cities to pay the high ransom to Napoleon earned for Pomerania the reputation of "the most loyal Prussian province."

Known for its fine potatoes and livestock breeding, Pomerania remained an agricultural province during the nineteenth century. Its prosperity declined temporarily after the Napoleonic Wars, and only the port of Stettin experienced the impetus of the Industrial Revolution. Although the communications system was improved around 1850, the consequent restoration of export markets for Pomeranian products favored only the land-holding nobility, which succeeded in acquiring more than 55 per cent of the arable land of the province by 1895. This development was also encouraged by the arrangement that the peasants, in order to be liberated from serfdom, had to cede parts of their lands to the estate-holding nobles.[27] The social tensions inherent in this lopsided distribution of land were, however, less evident than in Silesia or other provinces. The Conservative party of Prussia had its political and intellectual mainstay in the province,[28] and only Social Democrat Francis Mehring of eastern Pomerania criticized the agrarian conditions of his province sharply. The flight of the population from the rural areas assumed great proportions; the people fled to the industrial centers or emigrated to the New World. Nationality conflict was unknown in Pomerania, where the only Poles were seasonal farm hands or residents of the districts of Lauenburg. Conflicts were less violent, even during the Wilhelmian era, than anywhere else in the Reich partly because Protestant charity work, more than social reforms, eased the burden of the Pomeranian farmer.

4. THE LANDS ON THE VISTULA IN THE MIRROR OF CENTURIES

The scene showing Emperor Frederick II of Hohenstaufen offering possession of Prussia to the Grand Master of the Teutonic Order at Rimini in 1228 is often described by German historians.[29] They remember with joy the Order's power, which radiated from its seat at the Castle of Marienwerder to the Lower Vistula region and to the Baltic provinces. Polish authors, in turn, like to describe the famous painting by the artist Matejko entitled *The Submission of Prussia*.[30] The picture shows the last Grand Master of the Order, Albrecht of Hohenzollern, already a Protestant, kneeling before the Polish sovereign, Sigismund the Older, who offers him the standard of the "black eagle" of Prussia. Polish historians accuse the Teutonic Order of having been the archenemy of the Polish state[31] and of having acted like wolves in the sheep's clothing of monks,[32] yet it is undisputed in Western historiography that the foundation of the Teutonic Order was one of the last great spiritual accomplishments of the Reform Christianity of Cluny, inspired by the great monk Bernhard of Clairvaux and by the military and cultural development of the century, and that the Order originally preserved its universalist and crusading spirit, which was based on the purest concept of the *miles Christi*.

The extreme fluctuations in judgment should not serve, however, to confuse the role played by the Order in the fate of these territories, which survived the decline of the Order proper and even the end of the Hohenzollern dynasty. Possession by the Teutonic Order not only of East Prussia but also of the present Polish Pomorze, the former German province of West Prussia, facilitated German colonization to such an extent that a significant German minority survived in Pomorze even after three hundred years of Polish rule between 1466 and 1772. The survival and subsequent strengthening of the German element by the Prussian government before World War I put this province, unlike East Prussia, into the focus of nationality conflict.

The Order came to East Prussia at the invitation of Conrad of Masovia, who was directly threatened by recurrent raids of major proportions by the Prussians, a pagan Baltic tribe residing in the area of the modern German province of East Prussia. The Prussians resisted all missionary efforts, which came in the eleventh century from St. Adalbert of Prague and in the early thirteenth century from Christian, Bishop of Chełmno.[33] In view of the Order's unpleasant experiences with King Andrew II of Hungary, Grand Master Hermann von Salza insisted upon securing the rights of the Order to the Chełmno Land and to any territories it might conquer in Prussia before moving to attack the bellicose Prussians in 1231.

The next fifty years foreshadowed the conditions which favored the early ascendancy of the Order and caused its final collapse. The gradual conquest of East Prussia, the many battles with Lithuanians and Slavonic Pomorze princes, and the increasingly worsening relations with the Crown of Poland influenced the policy of the Order on the international scene. Domestically, too, events followed the course set by the sharpening conflict between the knightly elements of utmost political and military importance, although a numerical minority in the state, and the burghers.[34] The latter were gradually strengthened by the establishment of cities in the wake of land colonization, contributing materially to the undoing of the Order. In the fourteenth century, however, the Order, based on a fine network of castles and communications, could expand easily to the west, where it took advantage of the conflict between Brandenburg and Poland to occupy the region west of the Vistula and to establish contact with the Reich.

Few events have been denounced by Polish historians more vehemently as has this move of the Order in 1309. They report[35] atrocities and arson in Danzig, together with the massacre of the Polish garrison of the city. German historians doubt the authenticity of the documents convicting the Order of such excesses and regard them as forgeries of the enemies of the Order.[36] Whatever the true story may be, the Order achieved the cession of West Prussia in 1343 in the Treaty of Kalisz and remained the most powerful unit in the region. With its power radiating into the Baltic States, the Order continued a large-scale colonization of West and East Prussia.[37]

Polish historians allege that the native Prussian population was massacred by the knights, but this account seems to be incorrect, despite the high losses the Prussians must have experienced in the fifty-year war leading to their submission.[38] The fact that the Prussian language was used in the province as late as the seventeenth century contradicts the Polish thesis, as do principles of economic feasibility, for German settlers began to arrive only at the end of the thirteenth century and the number of colonists never exceeded that of the native population, which became assimilated only gradually. Polish allegations calling the policy of the Order "an accommodation of German population surplus" and "the Germanization of East Prussia" are guilty of applying the principles of our era to the medieval world, where such doctrines were unknown.[39] The fact that even the children of German colonists were for centuries excluded from the Order, which governed the country's affairs, should dissuade any historian from regarding the Teutonic Order as representative of the German national idea.[40]

Colonization followed the principles of economic feasibility, military considerations, and the spreading of the Christian Gospel. About

1,000 villages were established in West Prussia during the 150 years of Order government in the province. Here, as early as 1309, the Order discovered significant German settlements founded by the Slavonic princes of Pomorze, such as Swietopelk, and by the Johannite Order. German colonization of the province made great progress under the Order. By 1440, not only did the cities have German majorities, but in the northern and central districts, not less than 122 villages out of a total of 400 used Germanic law.[41] While adoption of German Kulm law was not an absolute proof of German preponderance in the settlements, the land was well on its way to becoming German when the Second Peace of Thorn (1466) placed it under Polish suzerainty.

The unexpected collapse of the Order can be traced back to foreign-policy considerations, although the conflict between nobles and cities on the one hand and the Order on the other certainly contributed its share to the maelstrom of 1463. Next to its superior military organization and a steady supply of German, French, and Bohemian knights, the strength of the Order lay in its close relationship to the two world powers of that day: the Holy Roman Empire and the Papacy. Its existence was also favored by the absence of a statelike organization and the prevalence of paganism among Lithuanians and the presence of a weak Polish kingdom. All of these factors disappeared by 1400. The Empire and the Papacy lost much of their power and prestige, the Lithuanians adopted Christianity from Poland, and the two states were united after the marriage of Jadwiga of Hungary and Ladislas Jagello.[42]

The loss of the last pagan frontier converted the Teutonic Order into a mere state among many states. The first combined Polish-Lithuanian attack on the Order led to the famous victory of the former at Tannenberg in 1410, but the Order was saved by Hermann of Plauen in the First Treaty of Thorn (1411). The enormous reparation paid to Poland and the deepening rift between the Order and the new diet foreshadowed future disaster. The power of the Order was finally broken in the Thirteen Years' War (1454-66), resulting in the Second Treaty of Thorn. West Prussia, the bishopric of Ermland, and the area around Kulm were to be transferred to the Polish Crown, and on paper, the Grand Master of the Order became a Polish vassal.[43] Changes in the balance of power at first delayed the submission of the Order, but the independent position of the Lower Vistula state was destroyed. The process was completed by the submission of the Lutheranized Grand Master Albrecht of Hohenzollern to the Crown of Poland in 1525.

Steady interference of the Polish kings with the domestic affairs of East Prussia—at the request of the diet—characterized the history of the sixteenth and seventeenth centuries in the province. In 1604, however, both the diet and Poland accepted the succession of the Brandenburger, which gave impetus to the regaining of the independence of the dukes of East Prussia.[44] The Thirty Years' War caused little damage in the province, which now became the financial and military nucleus of the Brandenburg-Prussian state of the Great Elector, Frederick William, who had exploited the Swedish-Polish War of Succession in order to attain recognition of his sovereignty over Prussia by Sweden (Treaty of Labiau, 1656) and by Poland (Treaty of Wehlau, 1657). He also broke through the *ständische* administration, established a ducal bureaucracy, and curtailed the powers of the diet.[45]

In this context, the importation of the so-called Masurians must be mentioned. The Thirteen Years' War and epidemics decimated the population of the southern districts of East Prussia during the fifteenth century. In order to remove the existing wilderness at the Lithuanian frontier and to repopulate the abandoned villages, the last Grand Masters invited Polish nobles and settlers into the land. Many immigrants came to the province and settled around Allenstein and in the eastern districts as far north as Rastenburg and Goldap.[46] By choosing Lutheranism in 1525, the Masurian settlers soon lost contact with Poland because the Protestant movement was defeated there by the united efforts of Cardinal Hosius and the Jesuits. While losing their national consciousness this way, the Masurians became culturally Germanized, although their dialect has survived until the twentieth century.

The next ambition the Hohenzollern dynasty attained was the recognition, by the European powers, of Frederick I of Brandenburg, son of the Great Elector, as King of Prussia in the year 1701. Now the position of the Hohenzollern Prince was not only that of a *Reichsfürst* (Prince of the Empire) but also that of a sovereign outside the Holy Roman Empire. However, it was not until the second half of the reign of Frederick II that Prussian policy turned toward the east and involved the state in the subsequent partitions of Poland.

The fate of "Royal Prussia," as West Prussia was called, within the Polish State developed differently. Its autonomy was respected only until the Union of Lublin (1567), an unfavorable change from 1456, when the Prussian Union and Danzig called in the Jagellos in order to preserve their autonomy against the encroachments of the Teutonic Order.[47] The ensuing counterreformation pitted Germans and Poles, as Protestants and Catholics, against each other. The southern districts and the small towns regressed in size and were easily Polonized. In the sixteenth and seventeenth centuries, a large part of the nobility, too, became Polish,[48] but the cities and the Vistula Delta remained solidly German. As the Nordic Wars decimated the population, Polish nobles promoted colonization and a new wave of German and Huguenot immigrants came to the province. Historians have divided opinions about the percentage of Germans in Royal Prussia by 1772. German historians speak of 50 per cent,[49] while Polish writers testify that on the basis of treasury records, the province must have been overwhelmingly Polish.[50] The actual percentage must have been around 35 to 40 per cent, for in 1910, German statistics, reporting on West Prussia, excluding Danzig, claimed only 48 per cent Germans in the province.

When combined Russian-Prussian pressure resulted in the First Partition of Poland in 1772, both East and West Prussia underwent economic changes for the better. This was due to their unification under one ruler and to the subsequent centralist Prussian administration, which had promoted commerce and industry. After the bishoprics of Ermland and West Prussia were united with the Prussian Crown, Danzig and Thorn followed suit in 1793. The fate of the farmers was eased, and relations with the Polish subjects remained generally cordial, despite minor desertions from Prussian conscription in the southernmost districts.[51] It is therefore not convincing to read about the extremely hostile attitude of the Polish population in the years of 1806 and 1807 and about their share in Polish units of the French army.[52] The heroic hole played by East Prussia in saving the Prussian state after the defeats of Auerstädt and Jena was, however, an exemplary proof of a different attitude. The southern districts of West Prussia were attached by Napoleon to the Grand Duchy of Warsaw but were restored to Prussia by the Congress of Vienna, and there began an era of good feelings between the reformers of the Hohenzollern realm, such as Prince Karl August von Hardenberg, and the Polish population of West Prussia.

This co-operation was not seriously hampered until the 1840's, and no parting of the ways occurred until the Kulturkampf. Yet as early as 1848, signs of the coming storm of nationality conflict could be observed in the foundation of the Polish National League at Berlin and in the protest of Ignatius Lysowski against the incorporation of West Prussia into the German Reich at Frankfurt.[53] Surviving the oppressive years of Prussian absolutism, the province sent four to six Polish deputies to the new Prussian diets of 1861 and 1863. The demands which the Polish deputies submitted to the Prussian diet were modest, and no great riots occurred during the Polish rising of 1863.[54] It was only in the wake of the Kulturkampf that the nationality conflict erupted in the province, though it remained absent in East Prussia.

The Fateful Path to the Abyss

1. SILESIA IN THE SECOND REICH

BETWEEN the two World Wars, numerous works were published on the events leading to the plebiscite and the subsequent partitioning of Upper Silesia and on the question of its ethnic character and economic value to Germany and Poland.[1] Although the explosive character of the problem was mitigated by the Geneva Accord of 1922 and by the meticulous observance of impartiality of the Mixed Arbitrary Tribunal, mutual recriminations contributed to the worsening of relations between the two countries.[2]

The origin of the dispute can be traced back to three different political, migratory, and socioeconomic trends of the second half of the last century, to wit:

(1) The tendency of the Reich government, under the chancellorship of Otto Fürst von Bismarck, to reduce the influence of the Roman Catholic church on the social and economic course followed by the government and the subsequent persecution of the Church in Prussia;

(2) The rise of the Polish intelligentsia in Posen and their infiltration into the province, creating centers of national Polish resistance;[3] and

(3) The grave social and economic inequalities surviving in the province, manifested by the estate-holders in their oppression of the agricultural and industrial workers, which led to the hatred of the Prussian system (identified with the rule of the estate-holders and industrial captains) by the masses, Germans and Poles alike.

These trends became apparent only gradually, and until 1900, Polish national agitation was absent from the province.[4] Karol Miarka's paper, *The Catholic*, denounced by Chancellor Bismarck as the precursor of the Polish party in the provinces, and even Napier-

35

alski's press[5] accepted the framework of the Prussian state. These men should be considered as protagonists of both German and Polish Catholics, protesting the May edicts and the abolition of Polish language instruction in the schools of Upper Silesia. Soon, however, the diligent and thorough methods of Prussian administration, calling for compulsory school attendance and promoting the building of libraries,[6] established literacy at an essentially higher level than in Congress Poland and Galicia.[7] This intellectual progress was then exploited by Catholic and national Poles. The articulateness of the masses could have been used either to save the province from Protestantism and Marxism by preserving its Catholic character, regardless of the language question, or to introduce the nationality question into the religious conflict, thereby splitting the unity of the Catholic camp.[8] The Poznanians, well versed in the techniques of nationality struggle, entered the province around 1890. Their fanatic adherence to Poland as a national community which had been crucified and buried but which would be resurrected[9] helped to arouse some native radicals. They questioned German superiority and demanded the introduction of Polish (not the native Water Polish dialect, which borrows many German abstract terms)[10] in schools and courts. They also strove for autonomy as a limited gesture toward national self-determination.

At this juncture, German-Polish unity within the clergy ended in the wake of national passions. The new leaders of the Upper Silesian Poles had, for the first time, become laymen instead of priests, and the religious issue played an increasingly smaller role, to reappear again only in 1919. The leaders of the prewar era were Wojtiech (Adalbert) Korfanty and J. J. Kowalczyk. For fifteen years, however, they failed to impress the masses. Korfanty himself was elected in 1903 to the Prussian diet and joined the Polish Club of deputies from Posen and West Prussia, but his colleague was defeated. It was not until 1907 that Polish candidates could, after persuading Polish Catholic leaders to co-operate with them, receive 40 per cent of the electoral votes in the province. That the votes of the plebiscite of 1921 and the elections of 1907 showed the same percentage in regard to national affinities[11] is significant.

The unexpected success of the Polish nationalists in a province which was known to be loyal to Prussia was in part due to the social-reform demands of the masses of industrial workers and peasants. The natural alliance of the state authorities and private vested interests in the liberal Prussian state placed a heavy burden on both the German and Polish workers in the region. Wages were considerably lower than in the Ruhr,[12] but it must be conceded that savings incentives and professional ambition among the Polish-speaking and bilingual workers were also at a much lower level than in western Germany. Overcrowded industrial settlements and slums like those of Königshutte promoted discontent and bred ignorance among the miners and foundry workers. Unequal land distribution also contributed to national antagonism. Fifty-two per cent of the arable land was in the hands of large estate-holders, and in 1910, seven of them owned a quarter of the entire province.[13] Thus nationality and social lines coincided to a dangerous extent. In the words of Miss Wambaugh:

> The landed aristocracy, the small professional class, in the industrial area, the business administration, technical workers, government officials, and employers, all German . . . the peasantry, miners and unskilled laborers mostly Polish-speaking . . . here was a fertile soil for the cultivation of national animosity.[14]

Yet it cannot be maintained that social conditions were inadequate everywhere. If compared to the conditions in Congress Poland and Galicia, the sanitation services, earning power, housing, and public health of the miners of Kattowitz were excellent and their food supply sufficient.[15] In the early 1900's, low-cost residential developments were built in the Industrial Triangle for miners and factory workers, many of them including gardens and relatively deluxe plumbing fixtures. Thus the improvement of housing conditions in Upper Silesia was praised by the Gainborough Commission of 1905-1906.[16] Furthermore, the ranks of the middle and lower bureaucracy and private officialdom were by no means closed to children of the workers, while veterans' organizations and social-service associations tried to ease the barren lot of the bilingual workers of the Triangle.[17] Even pro-Polish authors concede that nationality conflict would have been overcome and complete assimilation of the bilingual group by the Germans accomplished in two decades were it not for the Reich's defeat in the First World War.[18]

The imminence of the Russian danger, commonly feared by both Germans and Poles, made the two nationalities co-operate at the outset of the First World War.[19] During the war, however, conditions deteriorated in the province, and declining food supply and rampant inflation increased dissatisfaction with the Prussian regime. After the

victory of the Allied powers, voices were raised by the Korfanty group
and by Polish politicians in Warsaw and Poznań to urge a reunion of
the province with Poland.

The Poles triumphantly referred to the German census of 1910,
which reported 57 per cent of the population of Upper Silesia as
Polish-speaking or as both German- and Polish-speaking.[20] The Poles
were also favored by the aroused fears of the German and bilingual
Catholics of the province when, at the close of the November Revolution, a Social Democratic government was installed at Berlin. In addition, the new German government knew little or nothing about Upper
Silesia, while Polish elements succeeded in buying important newspaper plants[21] and increasing their propaganda activities. German
Catholics called for federalization and neutralization (*Bund der Ober-
schlesier*), pointing to the fact that for six centuries Upper Silesia had
been a German land and had lived and prospered even before the new
Poland was born.[22]

2. SILESIA OR ŚLĄSK?

At the Versailles Conference, the French delegation insisted upon
the cession of Upper Silesia to Poland. Its stand was accepted by a
commission of experts which favored Poland. President Wilson, who
declared that he would take the Polish side in any dispute between
Germany and Poland, supported the French position. Thus the automatic cession of the province was included in the draft treaty of May
9, 1919, only to arouse a storm of protest in Germany and Upper
Silesia.[23] The British Prime Minister, in view of German objections,
insisted on a plebiscite, though he, too, trusted Polish arguments and
considered the result of the plebiscite a foregone conclusion. He argued, however, that if the cession were the result of a plebiscite, the
Germans would acquiesce more readily.[24] Anxious to induce the Germans to sign the treaty and moved by the demonstrations in the province, Lloyd George persuaded his colleagues to write the plebiscite
provision into the final treaty. He faced the protests of Paderewski and
Dmowski, to whom he had remarked:

> "We have given freedom to Poland, Bohemia and Yugoslavia,
> and these are the countries which rebel against the idea of pleb-
> iscites. You are more imperialistic than the Great Powers."[25]

According to the statute, the plebiscite was to be held in one to two years, and German troops were requested to leave the province.[26] But before the International Commission (IK) arrived in Upper Silesia, the battle lines between the warring factions had already been drawn.

By May, 1919, the German population had recovered from the shock of defeat and founded the Free Association for the Defense of Upper Silesia (*Freie Vereinigung für die Verteidigung Oberschlesiens*) under the leadership of Dr. Hans Lukaschek.[27] The Association immediately called for demonstrations against the cession of the province. In July and August, the Poles expressed their sentiments in strikes and insurrections but were defeated by the German Reich Commissioner, Mr. Friedrich Otto Hörsig. The weakness of the Polish position had been revealed in the election of representatives to the German National Assembly in January, 1919, when most of the voters went to the polls despite Polish appeals for boycott,[28] and even the accumulated discontent of the war years failed to bring about a basic change of administration in the communal elections of November, 1919, though the Poles won in some communities.[29]

The administration of the IK was characterized by dissensions among the Commissioners themselves. Although the British and Italian Commissioners were mildly pro-German, they played only a limited role. The French Commissioner, General LeRond, was the expert who recommended to the Big Three the automatic cession of the province to Poland. He possessed full administrative powers and was assisted by the overwhelming French majority of the inter-Allied troops. After declaring that a "new era of freedom and justice" had been instituted, he confiscated firearms from the Germans and erected a new court of appeals to which sentences of German courts in the province could be appealed. Terror and counterterror became the order of the day, claiming many innocent victims. The well-organized and Polish-supported groups led by Korfanty, relying upon the mine-workers and peasants of the southeastern districts for support, appeared to take the political initiative. Korfanty promised economic and social reforms, a cow, and free land to every peasant and worker under Polish rule and was not beyond quietly supporting elements who assassinated Germans and pro-German or autonomist Silesians like Theophil Kupka.[30] In so doing, Korfanty could exploit former Prussian negligence and irresponsible German statements.

The second Polish riot, prepared in advance by Korfanty, caused the

breakdown of the traditional German safety policy (SIPO), and in-
junction was applied to any lockouts of pro-Polish agitators by German employers.[31] The results were increasing violence, especially in
the Industrial Triangle, and a corresponding improvement of the
Polish position, now organized under the Plebiscite Commissariat of
Wojtiech Korfanty. The German organization was also prepared for
the battle after having been reinforced by the creation of the Silesian
Committee and the German Plebiscite Commissariat under Dr.
Rudolph Urbanek.[32]

The results of the March 20, 1921 plebiscite failed to solve the basic
dilemma. Although the plebiscite showed that the majority of the
residents were in favor of German rule (59.5 per cent of 707,488 votes
for Germany and 40.5 per cent or 479,369 votes for Poland)[33] and that
the majority of the communities (792 in favor of Germany, 682 in
favor of Poland) voted to remain in the Weimar Republic,[34] the division of the area was a foregone conclusion.

The most significant result of the plebiscite was the high percentage
of the bilingual, or Polish-speaking, votes for Germany. The Reich
received 400,000 German-speaking and 307,000 Polish-speaking Silesian votes, while Poland received 5,000 German-speaking and 474,000
Polish-speaking Upper Silesian votes.[35] In not less than seven districts,
Polish-speaking pro-German votes exceeded Polish-speaking Polish
votes. All the cities voted German, as did the foundry workers, while
Polish votes were concentrated in the mines and certain rural areas.[36]
The Polish objection to the emigrant votes and to the inclusion of
the districts of Neustadt and Leobschütz in the plebiscite area is of
limited validity. There could have been at least as many Polish miners
living in western Germany and France among the returning voters
who had opted for Germany as there were former Prussian officials.
Furthermore, the plebiscite area was already reduced by the districts
of Grottkau, Neisse, and part of Neustadt in order to augment the pro-
Polish vote.[37]

The third Polish insurrection followed soon after the plebiscite.[38]
It was instigated by Wojtiech Korfanty, who reported in his newspaper
Grenzzeitung that the Allied Supreme Council was only going to cede
the districts of Rybnik and Pless to Poland and that even in the event
of a decision in favor of Poland for the Industrial Triangle the German owners would dynamite the mines and factories.[39] Both of these
statements were pure inventions by Korfanty, but they aroused the
workers. With the connivance of the French troops, whose commander

left for Paris, and with magnanimous support flowing across the Polish border, Korfanty soon gained control of the Triangle and eastern Upper Silesia to the River Oder and disarmed the German police. In answer, the Germans, too, organized self-defense units, and, after defeating the Polish insurgents at Annaberg, took the offensive, only to be halted by the Allies.[40] After many fruitless debates in the Allied Supreme Council, ambassadors of disinterested powers were asked to decide the exact frontiers of the province. The decision was strongly influenced by the results of the third Polish uprising and French pressure to transfer the industrial regions to Poland. When the final boundaries were drawn, 75 per cent of the territory and 57 per cent of the population were to remain with Germany, but the links between the cities and plants of the Triangle were severed, separating mines and factories, coke plants and blast furnaces. The smaller part of the industrial region remained in Germany, while the larger part, including Königshütte, Tarnowitz, Kattowitz, and the mines of Rybnik, became Polish.[41]

The economic losses of the province were great, despite the provision of the Geneva Accord for a fifteen-year regime of free exchange of goods between the partitioned halves. The Arbitration Tribunal and the Mixed Commission, set up in Beuthen and Katowice, were to struggle through a long line of complaints referring to the land expropriation decrees of Poland and to the activities of the German People's League and to school disputes, especially after the appointment of Mr. Grazynski as the Voivod of Śląsk (Silesia).[42] The economic prosperity of the area failed to decline permanently, however. Although the depression years caused misery in the mining areas, German economic expansion, following in the wake of National Socialist rearmament, assured a fair standard of industrial activity in German Upper Silesia. New Polish exports of Silesian coal to the Nordic states, a result of the long crisis in the British coal-mining industry in Polish Upper Silesia eased the crisis, but the vulnerability of Silesian coal mining to marketing changes, and the inability of Poland to expand production were proved between 1922 and 1939.

The distribution of nationalities underwent important changes in the interwar period. The German census of 1925 showed a decline in the number of Polish-speaking citizens in the province and a large increase in the number of those speaking both German and Polish.[43] The shifts were even more accentuated in the 1933 census. The overwhelming majority of those speaking both German and Polish seemed to have made their peace with Germany or were already German-ophile in 1921. The bickering about the schools for the Polish minority soon lessened as parents increasingly preferred to send their children to German schools.[44]

The unfair regime of Voivod Grazinsky caused even Wojtiech Korfanty to denounce Polish rule in Śląsk,[45] and it was no surprise that the Polish census of 1930 acknowledged the presence of only 75,000 Germans, though in 1921 their number in Polish Upper Silesia amounted to 264,000, in addition to 166,000 pro-German bilingual persons.[46] Economic and political pressure not only moved those speaking both German and Polish to register as Poles but also led to the "peaceful" expulsion of about 150-180 thousand Germans from Śląsk. All this in the name of national self-determination.

3. West Prussia or Pomorze?

Polish writers picture the situation prevailing in the Lower Vistula region as the resolute, gallant fight of the native Polish population against overwhelming, brutal, and imperialistic German aggression, a fight which still continues despite the German defeat of 1945.[47] By emphasizing the war guilt of Hitlerite Germany in regard to Poland in 1939 and the injustices committed by the German occupants, the Polish writers like to show, by the method of *post hoc quid ergo hoc,* the despicable character of German *Ostpolitik* and its aggressive imperialism directed against the Poles. This picture was widely accepted by British and American authors,[48] and it influenced many a British and American politician and statesman during the two World Wars.[49]

German writers, in turn, prefer to regard the question in the light of the decades before 1914, the "golden era" for all nationalities thriving in the region under the thorough and benign Prussian administration, through which they partook in the Reich, the leading power of its day. Though many writers are critical of the economic and social inequalities in Posen and West Prussia, they still consider the German element—which, in their opinion, fought a fair but losing battle against an increasingly subversive Polish movement which threatens to engulf the provinces and destroy the work of German settlers—to be the bearer of all cultural and economic progress in the provinces.[50] They place the emphasis on the ruthless, ultranationalist rule of Poland in Poznańia and Pomorze, which exerted an irresistible economic and political pressure on the German inhabitants of those provinces. The results are also cited: 512,183 Germans, more than two-thirds of the German residents of West Prussia, left that province between 1919 and 1926.[51] Thus German writers see in the interwar attitude of Poland toward national minorities and in her dealings with Danzig, resulting in more than one hundred appeals to the High Commissioner and the League's Council, the beginning of the cata-clysm which led to the murder and expulsion of the German element, not only in Poland, but also in purely German provinces.[52]

With the Poles recalling German atrocities during World War II and the Germans referring to the mass expulsions of 1945-47, it is evident that both nationalities have ample complaints against each other. Both the starvation trains of 1945-46, which carried the robbed and maimed German population of Silesia and Pomerania, and the concentration camps of Auschwitz and Belsen provide terrifying ex-amples of the base passions that can be produced in man by extreme nationalism. The argument advanced by both sides—that the other one started the chain reaction and that he himself was only a hapless victim—cannot be applied to the question any longer in view of the magnitude of the crimes.

The tragedy of the dramatic events of the last decades consists of the fact that despite the carefully nurtured arguments of Russian Communist and Polish propaganda, no historical, hereditary enmity has ever existed between Germans and Poles. With the exception of the early centuries, the only major struggle between the two nations, until recently, was the fight of Jagellonian Poland against the Teu-tonic Order, a heritage of the unification of the Polish kingdom with Lithuania. There was one single instance, between the demise of the Teutonic Order and 1772, when Brandenburgers fought Poles (1655), despite a number of wars over Baltic supremacy. These facts were em-phasized in some German publications as late as 1939. The defenseless position of Poland, which has brought the Russians to the neighbor-hood of Berlin in every war Prussia has fought against them, was men-tioned as the strategic reason for the occupation of West Prussia by Frederick II.[53]

In the twentieth century, replete with tragic suffering in German-Polish relations, politicians and scholars have tried to bridge the widening rift between the two nations, whose historic destiny was to defend Europe from the onslaught of the East and to raise the civiliza-tion of the peoples at the great European frontier. Wladyslaw Stud-nicki[54] and Marshal Pilsudski have realized that Poland can remain loyal to her destiny and retain her strength only if she is able to settle her differences with her western neighbor and to concentrate on defense against Russia. In Germany, too, voices of moderation have often been heard emphasizing the necessity of a common front against Russia, since 1917 under Communist domination. Yet the voices of *Gauleiter* Greiser, Koch, and Rosenberg and the propaganda of Roman Dmowski, who was reported to have ruled Poland dictatorially even after his death by his theory of Polish nationalism,[55] of Smogorzewski, Baginski, and Tymieniecki have influenced the fate of the two nations more than those calling for German-Polish reconciliation.[56]

While the dispute over Silesia was never an organic part of the 1772 heritage of German-Polish relations and represented a social and economic rather than an ethnic struggle, the history of the eastern marches of the Reich shows all the signs of a gradually developing fight for supremacy between Germans and Poles, ending in the defeat of the former in 1945.

In the Prussian province of Posen, there were some German enclaves and in the western part many German villages, but the basically Polish character of the province was never denied, even by Hakatist German writers.[57] To create a nucleus for a Polish independence movement, the Polish intelligentsia and estate-holders in Posen united to form a center from which money and agents were sent to other Prussian provinces containing Polish minorities and/or to Congress Poland. Pursuing a conciliatory course during the chancellorship of Caprivi,[58] the Posen Poles soon reverted to opposition within the state under Bülow while remaining loyal to the Crown. In December, 1918, however, aware of the Thirteenth Point of Wilson's declaration, the Posen Poles revolted against the German authorities and proclaimed their reunion with Poland.[59] After these events, the de-Germanization of the province, Poznań, gained momentum, and the percentage of the German element in the province declined from 28.7 per cent in 1910 to 9.0 per cent in 1926 and that of the city of Posen from 41.7 per cent to 3.5 per cent.[60] Even Hitler failed, prior to the conquest of Poland, to demand the return of Posen to the Reich.

The tragic story of an ethnically intimately mixed territory started to unfold in West Prussia with the founding of the Second Reich. Any state interference brought grave consequences to one of the nationalities, and Bismarck's *Kulturkampf* against Catholicism was here, too, accompanied by a struggle against Polish nationality. Polish instruction in the schools was abolished, and in 1886, a so-called "Prussian

Land Commission" was established, settling more than 21,000 German families in the province between 1886 and 1916.[61] It can be argued that these repressive measures, economic discrimination in the extension of credit to Polish farmers, and forced Germanization in the schools probably contributed to the Polish awakening rather than to the desired denationalization of the Polish element, the province having been ethnically divided since the fourteenth century. In order to counter German economic pressure, Polish banks and parcellization associations, which came into existence under the guidance of estate-owner Theodor Kalkstein,[62] succeeded in buying 29,079 hectares (71,-854 acres) for Polish settlers and peasants. Furthermore, the Kashubian districts of Putzig, Neustadt, Karthaus, Berent, Stargard, Strasburg, and Dirschau continued to elect Polish delegates to the Prussian diet.[63]

Yet because of the colonization and the superiority of cultural means and methods, the already substantial German minority succeeded in becoming a majority in the province. According to the 1910 census, 1,097,943 of the 1,703,474 people living in the province were German.[64] Overwhelmingly German areas were located around the mouth of the Vistula (the city of Danzig and the districts of Elbing and Marienwerder), in the western outskirts of the province around Flatow and Deutsch-Krone, and in the southern districts of the province between Schneidemühl and Graudenz (which connected the German-inhabited areas of Pomerania with those of East Prussia). In the districts ceded to Poland, too, 42.5 per cent of the population (421,033 out of 935,643) were Germans, and five out of eighteen districts had German majorities, while in another eight, the number of Germans exceeded 45 per cent.[65]

The problem of West Prussia therefore baffled the peacemakers at Paris. During the war, Polish demands for the province, including the city of Danzig and the district of Marienwerder, were registered by Polish leaders in the West, but France's support was forthcoming only after the collapse of the Russian Empire because of French concessions to Russia in regard to a free hand in Poland.[66] At the end of 1917, Paderewski interested President Wilson and Colonel House in Poland's problem of access to the sea.[67] An inquiry commission, whose Polish subcommittee was headed by Professor Robert H. Lord of Harvard, recommended to the President that "an independent and democratic Poland shall be established . . . and its boundaries shall be based on a fair balance of national and economic considerations, giving due weight to the necessity for adequate access to the sea." It was in the spirit of this document, signed by S. E. Mezes, D. H. Miller, and Walter Lippmann, that the Thirteenth Point of President Wilson's program was composed:

> An independent Polish state should be erected which would include the territories inhabited by indisputably Polish population, which should be assured a free and secure access to the sea.[68]

Less enthusiasm was aroused in Great Britain. British Prime Minister Lloyd George believed that the Poles were not especially suited to self-government, and many other voices in England entreated the government to favor the retention of West Prussia by Germany.[69]

The disputes over West Prussia and Danzig at the Paris Peace Conference were rooted in the ambiguous character of the Thirteenth Point of Wilson's famous program. Despite the "free and secure access" clause, the program failed to commit the American President to the cession of the Corridor and Danzig to Poland.[70] The Polish commission of experts (the Cambon Commission) favored the cession of the larger part of the province, including Danzig and the district of Marienwerder, to Poland.[71] The British Prime Minister immediately objected to the inclusion of not less than 2,132,000 Germans in the new Polish state. He declared in his memorandum of March 25, 1919:

> The proposal of the Polish Commission that we should place 2,100,000 Germans under the control of a people which is of a different religion and which has never proved its capacity of a stable self-government throughout its history must, in my judgment, lead sooner or later to a new war in the east of Europe.[72]

By March 25, however, Lloyd George had acquiesced in the formation of a "corridor" through West Prussia, giving the Poles territorial access to the sea. Yet a compromise was arrived at, with plebiscites to be held in the district of Marienwerder and the creation of the Free City of Danzig, instead of a cession of these areas to Poland. The results of the plebiscite at Marienwerder overwhelmingly favored Germany. Even Polish authors recognize that the Poles could not have won under any circumstances.[73]

The province of West Prussia was now cut into four parts, and two of them, Grenzmark and Marienwerder, were reallotted to Germany. The largest part of the province was awarded to Poland, while Danzig was to remain independent under League of Nations supervision but economically under Polish jurisdiction. The breakdown[74] was as follows:

Pomorze (Polish part): 935,643 persons (42.5 per cent German)
Free City of Danzig: 366,730 " (95.2 " " ")
Grenzmark,
   Marienwerder: 401,101 " (81.0 " " ")

The decision at Versailles separated East Prussia from the Reich, rendered transit from one to the other difficult, prevented the establishment of a stable economy in the province, and, by constantly irritating German pride and interfering with German economics, contained and nurtured the seeds of the Second World War. Yet, mention must be made of the fact that the part ceded to Poland had a slight Polish majority and that Prussian policy succeeded in alienating the new Polish middle class and large masses of farmers from the idea of living in any kind of a German state.

While Germanization was pursued by the Prussian authorities before the war, Polish authorities began to apply worse measures to promote Polonization. Denationalization progressed with unexpected rapidity. Anxious to remain under German rule and fearing the invasion of the Bolshevik armies approaching Warsaw in the summer of 1920, several hundred thousand people left Pomorze between 1918 and 1921 or were recalled by the German government as civil servants (e.g., railroad officials).[75] The majority of the emigrants, however, were not officials, for civil servants amounted to only 10 per cent of the German population of West Prussia and Posen.[76] Most of them were permanent residents who left in the wake of economic discrimination and the psychological effects of being condemned to live under what they called an "inferior" administration without the necessary legal and administrative protection.[77] The kind of rule the Poles exercised over the Germans in Pomorze can be gauged from the speech given by the Polish Minister of the Interior on November 26, 1924, in the Sejm:

"I am a resident of this land [i.e., Pomorze]. I know the Germans, their ways and methods, and I am [therefore] aware of the great danger menacing us from their side. . . . I consider it as a prominent task to induce every German whom we possibly can rid ourselves, to leave Poland."[78]

Simultaneously with the expulsion of the optants, German real estate was liquidated by arbitrary land reforms which hit German estate-owners in 90 per cent of the cases.[79] German firms were boycotted, provisions were made for the employment of a large percentage of Poles as officials in plants and enterprises,[80] and the pensions of retired people were reduced.[81] The detrimental effects of the land reform on German estates[82] can be summarized as follows:

Holdings (in hectares)	In 1926	In 1927	In 1928
German	44,960	38,673	32,108
Polish	4,223	12,328	17,000
			(approximately)

The cultural life of the German community was also interfered with, and German Roman Catholics were pressed to become Poles.[83] The famous incident of St. Francis Church at Poznań was only one of the many. German schools were also restricted, though not abolished, because the Minority Treaty which Poland had to sign with the Allied and Associated Powers in 1919 had restricted Poland's freedom of action in this field.

The results of the Poles' repressive policies were overwhelming. By 1929, only 117,251 Germans (12.4 per cent) lived in the province of Pomorze, and even the cities had lost their German character. The loss of 304,782 Germans in Pomorze and of 207,301 in the Bromberg-Netze area, formerly belonging to the province of West Prussia, was an open criticism of Polish minority policies.[84]

4. THE EVENTFUL YEARS OF THE FREE CITY OF DANZIG

The creation of the Free City of Danzig as a compromise failed to settle the difference between Poland and Germany with respect to traffic on the Vistula. The incorporation of Danzig into Poland would have provided for a more effective German argument with regard to the "corridor" because, after including the port city, the Polish Corridor would have possessed a clear German majority of 57 per cent.[85] The compromise solution was also attacked by Germany and failed to satisfy Poland. Therefore, Warsaw constantly attempted to reduce the independence of the Free City to paper formulas by "interpreting" the various documents providing for the statute of Danzig.

National passions were aroused before the Danzig Constitution was passed. A strike of the Communist and Social Democratic dock workers prevented the city administration from unloading ammunition needed to stem the Soviet Russian tide before Warsaw in August, 1920.[86] Although the armaments were delivered, with British help, without incident, Polish resentment against Danzig's attitude of "high treason" failed to abate for years and resulted in repeated attempts to maintain Polish military forces and munitions depots on the territory of the Free City.[87]

Polish attempts to introduce the prerogatives of sovereignty into the postal service of Danzig,[88] a right belonging, under international law, to the domestic jurisdiction of any state, led to a number of complaints by the Danzig Senate to the High Commissioner of the League and its Council and to some political-judicial compromises by the League and the Permanent Court of International Justice.[89]

The administrative disputes usually arose from the divergent interpretations of the Treaty of Versailles and the Paris agreement of the contenders. To the Senate of Danzig, the Free City was a sovereign state, a subject of international law, and the transfer of her consular and diplomatic functions to Poland and of economic rights on her territory had not impaired her sovereign jurisdiction.[90] To Poland, Danzig was a part of the state, though granted a large amount of home rule. And as a matter of course, economic conflicts soon followed legal and administrative arguments.

Unable to impose its sovereignty on Danzig, the Polish government soon decided to build a second port in order to exert more pressure on the Free City and to render itself independent of the port of Danzig in case of future hostilities.[91] Preparations began in 1920. There was a dispute as to whether the port of Tczew (Dirschau) should be expanded or a new port built at Gdynia.[92] The proximity of Danzig, the confused real-estate situation, and the risk of the shorter ice-free period militated in favor of the new port at Gdynia. The cost of the port at Gdynia was about one hundred million gold zlotys, but the port had a capacity of thirty million metric tons by 1935.[93] French capital contributed to the building of the port, which was actually finished by 1929. A Polish Senator expressed the aims of Poland as follows: "Our relations with Danzig have become so intolerable that only a radical solution could help."

The rise of a rival port had very dire consequences for the Free City. By 1933, Gdynia outdistanced Danzig in regard to the volume of goods. As a result, the collapse of the commercial enterprises of Danzig seemed imminent, and more than forty thousand people lost their source of livelihood.[94] This was a powerful factor in bringing the National Sozialistische Deutsche Arbeiterpartei (NSDAP) to power in the Free City. The final compromise, made under the impact of Polish-German *rapprochement* in the fall of 1933, resulted in a broad agreement. This guaranteed the transit traffic of emigrants and Polish state imports and exports to Danzig and provided for a near equality in the level of port dues. The compromise failed to oblige Poland to forestall the economic decline of the Free City by using Danzig at the expense of Gdynia, and the Hanseatic city was now continuously blackmailed by Poland rather than vice versa.[95]

Other disputes originated in Polish economic rights in the field of customs policy. Were the particular interests of Danzig to be considered by Warsaw in formulating its policies, even though they might be opposed to Polish interests in general? Should the definition of interests be made in Warsaw or by the Senate of Danzig? Danzig's decreasing share of customs receipts (1924, $4,132,000; 1933, $1,005,-000)[96] and disputes about currency problems were also subjects of international disputes.[97]

The rights of the Polish minority (estimated at from 5 to 9 per cent, depending on the nationality of the author)[98] were also to fill volumes of League of Nations proceedings, especially before 1933, for after the German-Polish nonaggression pact of 1934, minority conflicts receded.

The crux of the Danzig domestic policy consisted of the ambiguous position of being politically independent and economically tied to Poland. With respect to law, culture, and sentiment, Danzig was part of the Reich, and there was considerable interchange between Danzig and Reich civil services. Furthermore, Danzig followed very closely the pattern of the Reich's party politics, both before and after 1933.[99] The only difference between the platforms of the Danzig and Reich parties was that the Danzig center and leftist parties followed a more conciliatory policy toward Poland than did their brothers in the Reich.

National Socialism, too, arose in Danzig as the result of feelings of national humiliation aggravated by an economic depression. The Volkstag elections of November 16, 1930, gave the party of Greiser and Rauschning twelve of seventy-two seats, about 16 per cent of the vote as compared to 18 per cent in the Reich in the same type of elections in 1930. There was, however, a wide gap between Dr. Ziemach's conservatives and the National Socialist party, which clamored for participation in government.[100] It was only in the May 28, 1933 elections that the NSDAP scored 50.1 per cent, or 107,331, of the votes and won thirty-eight of seventy-two seats and that Dr. Hermann Rauschning was appointed President of the Senate.[101]

Under Herr Rauschning, Danzig's foreign policy followed the switch of Hitler's policy toward Poland.[102] Of course Hitler's change of mind was a result of his evaluation of the international situation, but that Rauschning clearly perceived the danger, in the form of Bolshevik Russian aggression, threatening both nations may be believed. It is small wonder that within three years Rauschning found himself in exile, denouncing the German Führer. His views serve as proof that even among German nationalists there were thinkers who, unaffected by the germ of hatred of Poland, were ready to co-operate with the new state against the Soviet Russian menace. It was a real tragedy for both nations that these views were silenced by the rise of the unscientific Rosenbergian myth of the Nordic race and by the corresponding German contempt of Slavs.

German-Polish relations continued to be cordial until 1939, although the "honeymoon" period had worn off somewhat by 1936. Hitler was anxious not to arouse Polish apprehension while engaged in the west and the south, but he reserved for himself the right to renew his demands for a solution of the Corridor and Danzig questions. The idea of building an *autostrada* was presented to Poland as early as 1935.[103] Foreign Minister Beck's policy was, in turn, affected by the defense-mindedness of the French, whose military alliance had become increasingly worthless, and by French efforts to draw Soviet Russia into the concert of European powers against Hitler. Fearing Russia's power, Beck was willing to deal with Hitler while gambling on an independent Polish policy in view of the alleged incompatibility of National Socialism and Bolshevism. Thus Polish foreign policy was based on the idea of keeping Germany and Poland in perfect balance. Although Poland had co-operated with Germany at the Munich crisis because of Teschen, she declined German offers to give Poland a free hand in the Ukraine in a future war against Russia. It was this Polish aloofness toward Germany and the Western bloc which caused Hitler to shift his policy toward the U.S.S.R. in 1939.

Between 1935 and 1937, Danzig was again put on the agenda of the League because of the many complaints emanating from the anti-Nazi opposition against the NSDAP regime.[104] With Poland only moderately interested, Geneva, rather than uphold its role as the protector of the Constitution, appeased Greiser in disregard of the oppressive measures of his government. It was not until the spring of 1939 that the German-Polish conflict over the Free City and the Corridor occupied the chancelleries of Europe. Yet at that time neither of the parties was willing to compromise.

Before discussing the events leading up to the Second World War, I should describe the interwar situation of East Prussia. The Allenstein plebiscite in the southern districts resulted in an overwhelming German victory because the Protestant Masurians were not in favor of Catholic rule, despite the fact that a Polish dialect was their mother tongue.[105] The Treaty of Versailles had detached only the district of Soldau, and it had been decided that Memel and the territories of East Prussia north of the river Memel should form another free state. The latter, however, was invaded and occupied by Lithuanian military forces in 1923 in open defiance of the League's directive. The economic crises of the province continued to result in large-scale emigration. The crisis was a composite result of unprofitable estates,[106] of the existence of the Polish Corridor, isolating the province and rendering it defenseless, and of the rapid rise in population. Agricultural subsidies had to be given by the Reich government, but the Poles have not contested East Prussia and the Masurians were rapidly Germanized in their outlook. Only extremist military writers in Poland considered East Prussia a knife in the flesh of their country, rendering the Corridor and Poland's access to the sea indefensible in case of hostilities, and advocated its conquest. Still, Polish designs on the province were not of an immediate or pressing character, and only a minority of Polish opinion supported such claims before 1939.

CHAPTER IV

German and Russian Designs on Poland

1. PRELUDE TO WAR

THE conclusion of the nonaggression treaty between Hitler and Marshal Pilsudski in January, 1934, represented an important milestone in Polish-German relations.[1] Danzig ceased to be a sore wound, German demands to the Corridor were stifled by National Socialist censorship, and the requests of the German minority in Poland went unheeded by Berlin.[2] Of course there was considerable compromise on the side of Poland as well, for she had not only to tolerate, but also to entertain, cordial relations with the National Socialist government in Danzig and to desist from supporting the justified grievances of the bourgeois and socialist groups in the city, which were eliminated by Dr. Greiser's unconstitutional acts. Furthermore, in Poland the organization of the Volksdeutsche under National Socialist leadership could only be delayed, not prevented, by Warsaw. Despite the sacrifices involved for Germany, the treaty was Hitler's first diplomatic triumph, one which rid him of a small but formidable foe in the east, an enemy capable of occupying Berlin before the completion of German rearmament plans. By means of the treaty (because any French guarantee to Poland in case of a German attack not directed simultaneously against France had become increasingly theoretical)[3] Hitler was able to tear apart the chains of the anti-German French alliance system in the east. By doing so, the German Führer acquired a free hand to concentrate upon the problems on his southeastern frontiers. Poland, too, gained by the agreement, which delivered her from a policy of complete dependence on France. This development enabled her to reduce her strength on the western frontiers and greatly strengthened her hand in relation to her great eastern adversary, the U.S.S.R.

A constant deterioration in German-Russian relations between 1933 and 1938 seemed to prove the validity of Marshal Pilsudski's and Foreign Minister Jozef Beck's theses that Germany would concentrate on a violently anti-Russian policy only if Poland were to display a benevolent or at least neutral attitude toward the Third Reich. Or, vice versa, a Poland strongly antagonistic toward Germany would always have to fear the possibility of partition as a result of a Russo-German alliance.[4] The basic weaknesses of the treaty consisted, however, of two deficiencies insufficiently realized in those years. These were:

(1) The German-Polish differences over Danzig and the Corridor, the solution of which was left for a later time; and

(2) The unwillingness of Hitler to permit an independent Polish policy toward the West, should he succeed in consolidating his position in the southeast, and his insistence on using Poland as an advance guard, completely dependent on German good will in conducting her Russian policy.[5]

These two weaknesses of the pact were reinforced by serious miscalculations as to the intention of the governments and the strength of public opinion in the two countries.

Marshal Pilsudski and Foreign Minister Beck were convinced that because of ideological antagonism, Germany would not have the opportunity to come to an agreement with the U.S.S.R.—in contrast to the days of Generals Seeckt and Schleicher. The assurances of Hitler and Göring[6] to this effect were taken at face value and caused Beck to pursue a policy of nonalignment until March, 1939, and only Hitler's march into Slovakia opened his eyes. However, his hasty actions between March and September, 1939, seemed to weaken the justice of his cause.

The leaders of the Third Reich also began with erroneous assumptions about the restoration of cordial relations with the Polish people through a nonaggression treaty without a simultaneous solution of the transit and Danzig dilemmas. Hitler's anti-Semitic policies and his oppressive restriction of fundamental civil liberties in the first years of his rule greatly increased the number of his enemies among the democratic elements in both the western European countries and in Poland and heightened their distrust of his intentions. The Poles were also aware of the tenacious character of German claims to West Prussia and Posen before 1934 and of the emotional storm the Upper Silesian plebiscite had aroused in the Reich.[7] They remembered the *Saison-staat* expression of Trevirianus and the assiduous German propaganda in the early thirties, which led Sir Winston Churchill to declare on November 22, 1932:

> If the English government really wanted to do something for the promotion of the peace, it should take the lead in revising the peace treaties, and should open up the question of Danzig and the Corridor.[8]

Or, to paraphrase Ribbentrop in his January, 1939 interview with Lipski, ninety-nine out of a hundred Britons or Frenchmen would consider Germany's claim to the Corridor as just.[9] The Poles have not forgotten Hitler's expansionist ideas, as expressed in *Mein Kampf,* either.[10]

The Poles were therefore determined to "solve" the question of the Corridor by means of a "voluntary" emigration of the German population. The anti-German feeling of the masses in the western provinces united itself with the anti-Nazi attitude of the opposition parties and Jewish elements. Poland was ruled in a rather autocratic fashion by Marshal Pilsudski and, after his death, by the Army, as represented by Marshal Edward Smigly-Rydz and Foreign Minister Beck. The role played by the pro-French Army leadership, a natural brake on Beck's foreign policy, which had been pro-German, and the courage of the Polish nationalists was greatly underestimated by the German Chancellor. Hitler also had an exaggerated idea of Beck's anti-Russian ambitions. Beck was little interested in another march on Kiev, especially since he did not want to give his western neighbor a chance to gain absolute hegemony in east central Europe.[11] Thus Göring's overture[12] and Ribbentrop's proddings in regard to the Anti-Comintern Pact and a common Polish-German policy toward the U.S.S.R. fell on deaf ears. The frequent feeble attempts to gain Polish consent to the construction of an *autostrade* through the Corridor were never answered *in concreto* by Warsaw, though the official rejection was not forthcoming until the January, 1939 visit of Ribbentrop to the Polish capital.[13]

Beck's policy, based on Marshal Pilsudski's concept that the security of the state should never be based on alliances but only on the military strength and political resources of the state, required, simultaneously, nonentanglement with the two neighbors and correct relations with them. This policy was based on three assumptions, to wit: (1) the attention of Germany and Russia could be diverted to other areas that interested them, a hypothesis which worked as long as the Japanese advance in China harassed the U.S.S.R., and the conquest of Czechoslovakia, preceded by the Austrian *Anschluss,* provided Germany with suitable objects of expansion; (2) the French army was superior to the Wehrmacht in the extent of armament (this was true only until 1938); and (3) a friendly policy toward Hungary and Rumania could be pursued, and such a course would result in neutralizing German influence because such a policy provided an alternative course to anti-Communists in the region.

Beck's policy enabled him, as an indirect consequence of the Munich Agreement of September 28, 1938, to appropriate some of the Polish-populated frontier districts of Czechoslovakia which the Czech government occupied during Poland's dark weeks in 1920. Poland actually helped Germany to win at Munich, since her troop deployments prevented Russian action during the crucial hours.[14] Although Beck attempted to proceed with a minimum of dependence upon Germany, his ties with the West were loosened, and relations with the U.S.S.R. were so strained as to be damaged beyond repair, despite the normalization attempts of February, 1939. It is ironical that by supporting the German adventure in the Sudeten crisis, Beck actually encouraged the very same German demands which triggered the Second World War and caused Poland's downfall.

On October 24, 1938, the German Foreign Minister mentioned to the Polish Ambassador to Berlin, Walter Lipski, that the Führer intended to effect a general settlement of Polish-German relations. The offers to Poland included the renewal and extension of the nonaggression treaty from ten years to twenty-five years, the guarantee of Poland's frontiers by Germany, and the addition of a mutual-consultation clause to the treaty, ostensibly to assure a common German-Polish policy toward Russia, the Jewish question, and the problem of colonies.[15] The German demands were detailed as follows:

(1) The Free State of Danzig should return to the German Reich;

(2) Germany should be permitted to build an extraterritorial highway and railroad through the Corridor; and

(3) Poland should accede to the Anti-Comintern Pact.

In return, Poland was to be granted an extraterritorial highway and railway and a free port in the territory of Danzig and a further guarantee of a free market for her goods in the city of Danzig.

The demands, though modest, have to be interpreted in the light of the Hossbach Document,[16] a record of Hitler's conversations with the military leaders of the Reich in 1937 wherein Hitler clearly foresaw that the eastern question could be solved only by a war enabling Germany to acquire sufficient additional territories. Therefore, any acceptance of the German proposals by Beck would have ultimately resulted in total Polish dependence upon the Third Reich, without the prospect of an equal or near-equal partnership.

In his instructions to Lipski concerning Danzig, Beck used uncompromising language.[17] He traced the development of the city of Danzig from its beginning and declared that Polish rights could never be guaranteed if the city were to form a part of the Third Reich. He finished the instruction with the categoric threat:

> In consideration of all these factors, and desirous of bringing about a stabilization of the situation, through a friendly understanding with the government of the *Reich,* the Polish government proposes to substitute a bilateral Polish-German treaty for the guarantees given and privileges enjoyed by the League of Nations. This bilateral treaty would guarantee the further existence of the Free City of Danzig in a form that would assure the freedom of the national and cultural life of its German majority on the one hand, and the rights of Poland on the other hand. Despite the complex character of such a system, the Polish Government is compelled to state that any other solution, especially the incorporation of the Free City into the *Reich,* would beyond doubt lead to a conflict. This conflict would not only cause local difficulties but would render Polish-German relations and understanding doubtful in its entirety.[18]

Lipski transmitted the threat to Ribbentrop on November 19, but the German Foreign Minister failed at that time to reject the Polish counterproposal. Berlin received another warning through the Polish Minister at Danzig, who told Dr. Greiser:

> The second national question was the sea. To the south the boundaries of Poland enjoyed the natural protection of the

Carpathians. In the east and in the west, there were two ideological walls with fixed boundaries which, by treaty, could not be altered. To the north was the open sea, toward which Poland and the entire Polish people were striving. And Danzig was included in this part of the Polish national question. Thus Danzig was a Polish national question less as a city than its role of providing free access to the sea. From this viewpoint and this interpretation . . . one would meet with resistance from every Pole, if one desired to cut off this access through any political action whatsoever.[19]

It seems that Hitler was anxious to come to a "general settlement" with Poland on his own terms. His desire was also frustrated by Ribbentrop's clumsy attempts to put pressure on Warsaw. Whether out of arrogant disregard of Polish interests or out of lack of resolution and a clear-cut decision, Berlin succeeded, through its handling of the Carpatho-Ukraine and Slovakian questions in the winter of 1938-39, in arousing Polish distrust and further antagonism,[20] despite the realization that even if Beck were willing to support German demands, he would still face a tremendous struggle with the Army and Polish public opinion.[21] The zig-zag policy on Carpatho-Ukraine (as Subcarpathian Ruthenia is incorrectly called in English) led to Polish normalization of relations with the U.S.S.R.[22] and rendered the pressure of the pro-British elements around the Army irresistible to Beck. Finally, Germany failed to profit by her pro-Ukrainian policy because she agreed, six months too late, to the Hungarian seizure of the area at the time of the liquidation of Czechoslovakia.[23]

At Obersalzberg, Hitler guaranteed to Beck that "in the future, political solution [i.e., the liquidation of Czechoslovakia] would never take place unilaterally; rather, all countries interested in Czechoslovakia would participate therein," only to renege on his promise two months later.[24] Despite Beck's opposition to German demands, Ribbentrop left for Warsaw on January 25, 1939, without any diplomatic preparation. The Polish Foreign Minister regarded his German colleague unfavorably: as a diplomatic novice who had close connections with the *Junkers* and the *Deutsch-Nationalen*. He also believed that the German Foreign Minister, often carried away by his ambitions, transgressed Hitler's instructions.[25] The only results of the conference were Ribbentrop's acceptance of Polish reasons for not acceding to the Anti-Comintern Pact[26] and the conclusion of a gentleman's agreement which provided that in case of the withdrawal of the League, the *status quo* would be maintained by both powers until a bilateral agreement on the Free City could be negotiated.[27]

Beck's position as a spokesman of the pro-German orientation of Polish foreign policy deteriorated in February and March. Student demonstrations in Danzig, regardless of whether they were aroused by fanatical National Socialists or Polish nationalists, led to several protest marches in front of the German Embassy in Warsaw.[28] Through the administrative decrees of Voivoid Grazynski, the remaining Polish-Silesian German estate-holders were expropriated, while their Polish colleagues were left almost untouched.[29] The minority question also reached an impasse,[30] and a detachment of Polish policy from Berlin in case of German rejection of the last Polish offer in the Danzig and highway question was prepared and a suitable alternative by far-reaching agreements with Britain sought.[31]

Yet it was Berlin, rather than Warsaw, which caused the final showdown. Hitler's march on Prague on March 14, 1939, shocked Beck into action not only because of the liquidation of Czechoslovakia, an artificial creation of the peacemakers of 1919, but also because a German protectorate had been established in Slovakia. German control of Slovakia endangered Polish security in the south, and although Beck's direct reaction remained moderate,[32] he considered Hitler's move a direct threat. His fears were reinforced by the German-Lithuanian treaty of March 22, 1939,[33] which created the precedent for the reincorporation of a free city detached from Germany at Versailles and illegally occupied by Lithuania in 1923. Moreover, the German move increased the pressure on Poland's northern frontiers by extending the Reich's influence over Lithuania.[34]

Beck now became the protagonist of a *rapprochement* with the Western powers in order to restore the balance. The fall of Prague had shocked British Prime Minister Chamberlain into undertaking immediate action,[35] so that the Polish *démarche* was heartily welcomed, since it had already been officially solicited earlier by Great Britain.[36] Yet British attempts to create an anti-German coalition, though successful in the case of Poland, lacked geographic cohesion in view of the progress of German rearmament and came too late.

The showdown in German-Polish negotiations came on March 26, 1939. Immediately after the publication of the German-Lithuanian treaty, Poland called some reservists to the colors in confirmation of the grave view she took of the developments.[37] German intentions to-

ward Poland were not peaceful either, though the prospect of an immediate military campaign was not foreseen by Hitler when he briefed
the commanders of his army.[38] Ribbentrop, surprisingly, continued to
underestimate the seriousness of the situation, even after his fateful
talk with Ambassador Lipski on March 26. After examining Beck's
counterproposal, which Lipski had submitted, Ribbentrop wrote:

> Poland would like to get off as cheaply as possible in the present
> discussions. . . . Poland's compromise proposal might not repre-
> sent the Polish Government's last word.[39]

After having been informed that the German government had rejected his counterproposals, Beck considered further German-Polish
negotiations futile.[40] He decided to visit London and conclude binding agreements with the British. Even before his departure, as a result
of the Sir Howard Kennard–Beck talks on the thirtieth of March,
Prime Minister Chamberlain gave his guarantee of Polish sovereignty
in the House of Commons:

> In order to make perfectly clear the position of His Majesty's
> Government in the meantime before these consultations are con-
> cluded [namely Beck's visit] I have now to inform the House that
> during the period, in the event of any action which clearly
> threatened Polish independence, and which the Polish Govern-
> ment considered it vital to resist with its national forces, His
> Majesty's Government would feel themselves bound at once to
> lend the Polish Government all support in their power. They
> have given the Polish Government all assurance to this effect.[41]

Hitler's reaction to the British moves and to Poland's acceptance
of the British offer on April 7 was typical. While on the one hand he
was afraid that the success of London's containment moves might prevent any further German expansion, he could not, on the other, believe that England and France would be willing to enter a German-
Polish war. His disbelief was nurtured by Ribbentrop, who earnestly
thought that the West would not fight. For a few months, Hitler remained cautious. He was satisfied with abrogating the German-Polish
treaty of 1934 and increasing the political and psychological pressures
on Poland. Yet the events of March 26 and April 7 caused him to
undertake an agonizing reappraisal of his foreign policy. The French

accession to the British guarantee of April 6[42] and renewed British moves to bring about a *rapprochement* with the Soviet Union necessitated a reconsideration of the position of the U.S.S.R. in the conduct of German foreign policy.[43] Stalin, too, was at that time weighing the advantages and disadvantages of both a Western and a German alliance. And Hitler had more to offer.[44]

The history of the next five months of Polish-German relations is replete with border incidents on the German side and brutalities committed against the minorities on the Polish side. In this respect, German charges of Polish oppression were exaggerated in order to serve as a smoke screen for the forthcoming invasion of Poland.[45] However, Polish impatience and intolerance and the propaganda of the Western Association contributed to the misery of the German minority in Poland during the summer of 1939.[46] Whatever the many cases of both loyalty and disloyalty among the *Volksdeutsche* in Poland before 1939, their ties with Poland were loosened by the attitude of the Polish authorities, who regarded them as an actual or potential fifth column, a view which was, at best, partially justified.

Regardless of the many frontier incidents, quite often provoked by Germany, and the minority complaints, well known in Berlin, Hitler had no justification for his attack on Poland, which involved not only the violation of the Kellogg-Briand Pact but also the certainty of a world war.[47] So when the German army moved into Poland, the National Socialist policy of conquest, determined to create German supremacy in eastern Europe, was clearly unveiled and judged guilty in the court of world opinion. This policy placed a very heavy burden on the shoulders of the German people and the Reich government and made the world forget the unjust blunders committed in the Treaty of Versailles, rendering the claims of the German minority in Poland inconsequential. By daring to place himself above international law and morality, Hitler brought severe retaliation upon both his people and himself. Despite the lofty principles of the Four Freedoms and the Atlantic Charter, the punishment meted out to Germany, with loudly voiced Soviet Russian approval, also failed to heed the precepts of international law.

2. The German "New Order" in Poland

One of the darkest chapters in the modern history of east central Europe commenced on September 1, 1939, when the German army entered Poland. The action not only precipitated the Second World War, plunging Europe into utter misery and transferring world power to the U.S.S.R. and the United States, but also destroyed the last chance for German-Polish and German–east central European co-operation against the intervening Soviet Russian power. Just as Polish-Ukrainian antagonism prevented the rise of an independent Ukraine in 1918-1920 and allowed the Ukraine's enormous industrial power and large population to serve the war machine of the U.S.S.R., so, too, did the German-Polish war of 1939 defeat all efforts to maintain a common front against Soviet Russian imperialism. Molotov expressed the position of the *tertius gaudens* in his speech before the Supreme Soviet on September 1, 1939:

> If those gentlemen have such an uncontrollable desire to fight, let them do their own fighting without the Soviet Union. We shall see what fighting stuff they are made of.[48]

The consequences of national antagonism in the face of the common danger were catastrophic for both belligerents. Poland and a large part of Germany ultimately fell prey to Soviet Russian power, and any semblance of a European balance of power disappeared.

The five years of German occupation form a continuous story of brutal terror countered by underground sabotage, which heightened the suppression exercised by the occupying power. A chain reaction which aroused the hatred of the Polish people against Germany to a degree where gentle emotions, religious convictions, and moral precepts yielded to murder and the other evil passions in man was thus started. The contempt shown and the political repression practiced by Hitler's Germany evoked a violent reaction in the Polish mind, for in view of the past events only a small impetus was needed to renew the struggle between the two nationalities with explosive violence.

The massacre of a part of the German population of Bromberg,[49] committed by excited Poles in the early days of September, 1939, as documented by the *Gräberstelle* Posen in 1939-40, provoked a mass murder of Polish civilians by the German armies invading the city, an evil portent for future relations between the two peoples. With the Wehrmacht came the German courts, empowered to pass their verdicts according to the German Criminal Code, although the offenses might have been committed before September 1, 1939.[50] On October 8, 1939, the German Führer decreed a new partition of rump Poland under German occupation. The pre-1918 German provinces of Posen, West Prussia and eastern Upper Silesia were reannexed to the Reich, as were the districts of Ciechanów, Lodź, Oświęcim, and the mining areas northeast of Kraców. These territories were to form the *Reichsgaue* of West Prussia and Posen. The latter was enlarged in the east and renamed Warthegau in the spring of 1940.[51] The annexed areas included about 35,100 square miles and 10,740,000 inhabitants. The remainder of Poland was organized into the *General Gouvernement für die besetzten polnischen Gebiete* (known as the General Gouvernement) and comprised 36,270 square miles and 11,484,000 people.[52] Discounting the area of Lodź, incorporated into the new Warthegau but excluded from the October, 1939 decree, the population of the annexed territories was as follows: Poles, 7,817,000; Germans, 597,784; others, 665,914.[53]

The tremendous disproportion of Germans to Poles could no longer be explained by Polish denationalization policies and voluntary or involuntary German emigration in the 1920's. For reasons of historical objectivity, however, mention should be made of the fact that in the territories annexed or reannexed the percentage of German nationals was almost 25 per cent in 1914.

The arbitrary character of the National Socialist leadership's "living space" policy was clearly manifested in the regulations of the government and the party sent to the new German authorities in the annexed areas (Ostgebiete).[54] Under wartime conditions, the expropriation of Polish estates and industrial and commercial enterprises proceeded several times as fast as the Polish take-over of German properties in the interwar period. In order to emphasize the German character of the annexed provinces, 850,000 Poles and Jews were deported from them to the General Gouvernement in the fall and winter of 1939 under very harsh conditions.[55] Economic and demographic considerations soon brought to an abrupt end the capricious expulsion procedures in West Prussia and Posen because German settlers were unavailable, except for a few "repatriates" from the Baltic States, eastern Poland, and Bessarabia whose homes were engulfed by the Red Army under the provisions of the 1939 treaty with Berlin.

The change in nationality distribution of the provinces of the Ostgebiete was also promoted by the use of the German People's List (*Deutsche Volksliste*), to which persons of German descent and children of mixed Polish-German marriages who had lost their national consciousness, as well as German nationals and members of the former

nationally conscious minority in Poland, were admitted. Acceptance
of the declaration of willingness to live in the future as Germans and
a fluent knowledge of the German tongue were conditions for admission.[56] A new category, unknown to international law, was created for
the so-called "Polonized" Germans and Poles, suitable for Germanization, who had never displayed any German national consciousness.
These groups could also be registered in the *Volksliste* and acquire
German citizenship *auf Widerruf*, which meant that their German
citizenship could be revoked. If not revoked, they could, however,
later acquire *Reichsbürgerschaft*, as full German citizenship was
called.[57] The German People's List was also extended to the General
Gouvernement, but with little or no success in recruiting future Germans. As Hitler told the German Reichstag, "the problems which have
to be solved there, will not be solved at the conference table or in
editorial offices, but only through the patient work of decades."[58]

By the end of 1940, order was restored in the annexed provinces,
which now contained a native population composed of Poles, German
repatriates from the east, and some German officials settling in the
provinces from the Reich proper. The percentage of the Germans now
amounted to from 22 to 25 per cent. The German character of the
provinces, though largely external and artificial, was emphasized by
the absence of any Polish journals, papers, or associations. Even Polish
sport clubs were forbidden by German authorities.[59] Polish schools
were practically nonexistent, save those of the underground, for the
education of the Polish people was to be restricted to an absolute
minimum.[60]

In the General Gouvernement, the National Socialist New Order
faced insurmountable difficulties. There remained no Polish officials
who were willing to assume the responsibility for local government.[61]
Furthermore, German plans called for economic and political dependence on the Reich and questioned the wisdom of establishing a
Polish administration which might lead to the creation of Polish
economic and cultural organizations, a danger to the German
Volkstum. While the accusation is often advanced by Polish writers
and their Western protagonists that the population of the General
Gouvernement was either to be Germanized or left to die quietly, no
satisfactory evidence has ever been produced to prove such a statement. It seems that, rather, the Germans were at a complete loss in
their search for a logical and unified policy in regard to this area. The
necessity of retaining German influence in order to implement racial

theories resulted in actions which aroused Polish suspicion of future Germanization or planned extermination. However, economic necessities, the difference between theory and practice in the east, and the ensuing German-Russian war mitigated German rule, and peaceful co-existence between Poles and the newly established German authorities proved possible in some districts.

Hans Frank, a fanatic National Socialist, became Governor of the General Gouvernement. Frank appointed the various district and provincial authorities, all of them German.[62] The presence of an oppressive foreign administration in a formerly independent country would have evoked popular resistance even if the oppressed had not been Poles and the hated occupants Germans. There is something of a conspiratorial character in the Polish nationalist mentality, formed and developed by the 125 years of Russian and Prussian oppression, which helped the Poles in 1939-40 to build up the most successful underground state in an occupied country during the war.[63] The underground state was formed by the representatives of the four political parties of the country, who wanted to uphold the sovereignty of the exiled government, located first at Angers and later at London, and to prevent any effective German rule. The impetus to form such an association sprang from the belief that England and France could not be defeated by the Wehrmacht.[64] German occupation would therefore be of short duration, and Polish forces were needed to fill the vacuum in the country once German troops were withdrawn. Although greatly hampered by both a large-scale deportation of the intelligentsia and a currency law that deprived every Pole of his savings two months after the arrival of the Russians,[65] the underground state also acted in Russian-occupied areas.

The tragedy soon began to unfold. The underground authorities condemned unco-operative Poles and brutal German officials to death, while the German Gestapo tortured and hanged Polish "bandits," who formed the rank and file of the underground. The valiant but merciless and cruel struggle carried on by the Polish underground against the German authorities resulted in tremendous suffering and losses. May three examples, as described in the book of an eminent scholar (who also served as the diplomatic courier of the underground), be quoted:

The case: Borecki, an underground leader at Warsaw who called the existence of any legal and political occupation nonrecognizable and declared: ". . . we cannot tolerate the existence of any Polish government co-operating with the occupants. If any traitors appear, we will kill them."[66] The man ". . . was dragged off to jail and submitted to the most atrocious Nazi tortures. He was beaten for days on end. His back was a mass of bloody tatters from an endless succession of blows administered with iron rods. . . . In the end, he was shot."

The case: Danuta, daughter of a Polish estate-holder in the Carpathians. She encouraged the underground to strangle a *Volksdeutsche* who was engaged in some Germanizing practices among peasants. A young girl, who looked innocent and inexperienced in the ways of the world, quietly planned the murder and even wrote the false suicide note which she put into the palm of the dead victim. The note contained Bulle's "confession" of being "a rotten German spy . . . repenting for all his 'crimes,' " cursing the Germans and asking the villagers for forgiveness. She kept the operation secret, even from another member of the underground who was used as a lookout. There were no pardons on either side.[67]

The case: Sophie Janusz of Stargard, who was sentenced to three months of forced labor because she wrote to her Polish girl friend in Germany that "it is pitiful in our Fatherland. Only a person who has lost his or her country, can understand what is meant by a lost Fatherland. We have our Fatherland in our hearts, but for what good should we work now."[68]

The victims of the resistance movement and the subsequent German retaliation formed a never ending spiral of terror which resulted in the frightful persecution of the Polish intelligentsia by the Germans, who were well aware of their leadership in the underground.[69] The chain reaction of brutalities was rooted in political antagonisms, as well as in the emotions of terror and revenge. This was not changed by the outbreak of the Soviet-German war. Although Wladislaw Studnicki might not represent the overwhelming majority of the Polish people in 1941, his writings on the subject remain significant in view of his anti-Communist beliefs and long-time observation of the Polish scene as a writer and historian. He writes:

> With tears of hope in their eyes, Poles listened to the broadcast declaring war on Russia. They thought hopefully that they would now regain their independence.[70]

And also:

Still, I assumed that German policy would undergo a substantial change, when Germany, under the impact of the war in the east and the west, became convinced of the absurdity of the annexation of such large Polish territories. I assumed that the entrance into the war by Soviet Russia would render the Germans willing to accept such ideas. I know that this war could end for us either in liberation or annihilation, but that a Soviet Russian victory would mean our annihilation, I had never doubted.[71]

These passages show that despite the imprisonment and murder of Polish patriots and sabotage by the underground, German-Polish relations could have been improved in the face of the common danger, except for the criminal mentality of Frank and the Nazi leadership in the *Reichskanzlei*. The German army, unconsciously remembering Bismarck's second dictum—that Poland had to be strengthened if hostilities with Russia could not be avoided—attempted to work in this direction, but to no avail.[72] The result of German haughtiness and rejection of Polish feelers in July, 1941, was more terror and hatred on both sides. Even Studnicki was thrown into prison, and the relative relaxation in the mistreatment of Polish prisoners, ordered by Frank in the spring of 1941, was again suspended.[73] Following Prime Minister Sikorski's instructions, the Polish underground continued its sabotage, which now clearly favored the Red Army.[74] The limited debate in the illegal Polish press on the proposed course of neutrality was buried in the face of continued German terror and the failure to extend an amnesty to Polish political prisoners. Such were the events in Poland at the time of Sikorski's signing of the Polish-Russian treaty of July 30, 1941.[75]

The German realization of the criminal stupidity of its regime of terror in Poland, including the repression of the Polish intelligentsia, came much too late. Individuals have often recognized the guilt with which Germany was burdening herself and her people by terrorizing and humiliating the Polish nation,[76] but Hans Frank could only find some conciliatory words for Poland after the German armies began their long retreat from Stalingrad and the River Don.[77] Of course the discovery at Katyn of the mass graves of Polish officers who were Russian prisoners of war had an important effect on the Polish population, for the exiled government failed to condemn the discovery as German propaganda. The events leading to a severance of diplomatic relations between the Sikorski government and the Kremlin at the latter's initiative, despite American and British pleas to Moscow, left the Poles worried about their future. At this time, however, Germany's star was declining, and there was no reason for the Poles to reconsider their former course. In addition, after the victory at Stalingrad and the Don, Russia, too, became active in Polish affairs.[78] Moscow created the new Polish People's Party (P.P.R.), which, though forced to restrict itself to limited actions because of its lack of personnel, set up its own partisan command and was successful in persuading the Polish underground to continue and accelerate its major sabotage actions. The results were devastating for the Polish people and for the underground. For every German killed, a large number of Polish hostages were shot. Of course the blood of the innocent cried out for revenge.[79] The London exile government, anxious to prove its good will toward the U.S.S.R., to preserve its domestic sovereignty, and to continue receiving British and American help in its losing struggle for eastern Poland, had also prompted the underground to commit diversionist acts.

The end of the struggle coincided with the appearance of the Red Army in eastern Poland, leading to the subsequent arrest of those underground leaders who revealed their identity. The trial of the sixteen high-ranking officials of the underground in eastern Poland became internationally famous in 1945, but many of the smaller commanders disappeared into Siberia and the Ukraine in 1944 without any notice in the world press. In Warsaw, in September and October, 1944, the valiant but illogical and betrayed revolt of the "Home Army," led by General Bor-Komorowski, was defeated by German armored divisions.[80] Before the Red Army expelled the Wehrmacht and the SS in January, 1945, more than one and a half million Poles had been shot, executed, or starved to death in Poland and in the notorious concentration camps of Dachau and Auschwitz. In addition, most of the three million Polish citizens of the Jewish faith,[81] the merchant and trader class of the country, were exterminated in pursuance of the fanatically irrational and criminal racial theories of Alfred Rosenberg.

Among the Poles, the percentage of university students and intelligentsia was disproportionately high and by 1942 had begun to affect the quality of the leaders of the resistance. With hindsight, the observer considers the blood toll exacted of the Polish nation extremely high for the relatively small and intangible returns, such as proving its adherence to Allied war aims, without any concrete return from the

Anglo-American powers from 1943 to 1945 to safeguard and guarantee Polish independence and territorial integrity against the imperialist designs of Soviet Russia. Polish courage in facing overwhelming odds and Polish patriotism, clinging tenaciously to freedom, were amply proved, but an adverse geographic position and Western indifference rendered the sacrifice futile. As a result of National Socialist policies, Germany, in turn, had to shoulder a large burden of guilt. This was to engulf millions of innocent Germans in the eastern provinces in a maelstrom of misery, expulsion, hunger, and death as the Poles, bent on revenge and imperialism and incited and encouraged by the U.S.S.R. in order to facilitate her annexation of eastern Poland, invaded the eastern provinces and applied their methods of oppressive terror. The life of misery forced on the Poles in 1939 failed to end in 1945, but as the fateful tragedy of east central Europe unfolded, it was shared from that time on by millions of East Germans.

3. RUSSIA AND POLAND, 1919–1943

Since the seventeenth century, Polish-Russian relations have been characterized by the continuous advance of Muscovy against the Polish-Lithuanian state, which had erected a frontier at Vitebsk and Kiev against the Golden Horde and its Muscovite successors. As the aristocratic constitution continued to weaken the executive and military power of Poland and as Peter the Great and Catherine II succeeded in eliminating Sweden and Turkey as power factors in the north and the south, Russian plans for the dismemberment of Poland entered a new and conclusive phase. The inborn drive of the Tsars to destroy Poland as a European power in order to remove the obstacle to Russia's westward expansion on the Continent contributed to Catherine II's decision to partition the kingdom of Poland. The acquiescence of Austria and Prussia in 1772 arose, on the one hand, from the deep-seated fear of Russian armies harbored by the philosopher-king of Prussia, who had recently experienced defeat at Gross Kunersdorf, and, on the other, from the emerging distrust of Russian intentions which was to characterize Austrian foreign policy in the nineteenth century.

Upon the occasion of the Third Partition of Poland (1795), the Prussian and Russian monarchs vowed that no Polish state would be resurrected or Polish nationality recognized,[82] and the Tsarist regime, with the exception of the rule of Alexander I (though even he refused to grant independence to Poland outside his empire), remained loyal to the promise of 1795. The brutal suppression of the revolts of 1830 and 1863, followed by an accelerated Russification policy, characterized the history of Congress Poland in the nineteenth century. The attempts to annihilate Polish nationality were the result of the Russian fear that if she were successful in forming a national organization, Poland might well become a successful contender for the loyalty of the peoples living between Moscow and Warsaw. This evaluation formed the geopolitical and diplomatic doctrine of Russian policy, while Chancellor Bismarck's anti-Polish remarks reflected only his views in regard to a particular political situation in the 1880's.

Both Tsarist Russia and the U.S.S.R. insisted on controlling Poland, basing their policies on the following considerations:

(1) Russian policy, under both the Romanovs and the Bolsheviks, was directed toward westward expansion and the absorption of peoples living between Moscow and the Germanic peoples, as the history of the past two hundred years demonstrates. The greatest obstacle preventing the realization of these aims has always been the presence, between Russia and Germany, of an unfriendly Slavonic state which both could and would promote the separatist tendencies of the Balts, White Russians, and Ukranians and thereby disprove the Pan-Slav theory in Russian (Soviet) propaganda designed to insure adherence of the Slavonic people to Russia (U.S.S.R.).

(2) The various directions of Soviet expansionist drives necessitated Russian control of Poland in order to provide for the security of the western flank during the periods when Russia was to divert her attention from central Europe toward the Mediterranean, central Asia, and Manchuria. The maintenance of control, therefore, had slowly emerged as one of the basic tenets of Russian foreign policy. Such a policy, however, could only be implemented if Poland or her temporary successor, the Austro-Hungarian monarchy, were weakened or destroyed and the Polish plains were under the control of the Tsarist or Red armies. It was only after the Dual Alliance of 1881 and the coming of Hitler, respectively, that Russia abandoned the policy of the Alvensleben Convention[83] and insisted upon the destruction of German power in order to further the security of her western frontiers.

(3) The Communist take-over in Russia failed to alter the old stratagems of Russian policy toward central and eastern Europe. Lenin's invasion of Poland, in answer to Pilsudski's aid to the incipient Ukrainian state, and Communist preoccupation with Poland, as a

natural glacis for an offensive against Europe, are cases in point. To the Soviet leadership, however, the conquest of Poland became part and parcel of a larger plan. In pursuance of its world revolutionary aims, the U.S.S.R. had a definite plan to wrest control of Europe and the Far East but found itself surrounded by groupings of hostile states. Therefore, the possession of Poland was, to Russia, more necessary than ever in order to break through the *cordon sanitaire* of 1920 and to remove French influence from east central Europe. As Germany recovered from the defeat and Hitler came to power, Poland's importance as a defensive glacis of Europe increased in the eyes of the Soviet Russian policy-makers as well.

The Communist quest for the occupation of Poland was unsuccessful at first. At the gates of Warsaw, the Red armies were defeated in August, 1920, and in the ensuing peace treaty signed at Riga, Russia had to accept a frontier which left large Ukrainian and White Ruthenian minorities in Poland, a grave danger to the Russification campaign conducted by Stalin in the Ukraine and Byelorussia.

Although it was not regarded as a Polish *Diktat* and was praised in the *Soviet Encyclopedia* as late as 1940, the Treaty of Riga dramatically exposed the weakness of the new regime.[85] The redressing of the balance of power remained a long-range aim of Moscow's foreign policy, but international developments, such as the replacement of French influence by German influence at Warsaw in the wake of the agreement of January, 1934, rendered short-term changes impossible. Faced with a powerful and aggressive Japan in the Far East, Moscow even initiated the request for nonaggression treaties with Poland and the Baltic States.[86]

Thus good fortune seemed to have struck when German demands for the return of Danzig and a highway through the Corridor were rejected by the Polish government,[87] thereby removing the threat of a combined Polish-German action against the U.S.S.R., an action which, repeatedly proposed to Poland by the third Reich, appeared to represent the primary aim of German policy between 1936 and 1939. The German-Polish conflict, which became known around March, 1939, permitted Stalin to take one of two courses:

(1) To ally himself with the Western powers, who were in full retreat in central and eastern Europe, in order to destroy the renascent German power and to secure Poland by friendly occupation, aiding her in her struggle against Germany;[88] or

(2) To revert to the policy of Tauroggen and Alvensleben,[89] which

would involve the diversion of German interests to southeastern Europe and Russian interests to the Middle East by arranging a *modus vivendi* with Germany at the expense of the destruction of Poland and the Baltic States.[90]

Both alternatives were to change the military and political *status quo* in Poland. Either Poland was to become a transit area for the Red Army fighting Germany, or she was to be annexed by both Germany and Russia. The Russian insistence upon the free movement of troops in Poland during the negotiations in Moscow with Britain and France in 1939 and their proposed advance on Lwów and Vilna showed clearly, in the light of the subsequent experience of the Baltic States, the intention of Moscow to obtain control of Poland in the event of a Western alignment.[91]

Largely motivated by fear of the Wehrmacht and the refusal of any British-French guarantees to attack the *Westwall* immediately in the event hostilities were commenced, Russia decided in favor of an agreement with Germany and thereby became the most ardent protagonist of the complete destruction of the Polish state. Although the Secret Protocol of August 23, 1939, did not necessarily preclude the further existence of a Polish state,[92] Molotov, after the entrance of Soviet Russian troops into eastern Poland, exerted pressure on the German Ambassador in Moscow, Count Schulenburg, to prevent the creation of a Polish rump state. He also insisted upon immediate negotiations on the subject.[93] The joint German-Russian communiqué mentioned "dissensions of the population living in its [Poland's] former territory" and spoke of the "creation of natural frontiers."[94] Stalin told Ambassador Schulenburg that "in the final settlement of the Polish question, anything that in the future might create friction between Germany and the Soviet Union must be avoided."[95]

According to Stalin's view, allowing the creation of an independent Polish rump state would be wrong. In the treaty of September 28, 1939, Russia and Germany expressly rejected "any interference of third powers in this settlement" and secretly agreed "to tolerate in their territories no Polish agitation which affects the territories of the other party" and "to suppress in their territories all attempts to start such agitation by taking suitable measures for this purpose mutually."[96]

The unnatural alliance of two expansionist powers with utterly hostile ideologies was to last for only twenty-two months. As Hitler proclaimed in his *Mein Kampf*:

The future aim of German foreign policy shall be *Ostpolitik* [an Eastern policy] aiming at the acquisition of necessary soil for our German nation, and not an Eastern or Western orientation.[97]

Also:

We will stop the eternal German migration to the South and the West, and we will turn our attention to the East.[98]

His hatred of the Jews, who, he mistakenly believed, dominated the Bolshevist movement, made him believe that the Soviet Union was on the brink of disintegration and that the end of Bolshevism would coincide with the end of Russia as a state.

We are predestined by fate to become the witnesses of a catastrophe which will become an overwhelming proof of the national theory of race.[99]

Despite the treaties of August 23 and September 28, 1939, ideological and imperialistic differences set the Third Reich and the U.S.S.R. against each other. The concrete point of friction lay in the Balkans. Hitler became increasingly convinced that Soviet Russia would, at an opportune time, attack the Third Reich, since Molotov continued to demand Rumania and Bulgaria. The alliance, contracted by both parties as *rebus sic stantibus,* bore tragic fruit. Compelled by fear of Russia, who, though concerned by the tremendous German successes of 1940, was still in favor of continuing the alliance temporarily, and angered by his inability to invade England in the fall of 1940, Hitler decided on December 19, 1940, to proceed with Plan Barbarossa, the code name for an attack on the U.S.S.R.[100] Such was the result of failure to agree with Molotov in November, 1940, on Russo-German interests in the Balkans and on the inclusion of Soviet Russia in the Tripartite Agreement.[101]

By the spring of 1941, Stalin realized the imminence of the German attack. He attempted mobilization, but his forces were inadequately prepared. Not only had the purges of 1936 and 1937 robbed Russia of qualified military leaders, but, in pursuance of the policy of the German-Russian pact, Red Army expansion was neglected until 1941 because Stalin was afraid of provoking Germany into premature action before Russia could attain a state of industrial and technological readiness.

The initiative did not rest with the Kremlin. Whether Stalin had planned a preventive war by August, 1941, as the Germans charged or whether his moves were purely defensive is still a subject for historical debate, for the Soviet Russians are not in the habit of exhibiting their archives. There is, however, little doubt about substantial German preparations for an offensive.[102] Hitler's decision to attack Russia, which he described as the most difficult of his life, also proved to be his most fateful move.[103]

The German invasion of Soviet Russia on June 22, 1941, invalidated all the settlements of 1939, and the U.S.S.R. became an ally of the Western powers and Poland. The Russian alternative of marching with Germany was shattered, and the Soviet Russian dictator, cognizant of the prospect of fighting a losing battle, transferred his capital from Moscow to the safety of Kuibyshev in November, 1941. Only the harsh winter, Anglo-American war matériel pouring in through Murmansk and Iran, and the disgust of the people, caused by brutal Nazi administrative measures, saved him from total defeat.

What was Stalin's attitude in those days of crisis toward his new ally, the Polish exile government at London? Among the immediate requirements of Russian foreign policy, the first was the acquisition of substantial military aid from the United States and Britain. The Polish government at London insisted upon the territorial integrity of Poland and had strong British and American support for its views. The British, especially, exerted pressure on both parties to come to an agreement, since Moscow could no longer regard the London Poles as an official enemy. To Moscow, the prospect of an agreement also meant potential aid to the retreating Russian armies by increased Polish underground activities, thus tying down a certain number of German divisions in the General Gouvernement. With the Red Army disintegrating under German blows, Stalin was in desperate need of allies.

Thus tactical considerations called for a *rapprochement,* in contradiction to the basic tenet of the Soviet Russian policy of domination of eastern and central Europe through control of the Polish plains. This tenet was not, however, surrendered by Stalin, even in the darkest hours of the war. In the July 30, 1941 agreement with the London Poles, the question of Poland's eastern frontiers was left undecided, though Russia renounced her claims, which were based on the Ribbentrop-Molotov treaty, and remained silent about the "validity" of the "plebiscites" undertaken under Communist control in the annexed provinces in November, 1939.[104] Despite this agreement and the new agreement of December 4, 1941, Stalin failed to arm General Anders' Polish army,[105] created within the U.S.S.R., and treated it as a hostile foreign unit which would be evacuated as soon as the German danger was temporarily averted.[106] The forced withdrawal of Polish troops and the failure to account for several hundred thousand deportees were visible proof of continued Russian *intransigeance*.

On a diplomatic level, Stalin soon injected the frontier dispute into his negotiations with Polish Prime Minister Sikorski. Stalin proposed, according to Polish sources, only a small change in the frontier at their December, 1941 meeting.[107] His demand was, however, preceded by a note to the Polish Embassy at Kuibyshev reaffirming the legality of the November 29, 1939 decree of the U.S.S.R., though granting Polish citizenship to Polish nationals of Polish descent domiciled in those territories.[108] The note was more important for the reason of granting Polish citizenship to Poles in the area only as an act of special grace by the U.S.S.R., revokable at the pleasure of the Soviet Russian government of its consideration of the non-Polish inhabitants as Soviet citizens. A month later, the Russian government made her demands even more precise. Answering Polish references that such action was illegal under the terms of the Fourth Hague Convention of 1907, the Soviet Russian government declared:

> . . . the assertion of "occupation" in respect to Western Ukraine and Western White Ruthenia is, in this case, devoid of all foundation alike from the political and international points of view, because the entrance of the Soviet forces into the Ukraine and Western White Ruthenia in the autumn of 1939 was not an occupation, but an attachment of the districts mentioned to the Union of Soviet Socialist Republics as the result of the freely expressed wish of the population of these districts.[109]

The political consequences of the Soviet Russian initiative on the Russo-German front after the Battle of Stalingrad in the winter of 1942-43 were unilateral actions in the Polish question. The first step consisted of a note on January 16, 1943, to the Polish government, which was accused of "adopting a negative attitude" to the note of December 1, 1941, by "refusing to take appropriate steps, putting forward demands contrary to the sovereign rights of the Soviet Union in respect to these territories."[110] According to a Polish author, the

Russians also argued that by accepting Soviet amnesty in the July, 1941 treaty, the Polish exile government at London had *de facto* recognized the conquest of eastern Poland.[111]

The next step was a campaign of denunciation, initiated by a member of the All-Union Supreme Soviet, Alexander Korneichuk,[112] and continued by the official Soviet news agency, Tass, which labeled the exile government a "regime of landlords and imperialists"[113] and expressed the conviction that "the present Polish ruling classes do not reflect the genuine opinion of the Polish people."[114] In this charged atmosphere the Polish government's request for an explanation of the mass graves at Katyn, found by the Germans, served as an excellent pretext for Moscow to sever diplomatic relations with the London Poles, accusing them of "contact and accord with Hitler."[115]

At this point, Stalin utilized the "Union of Polish Patriots," a Russian-created, pro-Communist committee. The Communist party's prewar leaders in Poland had been lured to the U.S.S.R. in 1936 and executed as Trotskyites and diversionists and could not, therefore, be members of the committee.[116] Instead, the Union was headed by Wanda Wasilewska, a well-known Polish novelist with Communist ideas, a daughter of the first Polish foreign minister; in 1940, she was elected to the Supreme Soviet Council of the U.S.S.R.[117] The military representative was Brigadier General Berling, a retired lieutenant colonel and known opportunist who had joined the Red Army in 1940. In 1941, he was assigned to the Anders army, which subsequently removed him because he was giving intelligence on the Poles to the NKVD.[118] Troops were organized into the Kosciusko division, which had to be staffed largely with Russian officers because the mass murders of 1940 and the evacuation of the Anders army in 1942 had left only a small number of officers of Polish origin in the U.S.S.R.[119] A congress was called on June 16, 1943, in Moscow. Proposing a democratic, moderately Socialist order for postwar Poland (the Trojan-horse tactics to be performed in the years to come in every occupied country), the congress called for the first time for recognition of the loss of eastern Poland and for the annexation of large tracts of German territories in the west (Upper Silesia, Danzig, and East Prussia).[120]

The next Russian move was the establishment of a second Polish underground subservient to Moscow. Comintern agents were dispatched into occupied Poland. Since their ranks increased very slowly, they concentrated upon organization rather than upon fighting the Germans. Another objective was the planting of seeds of dissension and confusion in the secret underground state, the Directorate of Civil Resistance.[121] Because the name "Communist" had fallen into utter disrepute in Poland, a group of agents led by Boleslaw Bierut established the Polish Workers' party as a cover organization. By the end of 1943, Bierut's counterunderground was transformed into a united "national council,"[122] which included the pro-Communist elements of the Socialists and many nonpartisans under Bierut's leadership. As Russian troops approached Curzon Line B, Osóbka-Morawski, the leader of the pro-Communist Socialists, was, on May 24, 1944, sent to Moscow to co-ordinate activities with the Union of Polish Patriots.[123] On July 22, 1944, Stalin finally unveiled his plans for postwar Poland. He sanctioned the Declaration of Chełm by the Polish Committee of National Liberation, an amalgamation of the National Council of Liberation and the Union of Polish Patriots, and four days later he transferred to them the administrative powers in any Polish territories west of the Curzon Line.[124] Now Poland's tragedy became a reality, despite repeated Western objections. Emboldened by the unhappy outcome of the Warsaw uprising,[125] which eliminated a considerable portion of the Home Army, and the visit of Prime Minister Mikolajczyk, which weakened the position of the London Polish exile government toward the Western powers,[126] the Soviet Russian government took another step, that of immediately recognizing the National Committee of Liberation after its reconstitution as the Provisional government of Poland on December 31, 1944.[127] Even the compromise reached at the Yalta Conference—recognizing the predominant part to be played by the Lublin elements in any future government—was violated by the U.S.S.R. The subsequent story of broken promises, the absence of free elections, and the Sovietization of Poland has been eloquently recounted by the late American Ambassador to Warsaw, Arthur Bliss Lane.[128]

CHAPTER V

The Russian Birth of the Oder-Neisse Line

1. SOVIET RUSSIA AND THE WESTERN FRONTIERS OF POLAND BEFORE THE TEHERAN CONFERENCE

In deciding to retain his wartime annexations of 1939-40 and to Sovietize Poland, Stalin needed to effect a settlement of Poland's western frontiers and the postwar position of Germany. His dilemma, which consisted of the priority to be attached to one or the other of his two contradictory projects, namely, the political control of Poland *versus* any future friendship with a new non–National Socialist German government, had to be resolved before the Teheran Conference of 1943.

Before 1941, Stalin committed grievous errors in his German policy. His equivocal attitude toward the destruction of the German Communist party from 1933 through 1936 and his incorrect estimate of both Hitler's domestic power resources and the ultimate direction of the Führer's foreign policy contributed to the isolation of the U.S.S.R. from the "decadent," imperialist countries, as the Western democracies were contemptuously called by the Russian rulers. Until June 22, 1941, Stalin failed to realize that despite Hitler's contempt for parliamentary democracy and his blundering into a war with England, the German leader had never hesitated to designate Bolshevism as a relentless mortal enemy that he would have to destroy in order to survive. Stalin's mistaken calculations of German military strength nearly resulted in the defeat of the Red Army in 1941. Subsequently, however, the Russian leader shifted to the other extreme in overestimating the German menace. The absence in Germany of any strong resistance movement against Hitler, together with the death-defying

78

fighting morale of the German troops and their contempt for the Communist system, awakened Stalin to the fact that the spirit of Tauroggen had been destroyed, not only by the propaganda of the National Socialist regime, but also as a result of Communism's unpopularity among the Germans. Accordingly, early plans for expansion of the German Committee of National Liberation were shelved, despite the chairmanship of this committee by the captured commander of the German Sixth Army, Field Marshal von Paulus.[1]

Another trend favoring a change in Stalin's policy was the increasingly anti-German attitude of the Western powers, particularly the United States. The Casablanca Declaration of January, 1943, calling for the unconditional surrender of Germany, removed the possibility of a separate peace between the Western powers and Hitler, a fear which had weighed heavily on Stalin's mind in 1941 and 1942. Under these circumstances, any Russian move designed to control a future Germany would be suspected by the Anglo-American powers as the forerunner of a Soviet bid for hegemony in Europe because the West was already aroused by Soviet Russian designs on Poland. Furthermore, Stalin was convinced that Germany would be basically anti-Soviet and anti-Russian[2] and that he had to exploit the present opportunity by enlisting the aid of the inflamed anti-German passions of the United States and Britain in order to destroy the power resources of his enemy.[3] Stalin probably assumed that complete destruction of German power by the Big Three would secure the emergence of Communism throughout the Continent. It looked as though, if Germany could be permanently weakened, Stalin would be sure of the undisputed mastery of Europe, for the strength of the French and Italian Communist parties, the countries of which were in the throes of grave economic crises, was growing steadily through the skillful manipulation of the prevailing atmosphere of anti-Fascist united fronts.

Recognizing these political trends, Stalin executed his political plans on Poland. To him, a pro-Russian Poland was the cornerstone of his policy, which was directed toward the destruction of German power and Continental hegemony. The obvious solution was, therefore, the strengthening of a pro-Soviet Poland through the acquisition of eastern German provinces on Poland's western frontiers. This move would both reduce German power and provide the basis for new demands to move the Western-Russian demarcation line in Germany farther west.

Even Stalin could not imagine the emergence of a pro-Russian Poland without large-scale territorial readjustments in the west, in view of the stubborn Polish insistence upon Polish sovereignty over the eastern provinces of prewar Poland. Therefore, he welcomed the so-called "compensation idea," which combined the issues of Poland's eastern and western frontiers.[4]

The compensation idea, of course, belonged to the semantics of pure power politics. Either Poland was entitled to the eastern provinces (a fact Stalin never admitted), for which she could not well be compensated with territories of a third power to which she had no ethnic claim (a fact again not admitted by the Russians, who called these territories historically Polish), or Poland was not entitled to the eastern provinces (as the official Russian contention maintained) and therefore had no valid claims for compensation whatsoever.

In order to prove successful, the compensation idea had to meet the approval of the Polish government and the Polish people and gain the support, or at least the acquiescence, of the Western powers. The first offers were made to the London Polish government before the latter categorically rejected any changes in the 1938 frontiers of Poland in the east.[5]

The Poles, who were already demanding certain changes in the Versailles frontiers, coveted Danzig, Upper Silesia, and part of the Baltic seacoast of Germany, including East Prussia.[6] By 1942, their claims had already been well publicized. In 1941, a publication of the Polish Research Center at London described German Upper Silesia as an area 60 per cent Polish with no economic future within Germany.[7] In a speech at St. James's Palace in London, the Foreign Minister of the Polish exile government, Edouard Raczynski, declared:

> They [the future frontiers] should, on the one hand, assure a wide access to the sea, a vital necessity for Poland, providing her with an adequate defense against foreign intervention, and on the other, secure an economic development for Poland which would take into consideration her expanding population.[8]

In his December, 1942 memorandum, Polish Prime Minister Sikorski[9] made a series of concrete requests for the support of the President of the United States. These were:

(1) Partition of East Prussia, the northeastern part around Inster-

burg to be allotted to Lithuania and the main part of the province, including Königsberg, to be attached to Poland;

(2) Frontier corrections which would favor Poland by moving Pomerania's northeastern boundary to the region of Stolpmünde; and

(3) Detachment of the Upper Silesian coal basin from Germany, either to be attached to Poland, to remain under international control, or to be partitioned between Czechoslovakia and Poland.[10]

Prime Minister Sikorski also demanded the strict military occupation by Polish troops of the German territories east of the Oder and western Neisse rivers, just as France, after the First World War, insisted upon French occupation of the Rhineland. The idea of Aleksander Bregman, that Sikorski did not dare to put forward the request for annexation of all German areas east of the rivers although he really wanted to attach them to Poland, is at best questionable in the absence of other supporting evidence.[11]

Thus there was a definite movement among exiled Polish elements to acquire those German territories claimed at the Versailles Conference by the leader of the National Democrats, Roman Dmowski. Still, the Polish leaders, aware of the necessity either to assimilate substantial German minorities or to colonize large areas, were unwilling to transgress certain limits in their demands. Their claims were relatively moderate, if it is considered that Poland was undergoing a period of ruthless German occupation and suffering heavy losses in life as a result of the fight between the underground and the occupants.

At first the compensation idea was turned down by every responsible Pole in the West and in occupied Poland.[12] The only dissenting voice was uttered by pro-Russian Ksawery Pruszynski, who had just returned from the U.S.S.R. He maintained that the Russian leaders wanted Poland to advance in the west to Stettin and Breslau,[13] emphasizing that he had received this information from Wanda Wasilewska.[14] In July, 1943, the Congress of the Union of Polish Patriots at Moscow demanded the Oder frontier. The assumption cannot be made, however, that the new frontier was Wanda Wasilewska's invention, for she had never previously been known to hold such views. Stalin had already mentioned the idea of limited compensation at his meeting with Sikorski on December 4, 1941,[15] and had selected Miss Wasilewska as his mouthpiece.

In the West, Stalin's compensation concept was promoted by British Prime Minister Churchill. Although aware of Russian intentions toward eastern Poland, the Prime Minister did not fully recognize Stalin's central European ambitions and decided to use the compensation idea as a bridge to restore relations between the London Poles and Stalin. The fact that not until the Teheran Conference did he expect Russian support for the Oder frontier for Poland reveals the limited extent of his knowledge of Russian intentions.[16]

Western compromises and Eastern *intransigeance* marked the negotiations concerning Germany and Poland which were conducted at Teheran between the United States, Britain, and the U.S.S.R. The path to tragedy was to be completed in common by the German and Polish nations. The warning of the Polish exile government, exposing the intentions of Stalin, went unheeded, but it is worth quotation for political clarity:

> ... even though the Soviet government should, in compensation, support Polish claims to some German territories in the West, these new frontiers would make Poland dependent on her eastern neighbor, and enable the Soviet Union to use her as a springboard for extending its domination over Central Europe and Germany in particular.[17]

At the Teheran Conference, Stalin faced little opposition because the West feared that if contradicted, he would not renew relations with the Polish government at London and would ultimately Communize Poland.[18] Therefore, Churchill appeared to be trying to "bribe" Stalin into renewing relations by agreeing to the Curzon Line as the eastern frontier of Poland and to the Oder River as the western frontier.[19] Churchill even insisted that the district of Oppeln should be allotted to Poland, to which Molotov and Stalin agreed only too heartily. The British Prime Minister spoke in glowing terms of the new Poland which Stalin was pleased to see developing into a powerful industrial state allied with Russia.[20] It is no wonder that Churchill, by showing his overeagerness to agree on the frontiers of Poland, could not attain the restoration of diplomatic relations between the Polish government and the Soviet Union. At Teheran, Stalin was not yet interested in the problem of exchange of population, but Professor Lange, on the basis of his long interviews with Stalin in early 1944, told Mikolajczyk in regard to the German population of the provinces:

> We'll find room for about three million of them in Siberia. Some of the others will be sent back into what is left from Germany,

and we'll find places for the rest of them—perhaps in South America.[21]

Only President Roosevelt raised the question of expulsions at the Conference and proposed to establish a procedure for executing them.[22] The connection between the removal of the Poles from the areas to be attached to Russia and their resettlement in the new western provinces of Poland was only vaguely mentioned. Finally, Stalin emphasized that he would not tolerate Western interference after his troops "liberated" Poland.

2. THE PATH TO WESTERN ACQUIESCENCE AT THE YALTA CONFERENCE

The Teheran Conference marked the end of the first and most difficult phase of Stalin's efforts to gain control of Poland and effect a settlement in central Europe in accordance with the interests of the U.S.S.R. Even Churchill's account showed that Stalin's inclination to deal with the London Polish government was considerably less than in October, 1943,[23] and that Stalin was aware of the conciliatory tone of the British Prime Minister, who had overestimated future Russian power on the Continent at the close of the war.[24]

The next phase for Stalin consisted of the establishment of a pro–Soviet Russian Polish government and the alienation of the Allies from the Mikolajczyk government in London. First, he united the two branches of his shadow government, the Union of Polish Patriots at Moscow and the National Committee for Liberation in the underground.[25] Then he used them as "representatives of the genuine intentions of the Polish people." These groups supported Russian claims to eastern Poland on the one hand and the westward expansion of Poland on the other. According to Churchill, the question of the Neisse frontier had not been raised at Teheran, since the only area west of the Oder to be attached to Poland consisted of a few districts around Oppeln in Upper Silesia.[26]

In Churchill the Russian dictator faced a devoted friend of the Polish exile government, especially since the British Prime Minister feared that Poland would be Sovietized at the end of the war and attempted several times in early 1944 to effect a Polish-Russian entente. Churchill's efforts failed because of the unresponsiveness of the U.S.S.R. to any solution without a settlement of the frontier question and acceptance of the compensation theory by the Poles.[27] To cede half of prewar Poland's territory remained, however, beyond the power of the exiled Poles, who were, at least to a certain extent, responsible to the violently nationalist Polish underground. In his attempts to break the deadlock, Churchill seemed to fight for the implementation of the Teheran formula by promising expulsion of the Germans from the provinces east of the Oder River if the London Poles would accept those territories in exchange for the eastern Polish plains.[28] Despite his great wartime achievements, the burden of responsibility for the advocacy of mass expulsions rests on Churchill, though he tried to evade this fact in his memoirs.[29]

During the winter months, the London Poles became aware of the weakening of Western support through Churchill's cool reception of Mikolajczyk and his failure to include in his proposals any real guarantee for the resumption of Polish-Russian relations.[30] Furthermore, President Roosevelt's promised invitation to Mikolajczyk to come to Washington was also delayed.[31] The exile government officials also feared that some agreement on the question might already have been reached at Teheran, and therefore they accepted Churchill's program only in regard to the western frontiers and to the removal of German minorities; they refused to agree to the Curzon Line in the east.[32] However, as early as May, 1944, Mikolajczyk retreated from the position he had taken in January, realizing that the acceptance of the Oder frontier gravely compromised Polish claims to Lemberg and Vilna.[33] His concern was reinforced by his talks with Professor Lange, an admirer of the U.S.S.R. who assured the Polish Prime Minister that there was a definite connection in Stalin's mind between the two frontiers. Lange warned Mikolajczyk that Polish acceptance of the Curzon Line in the east was unavoidable but added that in exchange, Stalin would be willing to support Polish claims to all of the territories east of the Oder, including Stettin, and possibly Königsberg as well.[34]

The two visits of Prime Minister Mikolajczyk to Moscow (July and October, 1944) afforded Stalin the opportunity to increase the split between the London Polish government and the Western Allies by discrediting the former in the eyes of Western public opinion. This was necessary, for both the President and the Prime Minister stiffened their positions and insisted upon a guarantee of the sovereignty of the London Polish government while acceding to Soviet Russian demands on the frontier questions. The attitude of Stalin toward Mikolajczyk was different on the two occasions. The first time, Stalin treated Mikolajczyk with respect, though he deceived him about the forthcoming Russian aid to the Warsaw insurgents. The second time, Stalin received the Polish Prime Minister with indifference and contempt.[35] The difference was caused by the annihilation of the Polish Home Army (A.K.) at Warsaw by the Germans between the two visits, with the corresponding loss of any military power by the London Polish government and the deportation to Russia or arrest by the Red Army of hundreds of the leaders of the Home Army in Russian-occupied territories of Poland.[36]

In order to further the annihilation of the Home Army by the Germans, the Russians concentrated their propaganda offensive upon Warsaw in the latter part of July. Viewing the immediate fall of Warsaw into Russian hands with concern, the Polish exile government consented to the implementation of Project Tempest, the code name for the uprising.[37] Stalin's part in the Warsaw uprising was an example of shameful duplicity. He could not immediately refuse assistance to the insurgents after Mikolajczyk had shown him the message vouching for the democratic character of the anti-German uprising addressed by Red Army Colonel Kalugin to the Soviet High Command and intercepted by the Bor-Komorowski forces.[38]

First, by refusing to believe the accuracy of the report of street fighting in the Polish capital, then by taking refuge in the presence of heavy German reinforcements and the overextension of Russian supply lines, Stalin hesitated long enough to see whether Mikolajczyk would desert his colleagues and accept the premiership of a reorganized pro–Soviet Russian Polish government at Lublin. In case of acceptance, Mikolajczyk would have to offer twelve of sixteen portfolios to the protégés of Stalin.[39]

On August 13, after the return of the Polish Prime Minister to London, Moscow began the systematic denunciation of the Home Army. Tass accused its leaders of failing to co-ordinate the uprising with the Soviet High Command. A month later, Stalin cabled Mikolajczyk, stating:

After a closer study of the matter, I have become convinced that the Warsaw action, which was undertaken without the knowledge of the Soviet Command, is a thoughtless adventure causing unnecessary losses among the inhabitants. In addition, it should be mentioned that a calumnious campaign has been started by the Polish London government which seeks to present the illusion that the Soviet Command deceived the Warsaw population.

In view of this state of affairs, the Soviet Command cuts itself away from the Warsaw adventure and cannot take any responsibility for it.[40]

The message provided a fine example of perverted logic. Lured into a fight by the provoking broadcasts of the Russian-supported Radio Kosciusko[41] and thereby revealing the identities of its members, the Home Army and the London Polish government were abandoned on spurious pretexts and even accused of slander and treachery, while the real traitors pleaded innocence. This procedure was to be repeated with increasing frequency in the months and years to come.

An important success for the policy of the Soviet Union had been achieved. With its leaders in eastern Poland under arrest and the Warsaw army of twenty-five to thirty thousand people killed or deported to Germany, the Polish underground could no longer offer any resistance to the Lublin Committee.

In order to reinforce the position of his puppets in "liberated" Poland, Stalin played his last card in July and August. The July 26, 1944 agreement, which had turned over administration of the Russian-occupied territories of Poland to the Lublin Committee, guaranteed the new western frontiers of Poland on the Oder and western Neisse rivers.[42] The demand for this frontier was then publicly and officially announced by Osóbka-Morawski at a press conference on August 8, 1944.[43] The last counterconcession was thus offered to the Poles in the form of new territories between the Oder and western Neisse rivers—as a reward for coming into the Soviet Russian sphere of influence under the rule of the Lublin Committee.

Mikolajczyk was invited to Moscow for the last time at the request of the British Prime Minister, whose anxiety about Russian intentions increased daily.[44] The negotiations failed because Mikolajczyk was unable to persuade his colleagues to accept the Curzon Line and because the Lublin Poles, encouraged by Stalin, were unwilling to let the London Poles assume any great importance in a reorganized government.[45] By October, Stalin had succeeded in shaking Churchill's confidence in the London Polish government. Sharp words and threats were exchanged between Mikolajczyk and Churchill.[46] Keeping his plans secret, Stalin insisted that the new Polish state be based on the theory of private enterprise, though he had already resolved to transform Poland into a political-ideological satellite of the U.S.S.R. at any price, as the practice of the Lublin Committee has shown.

Molotov's indiscretion in telling Mikolajczyk about the Big Three decision at Teheran on the Polish frontiers alerted the Polish Prime Minister to the seriousness of his situation.[47] Upon returning to London and submitting the proposal to accept the Curzon Line in order to save the London government,[48] he addressed some questions to the British government. These were:

(1) Does Britain favor advancing Poland's postwar frontiers as far as the Oder River and allotting the port of Stettin to Poland?

(2) Is Britain prepared to guarantee the independence and integrity of the new Poland in a joint declaration with the U.S.S.R.?[49]

The British answer, given by the Undersecretary of the Foreign Office, Sir Alexander Cadogan, on November 2, 1944, expressed British willingness to grant Poland all of the areas east of the Oder, including the port of Stettin. This was the only official British publication on the Oder-Neisse frontier until the Potsdam Conference. Estimating the prevailing situation correctly, Cadogan also said:

It is impossible to ignore the possibility that agreement might be reached on the frontier question and that it might nevertheless prove impossible to reach agreement on the other matter [i.e., guarantee of the independence and integrity of Poland].[50]

The Cadogan letter was obsolete at the time of its composition, for the basic assumption, that Russia would deal with and recognize the London Polish government, was proved erroneous.[51] Despair and defiance, two traits so characteristic of Poles at a time of trial, caused the Polish exile cabinet to forbid Prime Minister Mikolajczyk to accept the good offices of Ambassador Harriman at Moscow in order to settle the frontier question, as was recommended by President Roosevelt.[52] On November 24, 1944, Premier Mikolajczyk resigned.[53] Stalin no longer needed to fear Western *intransigeance* in the Polish question, for the Western powers were more anxious to secure Russia's accession to the future United Nations Organization and to facilitate Russian participation in the Far Eastern conflict than to defend the independence and integrity of the ally in whose defense they had entered the Second World War.[54] Disturbance of the unity of the Big Three was looked upon unfavorably in Great Britain and the United States in the days of the Yalta and Potsdam conferences.

3. THE CREATION OF THE ODER-NEISSE FRONTIER, FEBRUARY TO JULY, 1945

Stalin's recognition of the Lublin Committee as the Provisional government of Poland preceded the great winter offensive of the Red Army on January 11, 1945, by only a few days.[55] This caused a change in British policy toward the western frontiers of Poland, as expressed by Foreign Minister Eden to Secretary of State Stettinius at Malta:

> As regards Poland's western frontier, we and the Americans agreed that Poland should certainly have East Prussia, south and west of Königsberg, Danzig, the eastern tip of Pomerania and the whole of Upper Silesia. . . .

> We were prepared last October in Moscow to let Mr. Mikolajczyk's government have any territories they chose to claim up to the Oder, but this was conditional upon agreement then being reached between him and the Russians, and there was no question of our agreeing to the Western Neisse frontier. I also think that we should keep the position fluid . . . since we need not make the same concessions to the Lublin Poles which we were prepared to make to Mr. Mikolajczyk in order to obtain a solution of the Polish problem.[56]

The Yalta Conference has acquired a certain odium in American historiography. It might be argued that the sellout of central and eastern Europeans was made inevitable by President Roosevelt's statement that

> . . . he did not believe that American troops would stay in Europe much more than two years. . . .

And that

> . . . he felt that he could obtain support in Congress and throughout the country for any reasonable measures . . . but he did not believe that this would extend to the maintenance of an appreciable American force in Europe.[57]

Others contend that American diplomatic failure was the result of exaggerated fears about the strength and capacity of the Russian armies as presented by Harry Hopkins and some of the military to the President or that it was simply the consequence of a sick man's attempt to counter a ruthless and ambitious partner.[58] To Stalin, however, the conference constituted the climax of his career in international politics. Recognition of the London Polish government by the Western Allies was to be soon withdrawn,[59] although even at Malta, Eden and Stettinius had agreed that they would prefer the present deadlock to recognition of the Lublin Poles.[60] Whether the Western statesmen, especially Churchill, still believed in the integrity of the Russian promises about the future Polish government in the light of past experience remains debatable, but within six weeks, Stalin shattered the remaining illusions.

The aftermath of the conference, as far as the composition of the Polish government was concerned, amounted to little more than a farce. After several months of obstruction by Molotov, the intergovernmental group created at the Yalta Conference agreed, under Russian pressure, to appoint a "Polish Government of National Unity," consisting of Bierut as its president, Osóbka-Morawski as Prime Minister, and Mikolajczyk as Vice-Premier.[61] Fourteen of the twenty-one cabinet posts went to the Lublin group.

Before a description of the concrete steps taken by Stalin to effect a *fait accompli* at the Oder and Neisse rivers is given, the unilateral and illegal character of Stalin's procedure should be considered in some detail. Even at the Yalta Conference both Roosevelt and Churchill energetically opposed the Oder and Neisse frontier.[62] The Oder frontier was accepted by the British only in return for a Russian *quid pro quo* of a free and independent Poland.[63] Stalin, however, maintaining that Mikolajczyk had been delighted in October to agree to the western Neisse frontier, expressed his conviction that the new frontier was inevitable.[64] In implementing his program between the Yalta and Potsdam conferences, however, he could not have been mistaken about the unequivocal opposition of the West to the Neisse frontier. Therefore, he had to realize that any arrangements would remain provisional, based solely on power dictates, and would not, under international law, bind either Germany or any other European countries. The Oder-Neisse frontier was opposed by the Western powers, the Polish underground, and the London exile government.[65] Archizewski appealed to the Lublin Poles for its rejection as late as

December, 1944.[66] Therefore, Stalin did not succeed in persuading the majority of the Polish people to support his program at the time of the Yalta Conference.

It is evident that the detachment of 24 per cent of the territory of Germany from that country without her consent—in contradiction of the Atlantic Charter, as well as of the British-Soviet treaty of May, 1942—would never have bound the German government. However, the applicability of the Charter to Germany was openly questioned at that time. The conclusion remains that the measures of the Soviet and Lublin Polish governments, resulting in the incorporation of the territories *west* of the Oder, were executed *in open violation* of the Yalta agreement. By *further violating* the agreement with regard to free elections and the independence and integrity of Poland, the government of the U.S.S.R. and its Lublin allies lost any right they might have possessed to dispose of the territories between the Oder, the pre-war German frontier, and the region of Stolpmünde. A definite tripartite understanding existed only in regard to Upper Silesia, eastern Pomerania, and East Prussia, the Oder line being contingent on the formation of a free and independent Polish government.[67]

While the Yalta Conference was still in session, Stalin permitted Bierut to establish Polish administrations in German territories conquered by the Red Army. On February 5, 1945,[68] Bierut stated that administrative units had been created "in implementation of its [Poland's] large-scale program to extend the western frontiers of Poland to the Oder and Neisse rivers." Before February 12, Bierut extended his authority to southern East Prussia and Silesia, while a study group of the "Lublin Commission for the Western Territories" demanded the establishment of Polish administrations in Brandenburg and Pomerania up to thirty miles west of the Oder, thereby using the threat of further annexations to forestall energetic Western opposition.[69] On March 5, 1945, Osóbka-Morawski declared before the Polish National Council that the "recovered" territories would be returned to Polish "culture" and "the traces of centuries-old Germanization would be deleted."[70] He alleged that because the Germans had in the distant past "massacred" the greater part of the native Polish population, new residents would be settled in the area from the ranks of the "repatriates" of eastern Poland and the rural population of central Poland.[71] On March 14, 1945, even before the entire area was occupied by the Red Army, the pro-Russian Polish government decreed the creation of four new voivodships: Masuria, Upper Silesia,

Lower Silesia, and Pomerania. A fifth voivodship, Gdańsk (Danzig), was created after the capture of the port city by the Red Army on March 20, 1945. The relatively mild tone of the American protest of April 8, 1945, encouraged Stalin and Bierut to promote the flight of the German residents from the Russian armies entering the provinces by deliberately mistreating them and deporting the able-bodied men among the remaining German inhabitants.[72]

In order to formalize the *fait accompli,* Stalin concluded a "Treaty of Friendship, Mutual Aid and Post-War Co-operation" on April 21, 1945, with the pro-Russian Polish government at Warsaw.[73] The Treaty provided for mutual military assistance against any state which promoted the "German policy of aggression" and endangered "the territorial integrity and security of the High Contracting Parties."[74] It was the last link in the chain binding Poland to the U.S.S.R. and creating a situation in eastern Germany which could be altered only by armed intervention on the part of the Western Allies. Stalin's secret anxiety concerning Polish sentiment was demonstrated by his refusal to accept even a handful of London Poles in the new Polish government until the treaty was signed by Bierut. He also demanded at the Potsdam Conference the immediate renewal of the April treaty by the new Polish Government of National Unity.[75]

The American inquiry of April 8, 1945,[76] was answered by Molotov in a statement that the advance of the Red Army caused the Germans to leave large areas, which necessitated the establishment of local Polish authorities. The Soviet Foreign Minister maintained, however, that these measures were not in any way connected with the frontier problem.[77] The new American protest note of May 8, 1945,[78] denouncing Polish enforcement of Polish laws and settling Polish repatriates in the provinces, was not even answered in detail by Deputy Foreign Minister Vishinsky on May 18, 1945.[79] Vishinsky emphasized only that the Yalta decisions had presupposed the creation of Polish administrations in the area and in the Free City of Danzig.

4. RUSSIAN ATROCITIES AND THE FLIGHT
OF THE GERMAN POPULATION

One Russian move designed to change the status of the eastern German provinces was to permit the establishment of pro-Communist Polish administrations in the area. Another move consisted of the simultaneous brutal treatment of the population in the occupied area in order to cause the Germans to flee to the west and enable the Bierut government to repopulate the territories with Poles. Subsequently, Moscow also reached agreement with the pro-Russian Poles on the expulsion of nationally conscious Poles from Russian-annexed eastern Poland and their resettlement in the Oder-Neisse provinces.[80] Although human misery was a prevailing theme during the war and large-scale losses among the civilian population were incurred by frequent air raids, guerrilla warfare, and concentration-camp conditions, the magnitude of the losses involved, the fiendish atrocities committed by the Red Army, and the sufferings caused by inclement weather, tied-up routes, and blizzards distinguish the tragic fate of the eastern German population from any other national group, with the possible exception of the European Jews.[81]

When on January 12, 1945, Stalin's armies overran the weakened German front lines of the Vistula and the Narew, the quick advance of Russian troops sent the German population of the Warthegau and East Prussia fleeing westward. Since the attrition rate of the Battle of the Bulge had exhausted the German armored divisions and those not needed for defense operations in the west were not sent to the east on Hitler's orders, the German defense in the middle part of the front collapsed, and in the north and south, the German armies could only withdraw slowly under increasingly severe Russian attacks.[82] The evacuation of the districts and provinces was often undertaken on the orders of the Party authorities, but at many places the limitless optimism of the National Socialist leaders and their inability to grasp the imminence of catastrophe prevented a successful flight to the west.[83] Polish authors allege that the flight of the German population proved that they were not attached to their homelands and abandoned them in bad conscience, knowing that the provinces would become Polish, a government under which they refused to live. Nothing, could, however, be farther from the truth than this example of self-justifying Polish logic. The flight was, rather, based on the reasons which follow.

There was tremendous fear of the Red Army and its atrocities. The number of refugees would not have been half as large had the Russians behaved in an orderly manner in the communities of East Prussia which they occupied in October, 1944. These communities were retaken by the Wehrmacht, and the atrocities discovered were widely published by Goebbels, for they provided an excellent means of reinforcing the sagging morale of the nation against the enemy in the east. *The effect of the anti-Bolshevist propaganda with which the Germans had been indoctrinated since 1933 was heightened by the reports of German soldiers returning for furloughs. Their experiences in Russia had made them hate both Communism and its representative, the Red Army.* The veracity of the East Prussian atrocities was proved by two reliable testimonies. The first was given by Dr. Heinrich Amberger of Gumbinnen before the International War Crimes Tribunal at Nuremberg,[84] the second by a German *Volkssturm* soldier, Mr. K. P. of Königsberg.[85] The testimony reads:

An inn is located close to the ruins of the village toward Sodehnen-Nennersdorf. It lies on the left side of the street, and its name is *Weisser Krug*. To the right from the inn, there is a street leading to the neighboring farms. In the front of the first farm on the left of the street, we found a ladder-cart [*Leiterwagen*]. On this there were nailed by their hands, in a crosslike position, four naked women. In the back of the *Weisser Krug* toward Gumbinnen, there is a small square with a statue of the Unknown Soldier. Close to the statue, facing the street there is a barn. On both wings of the barn door we have found one woman each, nailed by their hands, hanging in a crosslike position. In the houses, furthermore, we have found altogether seventy-two dead women and children and a man of seventy-four years of age. Most of them were murdered bestially, with a few exceptions who were killed by a shot in the neck. Among the dead were infants whose heads were crushed with a hard object. . . .

The testimony continues, telling of the arrival of a native of the village, at that time a nurse at Insterburg, who identified the dead as native Nennersdorfers, including her own parents.[86]

The terror of Nennersdorf was repeated with methodical precision in all of the territories occupied by the Red Army in Germany before April, 1945. The atrocities fall easily into four categories: (1) the raping of women; (2) the whimsical execution of civilians; (3) random plundering and arson; and (4) the mass deportation of civilians to slave-labor camps in Russia.

Among the numberless testimonies published and communicated orally to the author upon the entry of Russian troops into the German east, there is scarcely a one which did not tell of the raping of women and adolescent girls. In view of thousands of testimonies, a critical examination of the reports leaves no doubt that the raping of German women and children by Soviet Russian officers and enlisted men was systematic and not just the raw lust of undisciplined soldiers in isolated cases.[87] The methodical character is proved by the fact that regular raids were made to procure women, that many women were repeatedly raped by a series of men,[88] and that rapings very often took place publicly.[89] Even aged women and children were not spared, this having a particularly repulsive and terrifying effect upon the German population.[90] Conceding the Asiatic mentality of some units of the Red Army, which regarded the women of the enemy as a personal prey, the fact remains, as captured Soviet Russian newspapers and pamphlets prove, that Russian officers and men were deeply influenced by the hate propaganda of Ilya Ehrenburg and other Communist journalists who regarded mass rapings as an act of revenge against the Germans.[91] The ease with which the Red Army put an end to these excesses at the end of the hostilities also points in this direction.

Summary executions instigated by political commissars attached to Red Army units after the denunciation of the victim as a Nazi or murders resulting from the careless use of guns and pistols by Russian soldiers while under alcoholic influence cost the lives of many innocent Germans, as well as of some prominent National Socialist functionaries in western Poland and the German east. Railway officials, civil servants, and firemen were mistaken for National Socialist functionaries, either because they were state employees or because they wore uniforms. They were summarily shot,[92] as was everyone who wore better clothing and was accused of the slightest mistreatment of Russian and Polish workers.[93] Murder victims also included fathers and brothers who had resisted the rape of their wives and sisters.[94] The number of victims of this kind of violence ran to about 75-100 thousand persons according to German sources.[95]

Looting and robbery were systematically promoted by the Soviet High Command.[96] The inhabitants of the cities were continuously driven from one neighborhood to another as their homes were looted, and often burned, by the Red Army.[97] Industrial equipment was transported to Russia, leaving the German population thoroughly impoverished and the land bare by the time the Poles were allowed to take over the administration.[98] This was the "price" of Soviet Russian support of Poland.

The blackest chapter of inhumanity was written by the Soviet High Command in executing mass deportations. The indictment of such practices[99] is substantially reinforced by the countless reports of the utter lack of food, medicine, and clothing among the wretched deportees, one-third of whom failed to survive the winter of 1945-46, by the arbitrary "quotas" given to Russian divisions and armies concerning "deportations," and by the inconsistency of regarding the victims of deportation as minor war criminals.[100] According to a pro-Polish British author:

> Another constant element in Soviet policy was the drive to acquire German slave labour to rebuild Russia. . . . Already in March, and systematically until the end of April, the Russian army commanders deported Germans they thought suitable to forced labour in Russia. . . . Possibly the biggest "haul" they made in eastern Germany was in Upper Silesia where many skilled workers had been kept at work until the very moment of the Russian conquest; from East Prussia it was mostly female labour which was deported. German authorities estimate that some 218,000 unfortunates were so victimized. Those who were sent off during the worst cold of the winter suffered proportionately and some of them died on the journey.

To maintain that the Germans, in deciding to flee such a fate, deserted their homeland is at best hypocritical, as was the accusation that they feared for their security because they knew about German atrocities in the east.[101]

The German people of the Oder-Neisse provinces were unaware of the fate decided for them at the Teheran and Yalta conferences. Doubt about the outcome of the war, quite prevalent in western Germany, was in the east restricted to the East Prussians after the near catastrophe of October, 1944, but they, too, fell victim to the Goebbels propaganda of secret weapons and believed that the Reich would escape unconditional surrender. They also believed that the past plebiscites would save the province for Germany, even in case of Allied victory. Had they known the decisions of 1943-45 and the fact that their stay might influence the postwar fate of the territories, the eastern German population would have remained under the rule of the Red Army and suffered humiliation, death, and deportation in order to save the provinces for Germany. *Evacuation is a common experience in wartime, differing greatly from either the permanent abandonment of their abodes by a population or their permanent expulsion.*

*The procedure of preventing the evacuated population of entire
provinces to return after the close of hostilities was unknown in
Europe before 1945. The return of 1,500,000 German refugees in May
and June of 1945 from Czechoslovakia and the Russian Zone of Germany to the Oder-Neisse provinces, despite the threats of deportation,
hunger, and further humiliations, showed the attachment of the eastern Germans to their homeland.*[102] Not less than one million Silesians
returned in the early summer of 1945, though the Polish militia had
closed the bridges on the Neisse as early as June 1, 1945.[103] The number of Germans in the provinces by July, 1945, at the time of the
Potsdam Conference, had again grown to 5,650,000 belying Stalin's
and Osóbka-Morawski's denials of sizable German groups in the provinces and American estimates of 2,200,000.[104]

It is almost impossible to estimate the losses caused by the flight and
the occupation. Together with the losses from expulsion, smaller but
still substantial, the casualties[105] were as follows:

Silesia:	874,000
Eastern Pomerania:	440,000
Eastern Brandenburg:	239,000
East Prussia:	614,000
Total:	2,167,000

Some authors try to minimize the losses by not recognizing the total
and by subdividing the losses into different categories.[106] But to ex-
clude the population losses incurred by the flight from the losses which
these people had suffered as a result of Russian policy in the area and
the decisions of the Teheran and Yalta conferences would be an
obvious attempt to mislead. One must also remember that expulsion
was not alone a work of the Polish people but was instigated by Russia and that the signal for expulsion in the field, as well as at the
diplomatic table, came from Moscow.

The only losses which could not be directly attributed to the
Russian policy of 1944-45 are the air-raid and battlefield losses of the
population, which, however, amounted to only 550,000 persons. *This
leaves the loss at 1,600,000 persons, in addition to about 100,000 residents of Danzig and 217,000 Germans living in prewar Poland. Altogether, 1,900,000 people.*[107] The only comparable record is that of
the Jews exterminated by Hitler. But the eastern Germans were not

victims of Jewish rataliation but of methodical Communist policy and Polish national hatred.

The flight of the German population and the subsequent establishment of Polish administration in the Oder-Neisse provinces greatly strengthened Stalin's hand at the Potsdam Conference. By the time he met President Truman, Stalin had already achieved the basic aims of his policy toward Germany and Poland. These were:

(1) To compensate Poland for the continued annexation of eastern Poland by the member states of the U.S.S.R., namely, the Soviet Ukraine and Soviet Byelorussia;

(2) To cement the ties binding Poland to the U.S.S.R. and to assure the continued dependence of Warsaw by eliminating the London Polish exile government and acting as guarantor of Poland's new frontiers;

(3) To deepen the antagonism between the nationalities in the area—now Poles and Germans regarded each other as mortal and bitter enemies. The extraordinary cruelty practiced by Germans and Poles at the time of the Polish uprising and the excesses of the Polish militia in Russian-occupied areas of Germany were proof of the success of the Russian policy. The hatred of the Poles for Ukrainians also grew, while the Ukrainians now possessed large slices of territories, formerly Polish, which were coveted by Poland. Thus the Soviet Russians had no fear that the situation of 1919-1920 in the Ukraine could be repeated; and

(4) To acquire northern East Prussia without any Allied opposition, thereby attaining supremacy over the Baltic Sea.

CHAPTER VI

The Western Appeasement Policy at Yalta and Potsdam

1. WESTERN INTERESTS AND THE GERMAN EAST

ALTHOUGH Russia and Poland were intensely interested in Germany's future eastern frontiers and were able to surmise the consequences of any changes made, the Western powers lacked both knowledge of the Polish and German problems and the urge of self-interest, except for their general aim of weakening German power. However, Secretary of State Hull's and President Roosevelt's policy differed significantly, even during the war, from Churchill's vacillating position in regard to Poland and the German frontier.

It should be noted that neither of the two governments were *eo ipso* interested in the question, as President Wilson had been, both politically and emotionally, in the Czech, Polish, and southern Slav aspirations for independence from the Habsburg and German empires in 1917 and 1918. That the Treaty of Versailles had not catered to German interests and that most of the territories in the German east were not even claimed by Roman Dmowski is generally recognized. Discussion of the problem has always arisen in connection with other regional and global problems, namely:

(1) British advocacy of the restoration of a strong Poland as a bulwark against Germany and Russia, a view held by His Majesty's government between September, 1939, and June, 1941, in direct continuation of the French concept of eastern alliances for the purposes of exerting pressure on Germany and Russia and thereby diverting their aggressive intention from the Atlantic area and the Middle East, respectively.

(2) British-American concern over Russia's uncompromising de-

mand for her 1941 frontiers, the fruit of naked aggression against Poland, undertaken with the connivance of Germany, combined with apprehension as to the U.S.S.R.'s future intentions in the Balkans and Poland proper.

(3) The problem of postwar Germany, which was not seen in the light of a reasonable balance of power but in the heat of war psychosis, was an emotional component which led to the many demands for unconditional surrender, the Morgenthau Plan, and other measures devised to keep Germany divided and permanently impotent.

(4) The general framework of Western-Russian alliance and the anxiety shown, especially in the United States, for the formulation of solutions enabling the alliance to survive in the postwar period; hence, proposals for the placation of Russia in order to reduce casualties and insure co-operation.[1]

These factors, which provided the framework for the discussion of Polish-German frontiers in London and Washington, rendered an agreement on a just frontier impossible. They also weakened the Western argument against a resolute Russian policy in the region, explaining Western appeasement at the Yalta and Potsdam conferences and the subsequent conflict over the interpretation of the Potsdam Protocol.

Since the days of the eighteenth century, the primary aim of British policy on the European continent has been to maintain a favorable balance of power, a course prescribed to the English government by its own *Staatsräson*.[2] Britain was a maritime power exercising control over most of the seas but patently incapable of withstanding a determined attack of the combined power of the European continent. The American War of Independence and the subsequent Napoleonic Wars impressed upon His Majesty's government the need for powerful allies in Europe and/or for the prevention of any coalition or the emergence of any power or powers which could gain supremacy over the continent.[3] Even in the period of "splendid isolation," English policy toward France, Austria, and Russia was characterized by attempts to prevent Russian preponderance by backing Austria and France and to thwart French hegemony by supporting Prussia and the Tsarist Empire. These considerations led to the fruitless overtures to Germany following the dismissal of the Iron Chancellor and, subsequently, to the *entente cordiale* with France and Russia in 1904 and 1907.[4] Concern about the balance of power also prevented London from energetically supporting the French system of alliances after

World War I, making Hitler, after 1933, a welcome ally of some British conservative circles, which assumed that the strengthening of Hitler's Germany would avert the danger of Russian preponderance.

Finally, after Hitler's march on Prague, his thrust against the European balance-of-power system, more than British disgust with his totalitarian methods and the humiliation at Munich underlay Neville Chamberlain's decision to turn against Germany in March, 1939.[5] The subsequent British courting of the U.S.S.R. in the spring and summer months of 1939, intended to assure a supporting arch in the east, ended in failure, leaving Britain and France exposed to the fury of German attack. While Russia became a German ally, Poland fought to the bitter end and was considered a reliable friend of the West in case of a negotiated peace and/or total victory. Therefore, Polish ambitions to attain wider access to the Baltic Sea became a British interest, too. As expressed in the Chamberlain-Sikorski talks:

> Britain and France agreed that it was essential for Poland to be a "powerful state in the Baltic area so as to maintain a balance in the future between Germany and Russia."[6]

Sikorski has defined the understanding as:

> They recognized as their supreme task efficacious participation in the war, to deliver the country from enemy occupation and to assure Poland—in addition to direct and ample access to sea-frontiers which would safeguard her security.[7]

Of course neither Prime Minister Chamberlain nor his successor, Winston Churchill, contemplated the extension of Poland's frontier to the Oder and Neisse rivers. They looked at the problem from a strategic viewpoint, under the impact of the premature collapse of Polish military resistance in September, 1939. They attributed the collapse to the superiority of German armor and the numerical supremacy of the Wehrmacht but realized that German possession of East Prussia rendered defense of the Polish Corridor ineffective and, almost from the first day of the war, severed the connections of Poland with the sea. The presence of the Polish minority in the industrial centers of Upper Silesia had not escaped the attention of British circles,[8] which realized the importance of Silesian industry to the German war effort.

Both German[9] and Polish[10] authors chastise the fluctuating and inconsistent attitude of the British government on the question of Polish frontiers between 1941 and 1945. Although they are morally and legally justified, they fail to grasp the tremendous change in outlook and composition that had occurred in the camp of the anti-Hitler coalition on June 22, 1941. Before that date, the war, aimed at the destruction of German power, was equally intended to contain Russian power. Thus before the entrance of the U.S.S.R. into the war, the struggle had the characteristics of the resistance of democratic forces against totalitarian philosophies. The war, however, was still fought with a politico-military question mark: the long-range position of the U.S.S.R. toward the belligerents. When the German attack on Russia decided this point, Britain, in order to restore the balance of power, hastened to the aid of the U.S.S.R. in order to enable her to contain German power on the Continent. It is characteristic that the same Churchill who, in 1918-19, actively supported intervention in internal Russian affairs to defeat the Bolsheviks offered, in 1941, all aid needed by and a close alliance with the same party, now in control of the U.S.S.R. In extending support to Bolshevist power in the east, Britain and other Western powers had to abandon their moralistic attitudes for tangible military advantages. Though a defender of Western values, Prime Minister Churchill, in order to defeat German power, became the ally of the most dangerous iconoclast in history, aggressively rebellious against democracy and other nineteenth-century Western achievements.

The defeat of Axis power proved to be an overriding consideration in the formulation of His Majesty's governmental policies. To this, the future consequences of a strengthening of Soviet Russian power were clearly subordinated. Von Clausewitz's valid dictum that war is only a continuation of diplomacy with other means was forgotten. The British attitude was dictated by the still-doubtful outcome of the war and the absence of any benevolent neutrals, except the United States, which was already committed. Churchill hoped that the forthcoming American participation in the war would strengthen his hand against the U.S.S.R., as well as against Germany. His confidence seemed to increase as a result of strong American protests against the territorial clauses demanded by Moscow in the draft British-Russian treaty[11] and his knowledge of the dependence of Russia on Lend-Lease aid.

Reappraisal of Britain's position in the war effected a reconsideration of her policies toward Poland, henceforth regarded as a secondary power in containing Germany. The U.S.S.R., whose armies were locked in a deadly struggle with the mass of the Wehrmacht, rather than the weak and unequipped Poles, whose resistance was broken by the Germans in a matter of days, was to be the guarantor of peace in the east. Therefore, Poland was called upon to make a compromise with Moscow, and any agreement about the transfer of German territories to Poland was to be dependent on Russian good will and support.[12]

While British policy often sacrificed the lofty goals of a world-wide democratic order for real or apparent military advantages, the United States had the reputation of defending the rights of small nations and of working for a stable world order based on justice and peace. American contributions to the rule of international law and arbitration, as well as the absence of any territorial demands of the United States against other nations, were guarantees that if any state could succeed in checking the imperialistic impulses of the Soviet Union, it would be the United States. Never was faith in the supremacy of democracy and the urge to conduct a crusade to save freedom in Europe and Asia stronger in the United States than in the early forties of this century. To the war-winning ideology of the Allied powers, President Roosevelt contributed the "Four Freedoms" and the stipulation of the Atlantic Charter on annexations, to wit:

> [The Signatory Powers] desire to see no territorial changes that do not accord with the freely expressed wishes of the peoples concerned.[13]

There is a tremendous responsibility inherent in any high-level pronouncement. Failure to implement its precepts results not only in serious disillusionment among actual and potential allies but also in a dangerous loss of prestige that has been defined as power that does not have to be used in order to achieve a certain political objective.[14]

The dicta of the Atlantic Charter, benevolent in intention, although produced largely for purposes of psychological warfare,[15] were naïve in the context of world politics as of August, 1941. There was no Western power both adequate and available to play *arbiter mundi*, and public support was lacking for any grandiose projects to create and maintain a just and stable world order by the American sword. Two powerful forces were at work frustrating a thorough involvement of the United States as the postwar world's defender of freedom and democracy against Soviet Russian encroachment. They were:

(1) The isolationist opposition which, even after the attack on Pearl Harbor, was only temporarily dormant. It considered both alliance with Russia and involvement in European affairs with horror.[16] While doubtlessly correct in its denunciation of the alliance with the U.S.S.R., the isolationists were thoroughly inconsistent in their denial of permanent American responsibilities, for, from the point of view of American national interests, active American participation and pressure were necessary to attain a peace that would insure American security by refusing to allow the U.S.S.R. such territorial and military expansion after victory as to enable her to launch aggression against the West.

(2) Leftist elements were very influential in the Roosevelt administration.[17] Though often without any formal connections with the Communist party, these elements agreed that the Communists, especially those in China, were only social reformers, more akin to liberal democrats than the "reactionary," imperialist Britons. The absence of a strict and adequate government security program and wartime co-operation with Moscow allowed undesirable elements to infiltrate the government and becloud the judgment of American policy-makers in regard to American self-interest. Here, too, the obsession with total victory was given priority over an objective appraisal of Russian strength and intentions. The argument of those favoring appeasement was either to emphasize the necessity for placating Russia or to give her unlimited Lend-Lease aid, regardless of her peccadilloes, in order to reduce American casualties. Their method of eliminating opposition often consisted of accusing of Nazi sympathies anyone who argued with their conclusions. The Harry Hopkinses and the Henry Wallaces thereby did a great disservice to the cause they were purportedly serving.

Under the honest and well-meaning Secretary of State, Cordell Hull, the United States began to resist unreasonable Russian demands. When the reports that Russia wanted British support for the Russian frontiers of 1941 and for the transfer of East Prussia to Poland were confirmed, Hull persuaded the President to support the British position of no wartime frontier agreements. He pointed out that:

The admission of the principle that post-war frontiers should be adjudged during the war would decisively weaken the association of nations opposed to the Axis . . . by the introduction among its members of mutual suspicion and by the efforts of various members to intrigue in order to obtain commitments with regard to the territory of other members.[18]

If the British governmnent, with the tacit or expressed approval of this government, should abandon the principle of no territorial commitments prior to the peace conference, it would be placed in a difficult position to resist additional Soviet demands relating to the frontiers, territory, or spheres of influence which would almost certainly follow whenever the Soviet government would find itself in a favorable bargaining position.[19]

There is no doubt that the Soviet government has tremendous ambitions with regard to Europe and that at some time or other the United States and Britain will be forced to state that they cannot agree, at least in advance, to all of its demands. It would seem that it is preferable to take a firm attitude now, rather than to retreat and to be compelled to take a firm attitude later when our position had been weakened by the abandonment of the general principles referred to above.[20]

The Secretary of State threatened the issuance of a separate American statement in opposition to wartime territorial settlements, should the British and the Russians include such a clause in their treaty.[21] It is interesting that this single instance of forceful American intervention in the territorial questions of east central Europe was very successful; it caused Russia to desist from including the clause in the British treaty. It also shows that even during the war, forcing concessions from the Soviet Union was not impossible if the West had the courage to insist.

Unfortunately, the firm stand deteriorated. The reasons for the deterioration have been touched upon before, but for an understanding of the reasons for appeasement, the ideas of American policymakers must be analyzed.

All of the leading Western policy-makers, including Secretary of State Hull, who at least was aware that Russian subversive operations in countries which had extended recognition to her had not been completely abandoned, were guilty[22] of disregarding the aims of world Communism. Under the influence of Roosevelt's great "design" to persuade Russia to work for international peace in the coming United

Nations, the Secretary managed to dispel the suspicion in his mind that Russia might ever return to an "isolationist" policy after acquiring certain territories in eastern Europe.[23] There is no mention, even in Hull's memoirs, of the possibility of a militantly aggressive Russia bent upon world domination, or at least upon the domination of Eurasia. The great illusion, reinforced by Roosevelt's ideas, influenced Hull to write: "We must be patient and forebearing. We cannot settle questions with Russia by threats. We must use friendly methods. We are constantly conferring with the Russians in a friendly way."[24] Again: "Consult them at every point. Engage in no cussin' matches. Explain to them, again and again if necessary, the principles upon which we felt peaceful international relations would prosper."[25]

The erroneous character of such a policy and the disadvantages accruing to the United States therefrom are clear today. Why, then, were they such a mystery to American statesmen in 1943? Russian ambitions were known to the government in those days, and American leaders could not be called uninformed. Still, they attempted to protect United States interests by a continuing effort to influence a foreign power that could not be persuaded.

The second reason for the "soft" policies of the American statesmen was the misinterpretation of the respective military positions of the U.S.S.R. and the United States. Fearing the conclusion of a separate armistice between the Soviet Union and Germany, the United States failed to attach any conditions to its Lend-Lease aid. Hull's argument that any conditions would have contradicted wartime requirements sounds unconvincing in view of the serious differences in the postwar objectives of the two powers and the impossibility of a German-Russian truce. The double reversal of alliances in 1939 and 1941 between the U.S.S.R. and Germany must have persuaded both parties of the impossibility of permanent co-existence. Thus Russian participation in the war, regardless of the conditions attached either to Lend-Lease aid or the strict observance of the Four Nation Declaration in the occupied countries, was assured for the West.[26] The complete preoccupation of American military and civilian leaders with tactical abridgement of the duration of hostilities and their appeasement of Russian military demands, even after the defeat of Germany, had become an accomplished fact that rendered the path of American postwar policy increasingly difficult.[27] The effects of the abandonment of the 1943 cross-Channel invasion of northwest France,[28] the opposition of General George C. Marshall to the Churchillian idea of a Balkan invasion in both 1943 and 1944,[29] and the extraordinarily defeatist evaluation of American and Russian military strength in 1944[30] paved the way for the American fiasco at the Yalta and Potsdam conferences.

A third important factor which erroneously influenced American policy in favor of Russia, with special emphasis on Poland and eastern Germany, was the so-called "Grand Design" of President Roosevelt.[31] Because the President considered Stalin a Russian nationalist rather than a Communist leader bent on world revolution, he believed that the Russian dictator, in view of the consequent political and economic advantages to Russia, could be persuaded to accept international co-operation, with its inherent limitation upon his freedom of action. Furthermore, the President also considered his personal diplomacy a great asset to the American cause. He believed that if given the opportunity, he could "convince" Stalin of the peaceful intentions of the United States and the advantages to Russia of implementation of the "Three Policemen" concept supported by the United Nations.[32] The Uncle Joe propaganda, Mr. Davies' *Mission to Moscow*,[33] and the subsequent press attacks on Secretary Hull, labeling him an anti-Russian, prepared the right psychological climate but probably trapped the President himself.[34] The results were most catastrophic in the Polish question and the eastern German provinces, for the continued insistence upon co-operation with Russia, in the face of her naked imperialist ambitions in Poland, made a strong stand impossible, despite the success of such an attitude in 1942.[35]

2. FROM THE BRITISH-SOVIET TREATY TO THE YALTA CONFERENCE

Secretary Hull's success in preventing British commitment to honor Russian claims to the Balticum and eastern Poland in 1942 has been mentioned. The flexibility of the British (and the inflexibility of the American) position on postwar frontiers underwent a change in 1943 as a result of improving Allied military fortunes. Russian victory in the Battle of Stalingrad and that of the Western Allies in the North African campaign destroyed the prospect of a negotiated peace.

Postwar planning was becoming the demand of the hour. Close British and American re-examination of the Polish-German frontier question, originally restricted to East Prussia,[36] was greatly influenced by the emergence of another issue—severance by the Soviet leaders of their relations with the Polish government-in-exile. The Russian action left the Western governments to search for a solution to Poland's eastern frontiers while the U.S.S.R. proceeded to make disturbing moves to create a second Polish exile government willing to grant to Moscow the coveted territories in eastern Poland.[37]

Although British propaganda favoring the exiled Poles was decreasing,[38] Secretary Hull expressed his willingness to defend Polish interests as if they were American,[39] and President Roosevelt was careful not to appease the Russians, lest the American voters of Polish descent turn against him in the 1944 elections.[40]

The Western powers began to look for a new approach in regard to the question of the Polish frontiers. Churchill believed that one could be found only if the compensation theory could be implemented, indemnifying Poland for the losses in the east. Although the idea of compensation was made the cornerstone of British policy at the Teheran Conference and thereafter, Churchill's solution[41] failed for the following reasons:

(1) The refusal of the U.S.S.R. ever to accept the London Poles, who insisted upon a pro-Western, independent course for Poland, as negotiating partners, and the Russian desire to dominate and use the country as the supply depot for their future occupation zone in Germany.

(2) The sacrifices demanded by the U.S.S.R. from the London Polish government were too great for the Poles to accept unless imposed upon them by a military dictate.[42]

(3) In relation to Germany, Churchill's proposal disregarded both the most elementary human right of any nation, whether aggressive or peace loving, to retain territories which are indisputably inhabited by its nationals, and the right of enemy nationals to remain in the home-land, even if a change of sovereignty should become inevitable.

The British "compensation" policy was, of course, a contradiction in terms. If Poland's claim to the eastern territories was valid, she certainly had no right to German territories; if she were compelled to cede territories in the east, she would become an aggressor in assuming the administration of other territories on the basis of their conquest and transfer to her by the aggressor against her. If, however, Poland's claim was questionable or nonexistent, as Britain's Russian ally maintained, she was not entitled to any German territories, save some small districts to enlarge her access to the sea. So the question remained: Should a wrong be done to correct one already existing,

as British opinion held, or should one to be done in order to calm the
Poles, rebellious over Russia's insistence upon recovering eastern
Poland, as Russian propaganda could be paraphrased?[43]

While the Prime Minister tried to save Poland's independence at
the expense of her territorial integrity, Secretary Hull vainly attempted to bring about a Russo-Polish reconciliation at the Moscow
Conference of Foreign Ministers in October, 1943.[44] He was told by
Foreign Commissar Molotov that the Polish question was one to be
settled by the Russian government, which would listen to what others
might say but would, in the end, do what was necessary to secure its
interests in Poland.[45]

President Roosevelt failed to understand the finality of the Russian
position and agreed to Churchill's compensation policy at the Teheran
Conference, including the acceptance of the Curzon Line, which, he
insisted, ran east of Lemberg.[46] He failed to press Stalin for a *quid
pro quo* on the question of restoration of Polish-Russian relations and
finally agreed to the Oder frontier *in abstracto* without receiving Russian guarantees of Polish independence and the disbanding of the
Moscow-supported Polish Committee.[47]

The result of the Teheran Conference was disappointing for the
West and Poland alike. Russia's uncompromising position on Poland
could not be shaken, while the abrogation of the principles of the
Atlantic Charter was to affect the central European balance of power
seriously by weakening Germany beyond the dictates of military necessity. These considerations did not, however, occur to President Roosevelt, who, at that time, agreed with Stalin that the fifty thousand
general-staff officers and engineers of the German army should be shot
summarily.[48] Whatever the horrors committed by the National Socialist regime of Germany, such retrogression to barbarian customs by the
President of the greatest democratic power on earth was to have grave
repercussions in the formative years ahead.

The decisions of the Teheran Conference can be deduced by researchers on the basis of available material, though the archives on
this particular Big Three meeting have not yet been opened.[49] According to Churchill, the transfer of East Prussia, the administrative district of Oppeln, and the German territories east of the River Oder to
Poland were decided at the Conference.[50] Sherwood was more cautious
in his presentation, as he mentions only that Stalin wanted to establish
a new frontier at the Oder, between Poland and Germany, to which
he requested Roosevelt's consent.[51] Simultaneous Western acquies-

cence to the Oder frontier and the Curzon Line amounted to the acceptance of Russian territorial demands without any *quid pro quo* as to the legality of the Polish exile government in London. Stalin, therefore, readily assumed that the British Prime Minister could easily induce the exile Poles to agree to Russian territorial demands.

Churchill's last illusions concerning postwar Russian co-operation were shattered at the Conference. He realized that the co-operation for which he professed to work would have to be based on a balance of military and political power between the two nations rather than on the good will of the Russian dictator. Therefore, the aim of the Prime Minister became to preserve as much Western influence in Poland and southeastern Europe as possible. However, his hand was greatly weakened by the fact that Poland would be occupied by Russia because the American military had rejected his Adriatic invasion plans in favor of the Normandy invasion, thereby depriving the British armies of the occupancy of east central Europe.[52]

Churchill's first move was to bring about a reconciliation between Moscow and the London Poles, at the price demanded by the Kremlin, in order to gain a solid bridgehead for Western influence in postwar Poland. He decided to accept the Russian solution to the frontiers and warned the London Poles of the consequences. His overtures in May, 1944, to Stalin and Roosevelt in regard to spheres of influence in the Balkans are clear proof that in the absence of formal agreements, he feared the establishment of Russian hegemony in the region.[53]

Churchill's next move was to negotiate with the London Poles. During his convalescence at Marrakech, he requested Foreign Secretary Eden to transmit the British proposal to Mikolajczyk, adding the thinly veiled threat:

> On the other hand, if they [the London Poles] cast it aside, I do not see how His Majesty's Government can press for anything more for them. The Russian armies may in a few months be crossing the frontiers of pre-war Poland, and it seems of the utmost consequence to have friendly recognition by Russia of the Polish Government and a broad understanding of the post-war frontier agreement agreed before then.[54]

In January, 1944, Churchill submitted his own program to the London Poles. It called for:

(1) Recognition of the Curzon Line as Poland's eastern frontier;

(2) The cession by Germany of Upper Silesia—and all areas east of the Oder desired by Poland—to Poland;

(3) Voluntary repatriation of Poles from areas east of the Curzon Line ceded to the U.S.S.R.; and

(4) Expulsion of the German population from the territories east of the Oder annexed by Poland.[55]

Mikolajczyk's government demanded more precise definitions. In regard to the border question, inquiry about a British-American, or at least a British, guarantee was made; the question of the sovereignty of the London Polish government in a Russian-occupied Poland was reopened; and a request for the participation of Western forces in the occupation was presented. The Poles wanted to make the cession of German territories part of a German armistice agreement and desired Allied support in uprooting the German population in the provinces and transporting them to Germany proper.[56] The British government evaded these issues by referring to the necessity of exchanging views with the other governments involved.[57] The Polish underground decided to reject the frontier changes in the east while demanding the cession of large German territories to Poland.[58] Mikolajczyk finally attempted a weak compromise by offering a "temporary demarcation line running east of Lwów and Vilna."[59]

Having reached a deadlock with the London Poles in early February, Churchill decided to persuade Stalin to accept some changes in the Curzon Line, for time had begun to run out when Russian troops entered prewar eastern Poland on January 4, 1944. His message to Stalin elicited a very rude reply from the Russian dictator, who reminded Churchill in no uncertain terms of the Teheran agreement and continued:

> Your message, particularly Kerr's [the British Ambassador to Moscow] statement, are interspersed with threats in regard to the Soviet Union. I should like to remind you that the method of threats is not only incorrect in the relationship of Allies, but is harmful, as it can bring about reverse results.[60]

Stalin turned down the Prime Minister's offer to postpone the frontier question until the end of hostilities and answered Churchill's warning to expose him in the House of Commons as follows:

> You are free to make any speech in the House of Commons. That is your affair. But if you make such a speech, I shall consider that

you have committed an act of injustice and unfriendliness toward the Soviet Union.[61]

In the opinion of Admiral Leahy, this was "the strongest and most undiplomatic document I have ever seen exchanged between two ostensibly friendly governments."[62]

With the failure of Churchill's efforts, the Polish problem became an increasingly American concern. United States interest was strongly expressed by Secretary of State Hull in October, 1943, but the course of events between Hull's departure for Moscow and Mikolajczyk's visit to Washington on June 12, 1944, caused basic changes in the American attitude.

President Roosevelt's belief in "personal diplomacy" survived its fiasco at the Teheran Conference. It is strange indeed that a man of great political astuteness and talent could fail to grasp reality and to recognize the objectives of the blunt actions of Stalin. The President did not realize that the Russian leader's refusal to recognize the London Polish government was based on his carefully laid plans to dominate that country. Roosevelt apparently assumed that once an agreement was reached on Poland's frontiers, the question of recognition would be solved automatically in favor of the London exile government. He voiced this opinion to Mikolajczyk,[63] and even at Yalta, where the political situation gave the U.S.S.R. absolute power over Poland and the choice left to the West was narrowed to either sanctioning or protesting against Russian control, he was misled that a free Poland would be created with Russian consent.[64]

Another basic change was Roosevelt's acceptance of the Curzon Line through his support of mutually satisfactory agreements between contending parties, thereby amending the American "no change" position of 1942.[65] The new policy, designed to extricate the United States from responsibility for unpopular frontier settlements, defeated its own purpose, for it was applied at a time when American self-interest should have dictated strong support for the efforts of Britain and the small nations in order to restrain Russian expansion in the region.

All of these factors contributed to the President's decision to support wholeheartedly the cession of large German territories to Poland, thus permanently weakening Germany. He was increasingly afraid of the effect of a public endorsement of the Curzon Line without large-scale compensation on the American Poles in the coming November,

1944 election.[66] By delaying the Polish Prime Minister's visit to Washington, the President missed the best opportunity to mediate before the Russians solidified their position in Galicia and built up a counter-government to the London Poles. Hull explains this erroneous policy by stating:

> The spring of 1944 was the period of preparation for the greatest military campaign in American history, the landing at Normandy. That landing had to be coordinated with Russian military movements in the east so that the Germans could not draw off too large a portion of their forces to meet us in the West. We could not afford to become partisan in the Polish question to the extent of alienating Russia at that crucial moment.[67]

It is a fact, however, that not until the Battle of Saint-Lô did the new Russian offensive in the middle section of the Eastern front force the Germans to withdraw sizable units from the Normandy front.

In view of the strongly pro-Russian tone of the propaganda in the Office of War Information's Polish program, the visit to Washington was of the utmost significance to Mikolajczyk, since possible American abandonment of the London government was brought into uncomfortable proximity.[68] The notes of the meeting were not published, but the Polish Premier's description of Roosevelt's reiteration of Russian good will toward Poland is hard to assess. Was the President sincere, or was he only uttering soothing words in order to free himself from detailed discussion of embarrassing problems? Thus, whether intentionally or unintentionally, the President deceived the Polish Premier by stating that Stalin was not an imperialist and that he did not desire to deprive Poland of her domestic freedom. He added a very deceptive phrase to his reassurance: "He [Stalin] would not dare to do that, because he knows that the United States Government stands solidly behind you. I will see to it that Poland does not come out of this war injured."[69]

Equally unrealistic was Roosevelt's estimate of his bargaining ability when he assured Mikolajczyk that he would act as a moderator in the Polish-Soviet dispute and intimated to him that:

> I'm sure I'll be able to manage an agreement in which Poland will get Silesia, East Prussia, Königsberg, Lwów, the region of Tarnopol, and the oil and potash area of Drohobycz.[70]

The statement can only be accepted either as a malicious deception or as a very sick man's delusion of grandeur in the light of the Teheran Conference and subsequent British-Russian exchanges, about which the President was kept informed.

After the Washington visit of Mikolajczyk, the transfer of the German territories east of the Oder River, with the possible exceptions of eastern Brandenburg and the area east of Stettin, seems to have been accepted by the Western powers, who regarded the agreement as a price to be paid to the U.S.S.R. and Poland in order to save Polish independence from Communization. Consent to the transfer also marked the ultimate acquiescence of the West to Russia's assumption of a predominant power position in the region, though seeking safeguards against its abuse for the subversion of existing regimes. Stalin was therefore surprised when, at Teheran, Roosevelt approached the question of Russian recognition of the London Polish government, with which he no longer considered negotiations necessary.

In this milieu, the crude betrayal of the Warsaw uprising failed to arouse energetic action by the Western powers. Churchill alone undertook some moves to save at least some of the politicians of the London government. By appealing directly to Stalin, he continued to espouse the compensation theory.[71] His position did not change, even after the supercilious reception of Mikolajczyk by Stalin in October, as the Cadogan Letter, which promised the Oder frontier to the London Poles, proves.[72] Only at the Malta Conference did Eden attempt to provide for a British retreat from the Oder Line position, in view of the deterioration of the Polish situation and growing American opposition.[73]

On the question of expulsions, Churchill told General Anders in August, 1944, that Germany ought to be able to absorb six million refugees and expellees.[74] The exile government, after voicing protests in the spring,[75] in late summer accepted the idea, representing the most sordid part of the Western-Polish deal, which, formulated to save Poland from Russian control, later came to naught.[76] The American government answered the Polish inquiry about the exchange of population affirmatively but placed the sole responsibility for any such action upon the Polish people and their government.[77]

The collapse of the Mikolajczyk government, resulting from the Cabinet's refusal to accept the terms the Premier brought back from Moscow,[78] sealed the fate of the London Poles. Relations with the Western power under the Archizewski government were correct but by no means cordial.[79] Overestimating their importance within the Allied coalition, the Cabinet rejected both the Curzon Line and fusion with the Lublin Committee. Although their action was morally justified, they were in an unenviable position, for in the fall of 1944, principles of equity were regarded as definitely inferior to the maintenance of cordial relations with Moscow. Thanks to the drifting appeasement policies of Teheran, the situation in eastern Europe could have been changed only by a new war against the Soviet Union. Churchill felt desperate and in his apprehension blamed the London Poles, rather than Moscow's greed, for the breakdown.[80] Although the Prime Minister's position seemed to be more understandable in December, 1944, it was a tragic one, since it consented to the creation of the tyrannis in central and eastern Europe.

President Roosevelt was now called upon to be the mediator, but Mikolajczyk's resignation saved him from the sad task of trying to solve the frontier issue. Any attempt would only have evoked the scornful rejection of Stalin at this stage. Still, the American government undertook further belated efforts to save Poland's independence and to bring about some small frontier corrections in the east in Poland's favor. The main effort was directed at freezing the *status quo* by preventing Russia from extending diplomatic recognition to the Lublin Committee as the government of Poland until the next Big Three conference at Yalta.

A message was sent to Ambassador Harriman to ascertain British views on the frontier and government disputes.[81] Then the American position against the new Soviet-Polish demand for the western Neisse frontier was strengthened and the Oder frontier subjected to a reexamination upon the recommendation of Ambassador Harriman, who reported:

I am somewhat concerned over the expanding concept of the Soviet Government in connection with the western frontier of Poland. . . .

When Mikolajczyk was in Moscow, he indicated that he was not at all certain that it was wise for the Polish boundary to go as far as the Oder, particularly to include the cities of Stettin and Breslau, as these cities and certain of the territories were almost completely German. . . .

Both the Lublin Poles and Mikolajczyk indicated in the October talks that they did not wish any German population to remain within Polish territories. . . . Churchill in his recent speech mentions the transfer of six million Germans. . . . The new suggested boundary to the Neisse would evidently necessitate the transfer of several million more Germans.

We have little information to appraise the consequences to European economy and stability if so large an area were to be occupied by Poles presumably evacuated largely from the backward districts incorporated into the Soviet Union. . . .

The question I have in mind . . . is whether, if we have reservations in the present case, they should not be registered on an appropriate occasion with the British and Soviet Governments before these concepts become so fixed that they are virtually a *fait accompli*.[82]

The result of the new diplomatic activity was two messages from the President to Stalin. The first, sent on December 16, expressed the hope that the Soviet Union would refrain from recognizing the Lublin government, "in view of the great political implications which such a step would entail," until a new Big Three meeting could be held.[83] The second message, an answer to Stalin's accusations against the London Poles, insisted uncompromisingly, on December 30, 1944, upon a postponement of Russian recognition of the Lublin Committee as the Polish government.[84] Stalin conveniently disregarded the President's message and extended recognition on December 31, 1944,[85] thereby demonstrating the absolute superiority of Russia over Western interests in Poland. The act was to have far-reaching consequences for the position of the Western powers at the Yalta Conference.

3. THE GREAT APPEASEMENT AND THEREAFTER

Probably no conference in American history has acquired the same odium as the meeting of the President with the Russian dictator and the British Premier at the Livadia Palace at Yalta in February, 1945. In the words of former Ambassador to Moscow William C. Bullitt:

At Yalta in Crimea, on February 5, 1945, the Soviet dictator
welcomed the weary President. Roosevelt, indeed, was more
than tired. He was ill. Little was left of the physical and mental
vigor that had been his when he entered the White House in
1933. Frequently he had difficulty in formulating his thoughts,
and great difficulty in expressing them consecutively. But he still
held to his determination to appease Stalin.[86]

Even more condemnatory is the judgment of John T. Flynn:

> It is the simple truth to say that Stalin outgeneraled Roosevelt
> at every point. Or perhaps, it would be nearer to the truth to say
> that Roosevelt had outgeneraled himself. Stalin had merely to
> sit tight, to make known his wishes and Roosevelt laid them
> in his lap with eager compliance, in the notion that he could
> thus soften Stalin. It is all the more incredible when we remem-
> ber that the things he was laying in Stalin's lap were the existence
> of little nations and the rights of little peoples he had sworn to
> defend.[87]

To excuse the appeasement leading to the decisions of the Yalta and
Potsdam conferences in view of the resultant chain reaction of events,
which loosed a terrible danger upon both the peoples of Europe and
Asia and the security of the Western powers, including the United
States, is impossible. In the Allied appeasement policy lay the seed
for the fall of China, the bloodshed of the Hungarian patriots, and
the present Russian threat to the United States and its allies in Berlin
and the Middle East.

Yet the Yalta Conference is not a magic code which, deciphered,
can explain all the ill that beset the postwar world. The concessions
were symptomatic of the inability of American foreign policy to
exploit a great military victory gained at a high price in manpower
and matériel. The tendency, in the Polish question, for example,
to refuse to resist trends in central Europe and elsewhere until they
became *fait accompli*'s and to minimize their impact upon American
national interests was a very serious shortcoming of United States
policy. In addition, the President's attempts to use "personal diplomacy" toward "Uncle Joe" resulted in compromises where the
Russian *quid pro quo* could be broken in weeks without any effect
on the course of American policy.

The restrictive interpretation of American interests in Europe at the Yalta Conference explains the President's remark that American troops could not be maintained on the Continent for more than two years,[88] which cost him more in the later course of the meeting than all his tactical and strategic retreats in the Polish problem. Roosevelt also entertained an exaggerated notion of Russia's power potential and the strength of her forces-in-being and displayed an irrational lack of military and political self-confidence, although American forces were at the peak of their power.

Churchill's lines, which describe the stupendous effects of the wave of hatred which the German aggression and Allied war propaganda unleashed upon Germany and her willing and unwilling allies, should also be kept in mind while groping for an understanding of the Conference:

It is a mistake to try to write out on a little piece of paper what the vast emotions of an outraged and quivering world will be either immediately after the struggle is over or when the inevitable cold fit follows the hot. These awe-inspiring tides of feeling dominate most people's minds, and independent figures tend to become not only lonely, but futile. Guidance in these mundane matters is granted to us only step by step, or at the utmost, a step or two ahead.[89]

Churchill, the classic representative of a past era when popular emotions aroused to a high pitch by mass-communications media were unknown or easily controlled, shivered apprehensively while trying to control the waves of hatred and passion he himself helped to create in the dark days of the Battle of Britain and which now seriously interfered with his concept of postwar reconstruction.

Such was not the case with the American President. At the first meeting, he told Stalin that he was struck by the extent of German destruction in the Crimea and that "all of this made him . . . more bloodthirsty toward the Germans than he had been a year ago."[90] Roosevelt was, indeed, riding the crest of a wave of popular passions, strongly convinced of their justification and propriety.

The extent of hatred for Germany in the Allied world was tremendous indeed. To quote the cautious comment of Professor John L. Snell:

The Germans opened a Pandora's box, and the floodtide of inhumanity which poured forth threatened to equal the one the Nazis had loosed over the rest of Europe. . . .[91]

Lord Vansittart's "Hate Germans" campaign pictured 75 per cent of the Germans as "incurably bellicose,"[92] and the majority of the American population, who had no use for the Germans, supported the "unconditional surrender" policy.[93] The question arises: Was an appeal to the base and irrational instincts of individuals necessary to defend the institutions which were regarded as the epitome of Western accomplishment? Did not such an appeal actually contradict the Allies' noble intentions and support the arguments of the cynics in Berlin and Moscow alike?

Even at the Yalta Conference the German-Polish frontier question was dealt with largely as an adjunct to the Polish problem. Only the British Premier raised the question under the heading of German frontiers[94] and reminded Stalin, who argued that most of the Germans had fled from the Oder provinces, that their resettlement in Germany formed part of the problem and posed insuperable complications in case further territories were detached from the Reich.[95]

The Western leaders were surprised by the stubborn Russian insistence upon the western Neisse frontier, which both Roosevelt and the British Premier energetically opposed. Churchill warned that "it would be a great pity to stuff the Polish goose so full of German food that it died of indigestion"[96] and said that the British people would never accept such a settlement. The President, displaying an unusual instance of determination in the face of Russian demands, included in the American proposal of February 8 on Poland the statement that "there would appear to be little justification for extending it [the frontier] up to the western Neisse."[97]

Yet even the American proposal of February 8 signified a substantial change in the American attitude since the Eden-Stettinius discussions at Malta, where, in the words of Mr. H. Freeman Matthews, Director of the Office of European Affairs of the Department of State, the United States favored only the cession of East Prussia, Upper Silesia, and certain territories up to the Oder.[98]

The reason for Roosevelt's adherence to the Oder frontier lay in the President's overoptimistic evaluation, on the eighth of February, of the chances for a pro-Western free Poland. In Malta, Line D was favored in anticipation of a Lublin-type, pro–Soviet Russian government in Poland, which, in the opinion of the Western leaders, should not be entitled to the same concessions as the favorite of the West, Mr. Mikolajczyk.[99] The February 8 meeting formed the real climax of the Conference. Stalin achieved a significant victory at the meeting by inducing the President to abandon the "Presidential Council" idea in Poland, to be composed of the neutrals and the London and Lublin Poles, and by persuading the British government to accept reorganization of the Lublin government rather than the creation of a new government.[100] Stalin's counterconcession was a flexible promise of free and prompt elections, which convinced Roosevelt that his "personal diplomacy" had proved successful and that the Russians would scrupulously adhere to their guarantee.[101] Russian willingness to enter the Far Eastern war and to drop the demand for recognition of the sixteen Soviet republics as members of the United Nations made Roosevelt conciliatory in the Polish question.[102] Only Churchill's continued warnings and the strongly negative attitude of the State Department on the western Neisse frontier prevented him from accepting this last Russian request.

The results of the Yalta Conference in regard to Poland and the German-Polish frontiers can be summarized as follows:

(1) The eastern frontiers of Poland, one of the most serious sources of disagreement between the U.S.S.R. and the Western powers, was settled on the terms demanded by Moscow.[103]

(2) The Western demand for recognition of the London Polish government was dropped before the Conference, and the Anglo-American request to form a completely new Polish government was abandoned during the Conference.[104]

No reorganization of the Lublin government that could have demonstrated successful Western interference with Soviet Russian hegemony in Poland took place. Moreover, Roosevelt and Churchill finally withdrew their request that "the Ambassadors of the three powers in Warsaw following such a recognition [of the new government] would be charged with the responsibility of observing and reporting to their respective Governments on the carrying out of the pledge in regard of free and unfettered elections."[105] They accepted the meaningless phrase "[They] will exchange Ambassadors by whose reports the respective Governments will be kept informed about the situation in Poland,"[106] despite Churchill's warning against a hurried, imprecise, and makeshift agreement.[107] Despite the agreement, the formation of a reorganized government was delayed until June, 1945, and the elections, which were considerably below "the purity of Caesar's wife," took place only in 1947.[108]

(3) Open conflict broke out in regard to the western Polish-German frontier. Driven by the fear of the permanent economic bankruptcy of a rump Germany in case of the cession of Lower Silesia to Poland and the corresponding loss of markets and economic aid to be provided to Germany, Britain assumed the leadership in resisting new Russian demands for the western Neisse frontier. Here the Prime Minister's hands were strengthened, both by the telegram of the British War Cabinet and by the able seconding of the President.[109]

(4) The decision in regard to the German occupation zones and the Reich's coming dismemberment, if executed, was to have a catastrophic effect on the future stability of western Europe and its relations with the Soviet Union. To Stalin, the Conference, which called for the destruction of German power and semi-permanent occupation of half of the Reich's territory by the Red Army,[110] must have appeared a complete success.

The Yalta decisions were not, however, implemented in their entirety, partially because flagrant breaches of good faith by the U.S.S.R. occurred too soon after the initialing of the Yalta Agreement. Stalin's irreconcilability in the Polish-government question and the *fait accompli*'s in the German east and east central Europe convinced even President Roosevelt of the impossibility of American-Russian co-operation.[111] He died, however, before deciding upon an alternative course.[112]

His successor, Harry S. Truman, was confronted with a difficult choice. Between February and April, 1945, in the German eastern territories and Poland, unilateral actions were undertaken by the Soviet Union. Polish administration was introduced into large parts of the contested provinces, and shortly after Truman assumed the Presidency, Stalin cemented relations with his puppets in Warsaw by concluding with them a mutual-assistance and friendship treaty.[113] The ambassadors at Moscow failed to make any progress on the projected "Government of National Unity." Truman also lacked a thorough knowledge of American military and foreign policy because, until his accession, the Vice-Presidential office had been neglected in American politics, and finally, the tradition of the Rooseveltian pro-Russian policy prevented him from taking energetic action that would result, in the hour of victory, in the disintegration of the wartime coalition.

The coalition had been disintegrating for the past year. The sole purpose, calling for the subordination of particular interests, faded with the surrender of the Reich, and the consciousness of separate interests after victory was to defeat this coalition as it had other coalitions in the past.[114]

President Truman's first action in the Polish question revealed his resistance to Soviet Russian moves to a degree unknown in the Roosevelt administration. Truman told Molotov in no uncertain terms that he would rather accept Russian absence from the San Francisco Conference, called to sign the United Nations Organization Charter, than to invite the present Warsaw regime.[115] Twice he protested the establishment of Polish administration in the Oder-Neisse provinces. The President's moves were unsuccessful, however, and he acquiesced in postponement of the discussion until the next Big Three conference.[116]

When the three victorious powers met amid the ruins of Potsdam, in the court town of the Hohenzollern, near Berlin, on July 17, 1945, the atmosphere was dominated by the growing fear that a new, basic conflict between the two blocs could not be avoided. Churchill expressed this fear, which was rapidly becoming reality, when he sketched the effects of Russian *intransigeance* in the Polish question in a message to Stalin on April 29, 1945:

There is not much comfort in looking into a future where you and the countries you dominate, plus the Communist Parties in many other States, are all drawn up on the one side, and those who rally to the English-speaking nations and their associates or Dominions, are on the other. It is quite obvious that their quarrel would tear the world to pieces and that all of us leading men on either side who had anything to do with that would be shamed before history.[117]

To Stalin, however, the meaning of history was contained in the coming victory of Communist world revolution supported by Russian military power, not in the moralistic denunciations of dissenters and aggressors.

The events of May and June determined the outcome of the coming conference of the Big Three. The Russian *fait accompli*'s in Poland and the Oder-Neisse provinces became obvious. The question was: What countermeasures could be employed? Churchill urged President Truman to refuse any withdrawal of British and American troops to their zonal frontiers in Germany until the outstanding problems with Russia had been settled at Potsdam in order to keep these territories in central and northern Germany temporarily as a bargaining weapon at the conference.[118] His letter to the President of June 4, 1945, was almost prophetic in the light of subsequent events:

> I view with profound misgivings the retreat of the American Army to our line of occupation in the central sector, thus bringing Soviet power into the heart of Western Europe, and the descent of an iron curtain between us and everything eastward. I hoped that this retreat, if it has to be made, would be accompanied by the settlement of many great things which would be the true foundation of world peace.[119]

The Prime Minister was turned down by the President, who feared the effects of a delay on Soviet-Western relations, and American withdrawal[120] began on June 21, 1945, not only causing a widening gulf between Poland and the western Russian demarcation line, but also permitting the area between the two Neisses to be allotted by Russia to Poland without reducing the size of the Russian occupation zone in Germany to less than those of the British and Americans, which Russia would have difficulty in accepting for reasons of prestige. Furthermore, the Red Army came into possession of the Thuringian Mountains, a perfect springboard for armored attack against the Rhine and the Low Countries, and ruled the second largest German industrial region, the precision industries of the triangle Leipzig-Chemnitz-Jena.

Still, the American attitude at the Potsdam Conference differed greatly from the Rooseveltian approach. In the Oder-Neisse question, the exact frontier line was the bone of contention between the United States and the U.S.S.R., but the accent was now transferred to the legality of establishing any Polish administration in the area before a peace conference and to the competency of the Conference to deal with the frontier question as such.[121]

While Truman succeeded in persuading Stalin that Germany, as of December 31, 1937, should form the basis of discussion,[122] his efforts to dissent from the Oder–Western Neisse Line were countered by Stalin's objections that prevailing conditions prevented any turnover of the area to the Germans.[123] Stalin also used a deceitful game in regard to the number of Germans left in the area, by maintaining that all of them had fled.[124] This failed to deceive Truman, but the President was certainly hardly aware that more than four and one-half million Germans were still living in the Oder-Neisse provinces.[125]

Prime Minister Churchill also fought the acceptance of the Oder-Neisse frontier and maintains in his memoirs that he would have preferred to risk a complete break with Russia than to agree to the present line, even provisionally.[126] The elections of July 28, however, removed him from the political scene. Clement Attlee became Prime Minister, while Ernest Bevin succeeded Foreign Minister Sir Anthony Eden.[127] Though Bevin continued, in pursuance of his instructions, even on July 30, 1945, to refuse the western Neisse frontier, the decision now rested with the President, who, anxious to return to Washington, saw a possible solution in the combination of the German-Polish frontier question with other outstanding problems. After Molotov rebuffed an American attempt to recognize the principle of provisional administration by Poland of the areas east of the Oder and the Glatzer Neisse,[128] combining the Oder-Neisse issue with the request for freer, Western access to countries now under Russian occupation led to the compromise of July 31, 1945.[129] The proposal of July 31, however, mentioned provisional administration of the area east of the Oder and western Neisse.[130] The reasons for the American compromise can only be partially understood on the basis of the present source material, for there is no explicit information on it. The Russians accepted a smaller percentage of the reparations, in the form of German machinery and equipment, from the Western zones than originally requested and agreed to Western control of the Ruhr.[131] Furthermore, the Red dictator gave paper concessions to the West in regard to wider access to eastern Europe and to free elections.[132]

On the principle of the competency of the Conference, however, the American position remained that the frontiers could be fixed only at the coming peace conference. In Truman's words, "cession of territory was subject to the peace treaty and . . . the American plan concerned only the temporary administration of the area."[133]

Thus by agreeing to a provisional Polish administration, the President extricated himself from the agreement Roosevelt had made at the Yalta Conference on the "Line of the Oder." In view of the fact that the Communization of Poland was making steady progress, despite Bierut's reassurances to Churchill to the contrary at the Potsdam Conference, to which he had been invited with other members of the "Government of National Unity,"[134] revision of the American position along the line of the Malta discussion became a matter of time.

To Stalin, the results of the Conference represented a marked advance. Poland no longer formed a topic of discussion, and Churchill's only objections were to the subordination of the Anders Army to the Bierut government, which was to be implemented with active British help. The Premier, however, considered that British participation would be a breach of honor.[135] The German-Polish frontier on the Oder and western Neisse was not agreed to but was at least tolerated by the West, and an open break was avoided. The Iron Curtain had not yet descended over central and eastern Europe with the same steel-traplike quality as in 1948, but Stalin had the stage set in Potsdam. The Western governments agreed to recognize the puppet Rumanian and Bulgarian governments,[136] and in Hungary and Czechoslovakia, no significant Western influences remained. The destruction of German power was completed, no German government survived, and looting of the Soviet zone of occupation could be continued for another six months.[137]

Yet at the Conference, the limit of unopposed or tolerated Russian expansion in Europe was demonstrated for the first time. The Allies' insistence upon control of the Ruhr, their energetic stand on Austria and the food needs of the German people, and their stiffening position toward Tito were welcome signs of strength.

More important for world politics was the changing tenor of the American government. President Truman lacked Roosevelt's wartime friendship with the Russian dictator and the latter's "Uncle Joe" complex. Harry Hopkins had followed his benefactor to the grave, and the new American Secretary of State was to play a more formidable role than either the absent or ill-informed Cordell Hull or the businesslike Stettinius. The sight of ruins, the penniless, hungry eastern German refugees, and the unchecked looting process in the Russian zone of occupation could not help but influence the President and the British leaders as well.[138] American public opinion, too, was affected, and doubts about the feasibility of co-operation with Russia multiplied as signs of oppression, breaches of international agreements, and unfriendly acts revealed the true intentions of the Kremlin. There could be no question in the mind of Stalin but that a continuation of the present course would lead to a break with Washington and London. He therefore had to consolidate his gains in central Europe while using the Communist parties as a wedge to gain control of southern and western Europe. It was this aim which animated Russian policy until 1949.

CHAPTER VII

Polish Administration in the Oder-Neisse Provinces

1. THE EXPULSION OF THE GERMAN POPULATION

THE ultranationalist and agnostic movements of this century have led to the full triumph of the concept of the nation-state with unlimited sovereignty. After the First World War, oppression of ethnic minorities was widespread in all central and eastern European countries, for ethnic homogeneity in the state was considered the ultimate political goal. Economic pressures, discrimination in employment, and the business boycott became weapons in the hands of the state. Those who formed the ethnic majority within a nation were pitted against the minorities in order to assimilate them or to destroy the bases of their politico-economic power. For the less docile and better educated elements of the minorities, voluntary migration to the mother country was offered as an escape from the restrictive measures of the government. These forces were at work in both Germany and Poland before 1939 and even before 1933, though the Germans in Poland, as the wealthier and better educated minority, suffered relatively more under the impact of the repressive measures.[1]

The coming of Hitler and his doctrines was to increase the severity of the nationality struggle.[2] Two new weapons were added to the arsenal of nationalist oppression: the claim of the Führer to the allegiance of the German ethnic minorities in other countries, despite their non-German citizenship, and the right to resettle German minorities, as practiced in the Baltic States and Bessarabia after the Ribbentrop-Molotov agreement of August, 1939. Furthermore, after the victorious end of the Polish campaign, the Third Reich undertook to evacuate the Polish citizens from a large part of the Warthegau, a purely Polish province.[3] Although economic consideration and the lack of "resettlers" prevented the Germans from implementing the plan, some 700 to 800 thousand Poles were moved, creating a fateful precedent for the East Germans after the war.

While National Socialist use of the ethnic Germans in central and eastern Europe poisoned the relationship between the minority and majority nations,[4] the acuteness of the problem dates from the inhuman and criminal German attempt during the occupation of Poland to exterminate the rebellious elements of the Polish intelligentsia and the Polish Jewry. The records of Belsen and Auschwitz and the Warsaw Ghetto uprising form eloquent indictments of the National Socialist relapse into barbarism that rendered a wave of Polish revenge after the war almost inevitable.[5]

In Hitler's policies and in those pursued by Poland from 1945 to 1947, the idea of the nation-state was led *ad absurdum,* and the question arises: Was not immorality and mass murder too great a price to pay for the creation of a homogeneous state and the glory of the nation? To any Christian, the answer should be obvious.

Russian excesses against the German population after the invasion of eastern Germany by the Red Army have been related before. The official character of the short-lived but thorough terrorization of the native population, carried out in order to induce panic and flight, has also been sketched. Although by the summer of 1945 Russian behavior toward German civilians became civilized, this cannot be said of the Polish attitude toward the remainder of the German population of the provinces. Like Hitler, the Poles, under Bierut and Osóbka-Morawski,[6] without any protest from Mikolajczyk,[6] augmented the nationality struggle by adding several unlawful methods. The German population was thoroughly and systematically looted, forced to heavy physical labor for little or no compensation, and then expelled, strictly on the basis of its ethnic origin. At this point, another question arises: Was the death of over one million persons, the expulsion of another three and one-half million, and the refusal to readmit about four and one-half million who were evacuated from the battle zone, mainly on orders of their government, morally or even politically justified in order to attain the goal of an ethnically homogeneous Polish state? Can Poland still appear before the world as the martyred, heroic nation defending Western culture and principles of morality against Nazism and Communism? Did not the adoption of the worst and most despicable of the Nazi terror methods used by the Polish militia and

Communist-infested State Security Police besmirch the ideals in defense of which Polish youth had shed its blood so readily?[7]

The story of the expulsion of the German population will not be recorded on the glorious pages of Polish history. Polish rule over the German population of the Oder-Neisse provinces, lasting anywhere from a few weeks to from two to three years, was characterized by misery, oppression and the inhuman treatment of these people, most of whom were as innocent and peace loving as the Poles who ended up in Belsen or the jails of the Gestapo. The determination of Bierut to expel the German population and the acquiescence of Mikolajczyk after he accepted the line of the Oder has been related. Actually, the administration of the Oder-Neisse region was, in the first weeks, in the hands of the Russian Red Army. Only in Danzig and in the cities of the Upper Silesian industrial region was Polish rule immediate and effective.[8] In Gdańsk (Danzig), the troops of the Red Army were soon released by the Polish militia, and by April, "repatriated" Poles from the U.S.S.R. were settled in the old Hanseatic port.[9] The city was practically annexed by Poland when Polish laws, including the decree regarding the "Expulsion of Hostile Elements from the Polish Society," were made effective as of May 8, 1945,[10] and the zloty was introduced as currency on May 25, 1945.[11] These measures were followed by a written appeal to the German population to leave the city immediately.[12] When "voluntary" emigration did not produce satisfactory results, Polish militia simply evacuated large residential sections inhabited by the Germans,[13] who were then transported to Stettin in locked animal freight cars. They were usually looted on their way by Russian soldiers and Polish gangs.[14] With the constant use of such methods, only ten thousand Germans were left in Danzig by the end of 1945. The rest fled, were expelled, or were deported to forced labor camps.[15]

A month before the Potsdam Conference, expulsion of the German population commenced in eastern Brandenburg and the western counties of Silesia and eastern Pomerania.[16] Haunted by hunger, misery, and the plundering of the marauders, several hundred thousand Germans were compelled to carry their small baggage with them on daylong marches from their places of residence to the Oder and Neisse rivers.[17] Upon arriving on the German side of the rivers, they could find neither accommodations nor food, and wartime destruction and overcrowded quarters, a result of the former waves of refugees who still awaited their return to the Oder-Neisse provinces, made assimilation impossible.[18] The aim of this unauthorized expulsion was to create a 50- to 75-mile-wide zone west of the Oder Neisse Line in which no Germans were to be present in order to convince the arriving Western Allies that no Germans remained in the disputed provinces.[19] The abrupt suspension of expulsion by July 15 shows that it had created catastrophic conditions in the regions of the Russian occupation zone adjoining the Oder and Neisse rivers. The situation was getting out of the control of the Red Army, which feared Western revulsion at the sight of wretched, hungry refugee masses close to Potsdam. Thus the inevitable end was again delayed for the German population in the provinces.[20]

The appeal of the great powers to Poland in the Potsdam Protocol[21] to stop any expulsion until the submission of the plan of the Allied Control Council in Berlin providing for population transfers in "an orderly and humane manner" was disregarded by Warsaw. The next area of expulsion was Upper Silesia, where trains were filled with Germans, who were transported to the Russian Zone as early as August and September, 1945.[22] The method of expulsion was not humane at all. The population of entire villages and small towns was gathered in camps, usually consisting of military barracks or factory halls, and there the victims usually had to spend two to four weeks, without adequate food or accommodations, before they were transported to the West.[23] The same fate was experienced by the women and children of the German population in southern East Prussia and Pomerania. They, too, were subjected to expulsion orders within a few minutes, to long marches and camp life without adequate food and sleeping accommodations, to "baggage controls," as official looting by the militia was euphemistically called, and to the criminal plundering of Polish gangs during the trip to the West.[24] The number of dead, sick, and weak people arriving in the Russian Zone of Germany was unusually high.[25]

Until November, 1945 (the Allied Control Council plan for population transfer was not concluded until the seventeenth of that month), Polish authorities went to great lengths to prove the "voluntary" character of the departures.[26] The expellees were required to sign a declaration in the Polish language renouncing their right to return, bequesting all their property and wealth to the Polish state, and stating that they had left on their own initiative. The winter months of 1945-46, however, caused a sharp decrease in expulsions, as hunger and fuel shortages were prevalent in both Germany and Poland.[27] The German population was reduced in the Oder-Neisse provinces by more than one-half in 1945. From the remaining population, 650,000 Germans, mostly women, children, and aged people,[28] were expelled, with about 2,850,000 remaining in the provinces, while 800,000 to 900,000 more ethnic Germans lived in forced-labor camps and jails within Poland proper.[29]

By the fall and winter of 1945, the Polish government began the recruitment of "autochthons" in Upper Silesia and the district of Allenstein. This action served two purposes. First, if a relatively large number of residents were to accept Polish citizenship, this would help to justify Polish claims to the provinces and to support Polish accusations that there was a large-scale "forced Germanization" in the past. Second, these citizens could be used to rebuild the economy of the provinces. Especially desirable was the retention of skilled labor for the steel and coal industry of Upper Silesia. Consequently, the pressures exerted on Germans with Polish-sounding names were as outrageously cruel as those exerted on Poles with German-sounding names during the German occupation of Poland.[30]

The early expulsions in 1946 differed little from those of 1945, but the agreement of February 14, 1946, concluded between the British representative of the Combined Repatriation Executive and Poland, eased the lot of the expellees.[31] Of course regulations relating to baggage and currency remained unnecessarily rigorous, and the lack of proper accommodations and medical aid en route,[32] the arbitrary acceleration of the departure of the expellees by overzealous local authorities,[33] and the absence of adequate organization on the part of Poland in proper implementation of the Potsdam Declaration caused substantial hardship to the wretched expellees.[34] Operation Swallow, as the 1946 expulsions were called, was more humane in one respect, in that it afforded a direct route into the British occupation zone, thus eliminating the necessity of unauthorized crossings of the Soviet Russian zonal boundary by the expellees who wanted to live in western Germany.[35]

In the course of Operation Swallow, 1,375,000 Germans were officially expelled. To these should be added about half a million Germans who had to leave the Oder-Neisse provinces for western Germany without the benefit of organized transport.[36] By the end of the year, an exceptionally severe winter stopped further expulsions because the British refused to accept any transports after the occurrence of many cases of frostbite and death among the recent expellees.[37]

The last great wave of expulsions, which took place in the Oder-Neisse provinces in 1947, was directed against the skilled workers and those who had been working for the Red Army. The expulsions extended to all of the provinces.[38] Approximately half a million Germans left for the Russian Zone of Germany, for the British refused to accept them, maintaining that the Poles were not observing the "orderly and humane" clause of the Potsdam Protocol.[39] By the end of that year, systematic expulsion had ended, though small, irregular expulsions were executed as late as 1949 and many Germans left Poland and the Oder-Neisse provinces on their own from 1948 to 1950.[40]

The Polish Communist government also increased its pressure on the remaining Masurians and Upper Silesians, who spoke both German and Polish, to opt for Poland. In 1945 and 1946, these people often escaped the pressure by declaring themselves to be Germans, with the subsequent result of their immediate expulsion, but from 1947 to 1949, many of them were often literally compelled to accept Polish citizenship regardless of their protests.[41] Finally, in certain cities and regions, such as Waldenburg, Liegnitz, and districts of eastern Brandenburg, some Germans were retained because of their special skills and the lack of Polish settlers.[42]

In the northern part of East Prussia, allotted at Potsdam to the U.S.S.R., flight, deportations, and epidemics[43] caused heavy losses among the resident German population.[44] Moscow had no national interest in their expulsion, and such measures were not implemented until late 1947, when Russia decided to change her policy toward Germany. The surviving German population came to the West in 1948.[45] Only in the Memel area, now part of the Soviet Lithuanian Republic, have no expulsions taken place.[46]

In 1950-51, Operation Link ended the tragic path to Germany for the overwhelming majority of the population of the provinces. About 50,000 Germans, part of them members of families torn apart by flight and expulsion, returned to Germany. Only 1,100,000 of the native population were permitted to remain in their homes, and their real national allegiance is very hard to assess. Some of them are undoubtedly bona fide members of the former Polish minority in Germany, while others are bilingual opportunists who claim Polish allegiance because it helps them to remain in their homes. A third part consists of ethnic Germans who were forced to become Poles. If we assume that the proportion of the three parts are roughly equal, we have approximated the truth insofar as it is humanly possible in view of the lack of reliable statistics and the highly volatile concept of nationality among the bilingual Upper Silesians. That the former German citizens now opting for Poland do not lead a happy life has been shown by the frequency of their applications in 1957 to come to the West, to Germany, rather than to remain under the rule of their "brethren." Another evidence was given by the famous article which appeared in *Po Prostu* in January, 1957, describing the hardships and physical violence these people have to endure from self-appointed chauvinists from among the ranks of the new settlers.[47]

As mentioned before, despite the brutal Russian excesses and the hardships imposed by a lost war, the German population was willing to remain in the provinces or, if they fled during the hostilities, to return to them. Subsequent Polish terror, however, in the form of large-scale expulsions in 1945, arbitrary looting, torture and internment practices,[48] and the transfer of all German property[49] to the Polish state or to Polish settlers[50] broke the resistance of the population. Futhermore, the remaining Germans were forced to leave their homes and to live in quarters formerly inhabited by farm hands and maids or by animals. They had to work for a nominal wage for those who inherited their homes and farms. The bitterness and despair of the Germans and bilinguals can be gauged from their reaction to the possibility of departure from the Polish People's Republic after the coming of the Gomulka regime. More than one hundred thousand of them crossed the Russian Zone to the West in the official transfer action of 1957, and their number is still increasing.[51] The provinces thus lost their German character and were populated by Polish settlers from central and eastern Poland.

2. The Polish Administration of the Provinces: Population and Agriculture

The agricultural and industrial potential of the Oder-Neisse provinces was substantially lower when Bierut assumed the reins of government than in 1939. Although air raids were relatively infrequent, southern Lower Silesia, the western districts of eastern Pomerania, Breslau, and the coast around Danzig and Heiligenbeil witnessed pitched battles and the cities long sieges.

Even greater damage was wrought by wanton Russian destruction in the provinces. Arson, wholesale dismantling of factories, and looting led to many clashes between the Poles and the Red Army.[52] According to Polish humor, the Russians intended to return these territories to Poland in exactly the same condition in which they had been six hundred years before.

Polish statistics fail to distinguish between the two kinds of damage. Their estimate of the total of wartime and occupation damages is given below.

Upper Silesia: The Industrial Triangle remained largely intact, though the capacity of some of its industries was reduced as a result of wartime exploitation and the lack of sufficient, skilled manpower after the expulsion of German workers. Destruction of the cities outside the Triangle ranged from 30 to 75 per cent.[53]

Lower Silesia: Breslau was about half destroyed, and Glogau lost 90 per cent of its buildings. About 40 per cent of all the bridges and tunnels and 60 per cent of the railway engines and repair equipment was also destroyed in the battles in the southern districts.[54]

Eastern Brandenburg: Substantial destruction of towns—Küstrin, 80 per cent; Zeppen, 80 per cent; and Crossen, Guben (Ost), Sorau, Sprottau, Landsberg, and Sagan, 60 per cent, destroyed or damaged.[55]

Eastern Pomerania: Minor destruction of the countryside, with the exception of Stettin; only the town of Kolberg was substantially damaged.[56]

Danzig (Gdańsk): Statistics show that both the city and its industries were badly damaged or destroyed.[57]

Allenstein region: Substantial destruction in Allenstein and in the utility services of the area.[58]

In all the provinces, Polish sources estimate wartime and occupation damages (partial or complete destruction) at 27.5 per cent of all farm buildings and about the same percentage (117,824 buildings) in the towns and cities, together with an average reduction of 60 per cent in industrial capacity. The low production level of industry was, however, due to manpower and electric-power shortages rather than to wholesale destruction of machinery.[59]

More catastrophic economically than the destruction of housing and industry was the lack of settlers. The flight of the Germans has already been discussed.[60] The remaining four million were expelled at an accelerated rate. Resettlement was effected by two different methods: (1) by directing the "transferred" Poles from eastern Poland, now a part of the U.S.S.R., to the new provinces, a process which began as early as March, 1945, and reached its climax after the establishment of the "Ministry for the Recovered Territories" on November 19, 1945;[61] and (2) by inducing the landless peasants and some of the unstable city-dwelling elements in central and western Poland to settle in the Oder-Neisse region.[62] The latter process was facilitated by the fact that prewar Poland was suffering from hidden rural unemployment.[63] Thus the inhabitants of central and western Poland simply spilled over the frontier districts and appropriated German property,[64] while the repatriates were directed to Lower Silesia and Pomerania in order to build a cordon on the Oder and Neisse rivers against eventual German reacquisition attempts.[65] Hundreds of thousands of Poles living in Germany as displaced persons were also recruited to fill the vacuum in the provinces.[66]

By January 1, 1947, the number of Polish or "autochthon" inhabitants had risen to 4,822,000 in the provinces and to 150,600 in Gdańsk (Danzig). The cities of Wrocław (Breslau) and Szczecin (Stettin) again had a population of 170,656 and 72,948, respectively.[67] State direction of the process and the abundance of free, fertile land, farming equipment, and credit facilities slowly achieved the aim of consolidating the Polish population after the chaos of 1945. The Poles at that time have been aptly described by an American author as "people aimlessly wandering with their skimpy belongings in this war-scarred territory in search of shelter in the form of shell-torn or bombed dwellings formerly occupied by German families" and "facing an uncertain, miserable life."[68]

By 1947, the number of Germans had fallen to a small percentage of the population. Although Polish Communist statistics are considered unreliable in this respect, the number of Germans hardly exceeded 800,000, in addition to those who were regarded as "autochthons" by the Poles.[69] During the two years, Polish peasants took possession of 340,000 farms out of 413,000 (each under 220 acres), equivalent in area to 8,500,000 acres.[70] There were also 4,200 state farms, the successors to the eastern German latifundia and Junker estates. In eastern Pomerania and East Prussia, there was a large amount of wasteland left cultivated and some farms were still run by Germans. Despite the successes, the great westward migration of Poles had come to an end by this time, since the manpower reserves were exhausted. Out of the 393,100 families residing on the new farms, 180,400 came from central Poland, 158,000 families were repatriates from the east or from Germany, 38,000 were military colonists, and only 15,000 families were local farmers or farmhands.[71] As a result of the lack of new settlers after 1948, the intensive exploitation of the land was never achieved under Polish Communist administration.[72]

At first, agricultural production declined catastrophically, and the resultant famine conditions were not overcome until 1947.[73] Even today Poland is an importer of wheat and other grain and food staple commodities despite the great surplus production of the provinces before World War II, when the population was substantially larger.[74] Livestock figures declined considerably, thanks to wartime destruction and forced slaughtering of the livestock by the Red Army. A comparison of the number of livestock[75] in 1939 and 1946 shows:

	1939	1946
Horses	890,000	249,600
Cattle	3,541,600	588,600
Hogs	4,877,100	314,300
Sheep	903,800	98,800

The year 1947 was a turning point in the development of Poland and the Oder-Neisse provinces as part of Poland. First, the Communist take-over was completed with the elections in January, 1947. Premier Osóbka-Morawski was succeeded by Josef Cyriankewycz, the Polish Peasant party was dissolved, and Vice-Premier Mikolajczyk was forced to flee to the West.[76] Open breaches of the Yalta pledge began a year after the creation of the "Government of National Unity" when government authorities subservient to the P.P.R. falsified the returns for the abolition of the Senate in the three-point referendum of June 30, 1946. Ambassador Lane protested to the government:

> The method used in tabulating the ballots and reporting the vote has given rise to charges of serious irregularities, including the removal of the ballot boxes from polling places in contravention of the referendum law. . . .[77]

The referendum also asked the voter whether Poland should retain the Oder-Neisse provinces. In view of the *fait accompli* recognized by the U.S.S.R. in the east, the great majority of the population answered in the affirmative.

Internationally, in 1946 and 1947, the frontier question again became the object of negotiations but disappeared quickly as the deepening rift between East and West prevented the convocation of a German peace conference. On September 9, 1946, Secretary of State James F. Byrnes, applying a more realistic American approach to the desperate agricultural situation in the Western zones of Germany, demanded partial revision of the Oder-Neisse frontier at Stuttgart.[78] The Communist government alleged that his speech was proof of the hostility of the Western powers to Poland, while the role of the Soviet Union in defending the "regained" territories was friendly. Wladyslaw Gomulka declared that he preferred "open enemies" to "masked friends" and boasted that "international capitalism could in no way hurt Polish-Soviet friendship."[79]

The change of mind of the Secretary of State and his British colleague in regard to the question of Poland's western frontiers was not caused solely by the internal events in Poland, though to state that the deterioration of individual freedom and progress of Communization did not exercise a deterrent effect on the opinions of the Western foreign ministers would be biased. The story of the Moscow and London conferences will be related elsewhere.[80] Here mention must be made only of the Oder-Neisse question as one of the issues underlying the East-West breach over Germany. After disappearing from the agenda of international conferences, the problem became primarily a German-Polish one, though both the West and the Soviet Union have, by supporting the contestants, kept the issue alive. The administration of the provinces, however, remains in Polish hands and will be dealt with accordingly.

Poland annexed the territories east of the Oder and Neisse rivers by enacting a law in the Sejm on January 12, 1949.[81] This was the last of many unilateral administrative and organizational steps taken by the Communist-dominated government, beginning with the declarations of Bierut on February 10, 1945. On November 19, 1945, the government erected the "Ministry for the Recovered Territories,"[82] the portfolio of which was held by the First Secretary of the Party, Wladyslaw Gomulka, who led and actively supported the methods and procedures of the expulsion of the German population.[83] On May 24, 1945, the territories were organized into Polish voivodships. Southern East Prussia, with the exception of the easternmost districts of Lyck, Goldap and Treuburg, which became part of the northern Polish province of Byałistok, was renamed Ołsztyn (Allenstein). The easternmost districts of Pomerania, together with Danzig and the largest part of Pomorze, became the voivodship of Gdańsk (Danzig), while the remainder of Pomerania was transformed into the voivodship of

Szczecin (Stettin). The eastern Brandenburg territories were attached to the voivodship Poznań and Lower Silesia to the voivodship of Wrocław (Breslau). Upper Silesia was again united with the province Śląsk, with Katowice as its capital.[84] The new distribution of districts demonstrated the Polish intention to sever the historical connections of the German provinces by annexing them to former Polish territories, but the essential integrity of the provinces was preserved. In 1950, however, a further distribution took place, subdividing the area into ten voivodships. Some districts, formerly part of Pomorze, around Dzialdowo (Soldau) and Nowe Miasto Lubawskie (Lobau) were added to Olsztyn.[85] The voivodship of Szczecin (Stettin) was subdivided into Koszalin (Köslin) and Szczecin (Stettin), transferring the area of the former German district Köslin to the voivodship.[86] The northern districts of Grenzmark Posen remained with the voivodship Poznań, while the eastern Brandenburg districts, the southern districts of Grenzmark Posen, and the Lower Silesian districts of Zielona Góra (Grünberg), Nowa Sol (Freystadt), Głogow (Gloggau), Szprotawa (Sprottau), Zagan (Sagan) and Zary (Sorau) were united with the voivodship of Zielona Góra (Grünberg). Wrocław (Breslau) was again deprived of additional districts in the southeast, where Brzeg (Brieg) and Namyslow (Namslau) were incorporated into Upper Silesia. The latter again was subdivided into two voivodships, those of Opole (Oppeln) and Katowice (Kattowitz). The latter included, from the former German Oberschlesien, the city districts of Hindenburg, Gleiwitz, and Beuthen and the districts of Guttentag, Tost-Gleiwitz, and Beuthen-Tarnowitz, now renamed Gliwice (Gleiwitz) and Dobrodzien (Guttentag),[87] in addition to the former Polish voivodship Śląsk.

The restoration of population level made progress until 1949, only to decline in the fifties until the return of Poles from the U.S.S.R. in 1957.[88] The present population is about 7,000,000, over 2,000,000 less than in 1939, although the natural increase alone would have amounted to at least 1,200,000. Thus in comparison with other European territories, the provinces are still underpopulated. There especially exists a disproportion between large towns and rural settlements.[89] Only in Upper Silesia, where Polish settlement policies were based on the presence of a Polish or Polish-speaking population and where heavy industry led to large-scale Polish and Russian capital investment, has the population increased to the 1939 level.[90]

The new population is almost entirely Polish. About 5,000,000 represent new settlers, 1,100,000 "autochthons," who can be counted in part as Germans and in part as Poles, about 200,000 Germans, and the same number of Ukrainians, the latter mostly in Pomerania and Olsztyn. Individual expulsions took place even in 1949-50, and Operation Link reduced the number of Germans by another 50,000.[91] The present emigration, since the Gomulka regime has been in power, is reducing the number of Germans by another 150,000, officially leaving no Germans in the territories, though many of the so-called Upper Silesians and Masurians are Germans. New waves of Poles returning from Russian slave-labor camps after a decade or more of imprisonment are filling the provinces to some extent, though they would prefer to settle in prewar Poland.[92] Their number hardly exceeds that of the departing, among whom are often found members of the "autochthon" group, who can but despair at the oft-repeated promises of an economic progress to come under the Communist leadership of Bierut and Gomulka.[93] The German minority now enjoys some rights and, to a small extent, has its own schools and papers,[94] but the position of the "autochthons" is far from enviable. A courageous exposition of the mistreatment of the group was given on January 7, 1957, in an article by Andrzej Wydrzynski in the now-forbidden Polish paper, *Po prostu*. According to him:

Together with the legal representatives of the government, who took over the administration of the land devastated by the war, came a horde of plunderers, careerists and speculators into Opole. . . . Exploiting the ignorance and the justified suspicion of the officials of the native population at the time of the expulsion of the Germans, they began their barbaric plundering. Furniture of the "autochthons" was looted, wedding rings were ripped from their fingers, and greedy paws grabbed their houses and gardens. . . . Then came a new wave of destruction aimed at the national and freedom-loving traditions of the Silesians. . . . We have refused to accept the heart and hands of these people. . . . An official decree was passed that German-sounding names would have to be changed and those who resisted such changes were fired from their jobs.

In many localities where after the war Polish was spoken, the language today again became German. People, even those who themselves attended Polish schools, would like to send their children to German schools. A railway worker from Bytom who fought with us in the Silesian insurrection and married a Czech woman is teaching her German instead of Polish, for otherwise she could not get along in Bytom. In the streetcars of the mining area, young lads who were brought up in our People's Republic sing German songs, just as the salesgirls and schoolgirls do, who are attending Polish schools.[95]

The agriculture of the provinces suffered greatly under wartime devastation. After the bumper crop of 1949, amounting to 65 per cent of the 1938 harvest, collectivization,[96] inefficiency within the state co-operatives, and forced-delivery quotas led to a serious decline in productivity and in the extent of cultivated land in the provinces.[97] The *Zycie gospodarcze* article[98] of February, 1958, merely reconfirmed the statement that between 1939 and 1949, cultivated arable land in the provinces declined from 13,362,800 acres to 9,167,400 acres.[99] *Trybuna Ludu* mentioned the fact that productivity, as of 1954, was substantially below the 1938 level by 1,400 pounds per acre for corn and 14,000 pounds for potatoes, as compared to 2,000 pounds for corn and 165,500 pounds for potatoes under German rule.[100] Livestock increased to 1,814,000 cattle, 2,821,000 pigs, 1,121,000 sheep, and 516,000 horses,[101] but it still amounted to only about 60 per cent of the prewar number of livestock.

These figures, together with the great fluctuation in the population of the provinces and the small initiative of the new settlers to produce more crops, a topic close to the heart of the German press,[102] explain the necessity for the importation of 1,600,000 metric tons of American grain in 1957[103] and close to 1,000,000 tons of Russian grain since 1952.[104] As the reporter of *Slowe Powczechne* expressed the frustrated feeling of many Poles: "Why do they [the government] try to deceive us in regard to the agricultural production in the Western territories?"

The inadequate agricultural production of the formerly surplus areas is a poor accomplishment of Polish administration. It is due to many complex factors, such as collectivization attempts, unnecessary government interference and high delivery quotas, and the lack of mechanization and capital, but most of all, it is due to the lack of people and of zeal and stability in the population structure of the provinces.[105]

This short survey of Polish population and agricultural policies is not intended to be an indictment. The settlement in the provinces was, demographically, a great accomplishment of the Polish state, which provided homes, though often only transient ones, to the millions returning from the east and the west.

The settlement has solved the hidden rural unemployment problem within western and central Poland to the extent that fallow land again appears in the formerly overpopulated voivodships.[106] Yet because of the presence of a larger state territory than could be adequately populated by the given population resources, the need for a highly developed agriculture cannot be achieved by the Poles. One cannot avoid the conclusion that much of the land would be more productive and would, therefore, contribute more to the European economy if it were returned to seriously overpopulated Germany, which has been deprived of 24.4 per cent of its agricultural acreage.

3. The Polish Administration of the Provinces: Industry and Communications

Industry has suffered from Soviet Russian plundering and from the battles and sieges of the major cities of the provinces, especially Breslau and Stettin. Only the heavy industry located in the Upper Silesian basin escaped serious damage. While resumption of production was rather haphazard and carried out mostly by German slave labor in 1945, during the Three Year Plan (1947-49), both the Soviet Union and the Polish Communist government realized the utmost importance of the creation of an Upper Silesian combine on a regional level, including the Czechoslovak part around Morawska Ostrawa and Teschin and the Ukrainian iron-ore mines around Krivoi Rog, rebuilt in 1945-46 by the slave labor of Rumanians and Rumanian Germans.

This period of recuperation in Upper Silesia was full of difficulties originating in both the lack of skilled workers and engineers after the expulsion of the Germans and in the random direction of the development plans. These difficulties were only temporarily relieved by the Polish-Czechoslovak economic agreement of 1947, which permitted free transport of the coal of the Karvina Basin to Katowice and Bytom in exchange for Wałbrzych (Waldenburg) coal for the plants of Kladno.[107] Coal production failed to attain the 1938 level until the end of 1948.[108] Further expansion was still slow, the 1944 production figures being surpassed only in 1954;[109] in 1956, production increases were infinitesimal. The fact, however, that the coal basins of western

and eastern Upper Silesia were reunited enabled Poland to become
the third largest coal-producing country in Europe outside the
U.S.S.R. In 1956, some 95.1 million metric tons were mined,[110] but
production in the last quarter fell considerably, and any further expansion became contingent on a large-scale overhaul of the increasingly obsolete equipment of the mines[111] and on the availability of
additional skilled manpower, an eternal problem of the Communist
planners in view of the demands of agriculture in the low-density
areas of the Silesian plains.[112] As a result of the increased demands of
the new iron, steel, metal, and chemical plants, all of them requiring
large quantities of coal as an energy source, the exportation of coal
was drastically reduced from 23.4 million metric tons in 1955 to 19.4
million metric tons in 1956 and 14 million metric tons in 1957. Thus
the tremendous expansion of the 1948-55 period came to a standstill
at a time when the other parts of heavy industry were still expanding.
The Upper Silesian coal basin failed to fulfill the *Kombinat* idea of
the Russian Communist planners, who wanted to make Upper Silesia
the industrial suburbia of the Ukraine.[113]

Any evaluation of the results and failures of Polish administration
of the Upper Silesian area must include consideration of Russian
influence and investments in the development of the region since
1945. While one may either accept or reject Dr. Peter Heinz Seraphim's thesis of *Industriekombinat*, it would be illogical to assume
that Russia was not primarily interested in establishing a strong industrial combine in the area, which alone contains the necessary min-
eralogical, industrial, and manpower resources to supply the satellites
with adequate production of military and capital goods. Before the
war, Poles often called attention to the fact that Silesia was Germany's
largest arsenal, but their reference was to one part of the industrial
region only, i.e., to German Westoberschlesien. The potentialities of
the entire region, which, with the exception of Hitler's wartime empire, has never been united under one government, are of such importance that they represent a serious contribution to the economy of the
Soviet Russian bloc. It is maintained that Polish-Czech co-operation
has increased under Russian pressure,[114] and Seraphim's statements,[115]
reiterated in many press reports and strengthened by Gomulka's own
confession,[116] about the role of Russian investments support the validity of such a hypothesis.

The effect of the October, 1956 events in Poland on Russian control
of the Upper Silesian area was negligible. First, control over industry

was economic as well as political. The Soviet Union's provision of credits for the building of new mining installations, crude-steel plants, and power stations led to the mushrooming of the industrial area between Gliwice (Gleiwitz) and Tarnowice (Tarnowitz). Some of the new plants were directly connected with the Krivoi Rog mines by a water- (Vistula) and land-transportation system, including preferential railway freight rates, and in the last decade, Poland increasingly desisted from importing Swedish iron ore.[117] Second, complete control of the Czechoslovak part of the industry assured harmony in economic production of the area. A disruption or an eventual termination of Czechoslovak-Polish co-operation, which by 1955 included strong Czech interests in the technical and material construction of power plants and chemical factories, as well as exchange of coal and steel products, would have been disastrous to Upper Silesian industry.[118] Third, the marketing of Silesian coal also would have presented great difficulties, as only a minor percentage of the coal goes to the West, while the rest is consumed within the Communist bloc. Fourth, the question of repair parts of Russian machinery and equipment would also have dissuaded Gomulka from charting an independent course, even if he ever had any intention of freeing himself from the economic shackles of Russian overlordship.[119]

The coal crisis was not followed by a similar crisis in the steel industry because the absence of local resources hampered the creation of a major steel industry in the area after the Second World War. Decreasing iron-ore production resulting from depletion also restricted development. Only 1.64 million metric tons of iron ore were mined in Poland, including that taken from the mines of Częstochowa,[120] and pig-iron and crude-steel production for Poland, including that of plants outside of the industrial area in Upper Silesia, amounted to 3.5 and 5 million metric tons, respectively,[121] of which only about 80 to 85 per cent was produced in the former German and Polish Silesias.[122] These figures are much higher than those of 1938, but dependence on Russian iron ore makes production vulnerable to any changes in the economic and political ties between Russia and Poland. The military importance becomes clear, however, when the 1948 figures for rolled-steel production are investigated. By a production of only 960,000 metric tons, which was more than tripled by 1956, steel used for railroad equipment amounted to 196,000 metric tons. Forty-one thousand metric tons were cast iron and plate. Other military and capital goods parts production amounted to 434,000 metric tons, and the rest consisted mostly of wires of different sizes.[123] A similar expansion of zinc production also took place.[124]

Within Russian-Polish-Czech planning, production of the following goods of the steel industry was then substantially increased over the 1948 level:

(1) Tractors, harvest combines, and other agricultural machinery. Here again, the collectivization efforts of the Bierut government must be taken into consideration because the newly produced agricultural machines were mostly those used on big estates.[125]

(2) Production of mining and precision equipment and apparatus. The aim of the planners has been the production of machine equipment within Poland and Czechoslovakia sufficient for both domestic needs and large-scale export at low prices to the other satellites.[126] However, in 1957 it was reported that production of new machinery was wholly inadequate to replace the old, obsolete machinery, usually of British, French, or German vintage, and to provide for the spare-part requirements of the industry. Many reports also maintain that a large percentage of industrial machinery had to be supplied between 1952-56 by the U.S.S.R. herself.[127] Armament production, especially ball bearings, cannons, plates for tanks, and mortars, was also increased, though exact data are hardly available in view of Communist secrecy.[128]

The rest of the reoriented and reconstructed industries have shown a curve fluctuating between great progress in production capacity on the one hand and confusion and disorganization on the other. Through the construction of high-voltage plants in both Upper Silesia and the Grünberg (Zielona Góra) area at Dychow on the Bober,[129] electric-power consumption by industry and private individuals was increased to 19.5 million kilowatts. Cement production was expanded through the construction of a new plant and the resumption of production of the Opole (Oppeln) plants, which were among the largest factories in prewar Europe.[130] Although the actual Polish production in 1956 showed a slight increase over that of 1955,[131] Polish technical publications complain that the Opole plants can exploit only 50 per cent of their capacity because of the constant breakdown of Polish machinery, including the furnaces, which require twice as much coal for heating as in the prewar years.[132]

Nitrogen fertilizers played a great role in the agriculture of the Oder-Neisse provinces before the war, though most of the factories were located in the present Russian Zone of Germany. On March 8,

1954, the Polish administration opened a large plant at Kedzyierin (Heydebreck), which was hailed as a partial solution of the low acreage yield of grain and other crops.[133] In 1957, however, it was reported that serious bottlenecks existed and that the daily production of the single plants amounted to forty metric tons, as compared to the production capacity of sixty metric tons of the ammonia high-pressure process in similar plants in western Europe.[134]

The food industry never attained the 1938 level. Despite some increases over 1955, the 1956 meat production in the Oder-Neisse provinces amounted to only 120-127 pounds per capita, compared to 156 pounds in 1938, though the population of the provinces remained 2.2 million less than in 1938.[135]

Traffic facilities have been inadequately reconstructed, with the exception of those in Upper Silesia. The reorientation of transportation lines led to a reduction of the direct railway connections with central Germany and the West. Only the two lines, Berlin-Poznań-Warsaw and Zgorlelec–Wrocław–Jelenia Góra (Görlitz-Breslau-Hirschberg) are maintaining through traffic.[136] While all the railway connections between the provinces and Poland were kept intact or were rebuilt,[137] the railway net in the northern provinces of Pomerania and southern East Prussia is still substantially under its prewar level. The position of Szczecin (Stettin) is a case in point. Though the connection with Gdańsk (Danzig) is maintained,[138] the Szczecin-Kostrzyn-Tczew-Elblag (Stettin-Küstrin-Dirschau-Elbing) line has no direct connections, and many of the East Prussian lines, severed by the Polish-Russian demarcation line, are no longer in service.[139] According to Polish sources,[140] approximately 1,778 miles, or about 20 per cent of 1938 mileage, of the railway tracks required reconstruction. Damage to the railway net was definitely greater after the wholesale dismantling of lines by the victorious Red Army.[141]

Hardly any reliable reports are available on the condition of the highways, but the assumption can be made that the damaged first-class highways were reconstructed. But in the words of an eyewitness:

Local roads are like mud-tracks, like land ploughed for the first time, or rubble-piles, and even highways have not been repaired for years.[142]

The acquisition of the Oder Line opened great opportunities to Polish water traffic. Ten and a half million tons of goods were transported via the Oder in 1929, but by 1956, the tonnage was only 60 per cent of that figure.[143] Szczecin's sea traffic in 1954 was 6,280,000 metric tons, as compared to 8,331,000 metric tons in 1937, and until the end of 1957, the port, now administered separately from the city, lacked drinking water for ships.[144] Expansion of the Polish merchant marine has also come to a standstill. More than 36 per cent of the vessels, mostly German ships given to Poland as war reparations, are more than twenty years old, and the gain in ocean-shipping tonnage in 1956 was only 5,300 BRT.[145]

It can therefore be stated conclusively that by 1958, Polish industrial activities in the Oder-Neisse provinces reflected the inadequacy of both manpower resources and investments for the building of a balanced economy. Investment in the consumer-goods industry has not occurred to any satisfactory extent. The sharp decline of sugar production, halted only by an exceptionally good harvest in 1957;[146] the very slow rate of reconstruction of residential buildings, leading to the creation of slums, not only in the Industrial Triangle, but also in small rural towns, such as Osterrode in East Prussia;[147] and the insufficient agricultural production show that the tremendous problem was only partially solved by raising heavy-industry production in the provinces and by the construction of new electric-power, fertilizer, and steel plants.

The failure to secure a sufficient number of settlers among the repatriates from the Soviet Union during 1956-58 demonstrates that Bierut's problem persists unabated under Gomulka.[148] The new settlers' feeling of insecurity and of a lack of permanent roots remains an imponderable obstacle to Polish planning, despite the undeniable accomplishments of the last decade. The standard of living of the new settlers is far below that of the former German population, a result of both inadequate exploitation of the resources and of Communist inefficiency and misplanning.[149] Light and shadow fall equally on the provinces, even after twelve years of Polish administration and reconstruction. Polish voices condemning the neglect and backwardness of the provinces are frequent. *Po prostu* has pioneered in Polish self-criticism, as did most of the local press. They have exposed economic crimes, discrimination, embezzlement, and the lack of interest of the Warsaw government in providing for a higher living standard.[150] The result has been the creation of the Society for the Recovered Territories and new publications by the revived Instytut Zachodni at Poznań.[151] The meager results achieved by the Society were summarized by a memorandum of the commission of the Society itself:

> The conditions have changed only insignificantly since October, 1956. Positive and negative phenomena neutralize each other, while before the undertaking of the travel for study purposes [by the Commission], it was assumed that positive phenomena in the political, economic and social life of the provinces would prevail.[152]

Even more optimistic Polish exile writers can observe improvements only in the agricultural sector.

The negative phenomena are summarized as follows: (1) The native population does not take the initiative in improving its economic lot. (2) Rumors and whisperings prevail and cause a certain feeling of insecurity in the provinces among the population, which still fears eventual reattachment to Germany. (3) Criminality, especially juvenile delinquency, occurs at a higher rate than Polish-press reports would indicate. (4) Outright theft of government property is on the increase, probably because of unkept government promises of better provision of consumer goods. (5) The problem of repatriates as new settlers was solved very unsatisfactorily, and emigration tendencies are increasing, despite the awarding of large credits to settlers. (6) Finally, in many districts, especially in the northern provinces and Lower Silesia, the members of the Commission noticed much apathy among the population. (7) As a result of West German–press exploitation of Polish criticism of the conditions, the local press is afraid to expose the real shortcomings.

4. THE POLISH ARGUMENTS FOR THE *Status Quo*

To believe that the harsh words of self-criticism expressed in speeches and articles by Polish journalists and politicians on both sides of the Iron Curtain means abandonment of the Polish claims to the provinces would be erroneous. While Polish emotional attachment to the different Oder-Neisse provinces may vary in intensity, the political and economic repercussions of any frontier revisions unfavorable to Poland induce Communist and anti-Communist Poles to repeat the Moscow dictum of the Oder-Neisse Line as the "peace

frontier." This attitude is not necessarily due to the ideological position taken by the individual Pole but, rather, to a conglomerate of his
political obsession with the "German danger"; to his realistic estimate
of power relations in central and eastern Europe as of 1959; to his
overconfidence in Poland's own economic, demographic, and military
resources; and to his partially unjustified belief that Poland's cause
would, in the long run, have Western support because Poland, and
not Germany, is the "historical friend" of the Western powers. On
the basis of these tangible arguments and imponderable feelings,
Polish writers advance several historical, political, economic, and
demographic reasons which, in their minds, "justify" the annexation
of German territories and the expulsion methods of 1945-47.

Perhaps no other people in Europe harbors the seeds of nationalist
hatred of Germany to the extent that the Poles do. So it seems, at
least, from reading the official and semi-official publications in Poland
and of the Polish exiles. Yet most German visitors report a friendly
reception from the Poles at the present, and there were many instances of personal charity and assistance rendered by Poles to the
persecuted German minority. But the number of friendly Poles was
trivial when compared to the Polish militia, adventurers, and de-
nouncers committing many common crimes as a revenge. To the Poles,
therefore, there exists a need for a preoccupation with Nazi crimes as
they draw a veil of silence over Polish excesses. This need can be
gauged from the remarks of a member of the United States House of
Representatives, Congressman Thaddeusz Machrowitz, who is of
Polish origin.[153] He said:

> I would wish to strike a note of warning. It is true that words
> cannot shift frontiers. But careless talk here might only nourish
> dangerous illusions in Germany. It could embolden the extrem-
> ists among the Germans and distil the heady spirit of German
> nationalism which has cost the world much.[154]

Stephen Arski, a member of the Lublin government's embassy staff in
Washington, was more outspoken in 1947:

> To open the question again and make it subject of bargaining
> would be to awaken the spirit of German revisionism and en-
> courage the growth of German nationalism.[155]

Also:

It would bring humanity to certain disaster if we were forced to fight Germany for the third time to thwart her repeated efforts at conquest and domination. Before we find ourselves joined again in armed encounter with Germany, the German problem must be solved once and for all.[156]

According to him, in the Polish mind:

. . . from the beginning, the modern German *Reich* was governed by the standard bearers of militarism and feudalism, lusting after power.[157]

To Arski, re-education was considered possible only after the East German *Junkers*, who were supposed to be devils incarnate, were deprived of their economic base, Silesian industry detached, and the arable area of Germany reduced by the new frontier, making autarky impossible.[158]

The past decade of stable, democratic government in Germany under the leadership of Chancellor Adenauer failed to convince Polish leaders, Communist or anti-Communist, of the decline of the German menace.[159] Yet in the age of the two super powers armed with ICBM's, H-Bombs, and space satellites, the German danger is largely imaginary, for Germany is only now building an army—smaller than Poland's. The psychological distortion of reality which pictures Germany as a world power bent on conquest would be more understandable if no more immediate dangers were menacing Poland. This is, however, not the case; Russian imperialism exercises a firm rule over that country and has in the past inflicted heavier casualties and damages on Poland than has German nationalism.

The only explanation of this distorted attitude is that the Poles realize, more than ever since the Polish acceptance of the Oder-Neisse frontier in the west and the establishment of Russian supremacy in the region, the impotence of Poland in relation to the U.S.S.R. Any geographic shift of Poland to the west was equivalent in 1944-45 to a corresponding eastward shift in political allegiance. Now, unable to secure any revision of the eastern frontier, Poland refuses to release, or even to consider to release, the annexed territories without receiving compensation from the east. However, such a compensation would be unobtainable under present balance-of-power conditions.

Furthermore, the Polish people realize that despite their ideological feelings, they cannot afford to alienate the U.S.S.R., either by following an independent foreign policy which would acknowledge the provisional character of the Oder-Neisse "peace frontier" or by a renewal of their claims to Vilna and Galicia. Under such circumstances, the hope, often expressed by Americans of Polish origin and even by people in the State Department, that a change in Polish policy toward the West might occur without incurring immediate Russian retaliation and that the Polish stand on the frontier issue might be altered without a change of the regime is unrealistic. After losing millions of her citizens to German and Russian terrorism while awaiting a Western liberation that never took place, Poland's leaders, regardless of their ideology, cannot abandon the Russian alliance without effective Western guarantees against Russia and a partial revision of the Curzon Line. The West is, however, not prepared—and is perhaps also unable—to promise fulfillment of such Polish desires. And so the dilemma remains.

It is the combination of an almost irrational fear of the Germans, frustrated hope in the Western powers, and willingness to compromise with Russia that makes Polish contentions that Poland is a major European power incomprehensible. Not since the age of the Jagellos and Vasas has Poland been a European great power. For 125 years, the state of Poland existed in the mind of enthusiastic patriots, but not on the maps of Europe. Her re-establishment in 1918-21 was largely due to French interest in creating a new adversary to Germany in the east, a heavy mortgage on the foreign policy of the new Polish Republic. Yet Gomulka and his aides on the one hand and the exiled Poles on the other consider Poland a great power in her own right, a guarantor of the peace and an effective check against "German aggression." In the words of Witold Nowosad:

> The Poles feel instinctively that something basic in their destiny has changed in the last twenty years . . . in some respect we have become a world nation [narodem swiatowym] with great and unlimited interests, and now we have the duty to adjust our political thinking to this fact.[160]

For Western political consumption, non-Communist Poles emphasize that the future of Poland, rather than the future of Germany, will decide the coming order in central and eastern Europe, and, consequently, their position should be given priority. As Representative Machrowitz expressed it:

> Divided Germany is undoubtedly one of the big problems of our day. But it is only part of a still bigger dilemma which is awaiting a bold and constructive solution. . . . The two problems: the reunification of Germany and the liberation of Central Eastern Europe are closely interrelated. . . . It is, therefore, neither politically wise just to separate Germany [sic] problem from the whole problem of Eastern Europe, still less to give it a definite priority over the needs and sufferings of our true allies to whom we owe considerably more.[161]

For an exile opinion, let Mr. Krakowiac in France be quoted:

> . . . the destruction of the aims of the German revisionists should be regarded as an absolute condition for the preservation of peace. We all have to cooperate in order to attain the recognition of the Western Powers of the Western frontiers of Poland.[162]

Overconfidence in the West's "traditional friendship" and in the demographic accomplishments of the high natural birth rate of the Polish settlers in the provinces are favorable topics of both Polish and pro-Polish authors.[163] Successes in the field of heavy industry and the increased birth rate are the arguments advanced to show that Poland has both the technical skill and the manpower resources needed to populate and revitalize the provinces. Moreover, the argument is pressed that in order to avoid a "second Rapallo," the West would benefit by "pinning down" Moscow permanently to a guarantee of the new frontiers.

To accept the thesis of adequate manpower resources and economic means, however, would be to show open bias. Despite the great achievements with limited means, the population fluctuates greatly,[164] villages and small towns are often deserted and even erased from the map,[165] and, regardless of which population figures are considered correct, the present population is at least 1.7 to 2.7 million less than in 1939.[166] The failure of the 1956-57 settlements of repatriates in the provinces and the fact that the Polish intelligentsia still considers a transfer to the central and northern provinces a disciplinary measure does not predict any easy solution of the manpower problem.[167] The growing financial and economic dependence on the U.S.S.R. and the additional need for American credits and agricultural products raises the question of the availability of Polish means for the exploitation of the provinces as well.

Whether or not based on facts, these arguments are lately broadcast with increasing intensity from Warsaw. They include:

(1) The Oder-Neisse Line is a "peace frontier both for Poland and the European community of nations." Twelve years ago, this was written:

> The pre-war German frontier stretched for approximately 1,200 miles . . . and Poland found herself encircled by Germany. . . .

> The Oder-Neisse line shortens the Polish-German frontier to approximately 400 miles and eliminates two dangerous bulges. . . . But the consequences are more far-reaching. By means of this territory Germany endangered the whole of Central and Eastern Europe and the Balkans. With the Potsdam decision on the German-Polish frontier, the security of the whole region has been strengthened materially.[168]

A second argument emphasizes that only the possession of the provinces enables Poland to remain an economically viable state. In the words of Arski:

> Although even with the gains in the West, Poland now has a territory 21 per cent smaller than that of 1939 [?], she has greatly improved her political and strategic position and finds herself favorably situated to develop as an independent nation with a balanced economy.[169]

The "peace frontier" is a just historical settlement of the problem.[170] In dealing with medieval and modern history, Polish and pro-Polish writers characterize Prussia (Germany) and Poland as two irrevocably hostile powers fighting relentlessly for the land of the Oder-Neisse provinces. In this struggle, the Poles have been retreating for centuries. This Polish view is maintained under the impact of a sinister Prussian regime oppressing and harassing them in every way in order to induce them to become Germans. Although Prussianism might not be the *ultima ratio* of Western political development, and autocracy invariably breeds discrimination, the Polish view remains seriously distorted. No greater service could be rendered to the cause of Soviet Russian imperialism by the Polish Communist leaders than to perpetuate in the minds of Polish youth the myth of a long-suffering, innocent Polish population in these provinces forcibly Germanized or expelled by a sinister and cunning Prussian (German) regime.

(2) It is argued that Poland could not survive without the Oder-Neisse provinces. Radio Warsaw used this argument several times.[171] Demographically, this argument makes little sense because the number of repatriates from the U.S.S.R., including those who have arrived in the past two years, hardly exceeds 1,650,000. On the contrary, 500,000 Ukrainians and Byelorussians have voluntarily returned to the U.S.S.R. from western Galicia and Province Byalistok, leaving a population surplus of only 1,150,000. Now the number of ethnic Germans in Poland proper was at least 800,000, and they either were expelled or perished in the dungeons and at the trials of the "traitors to the nation." Thus the net gain of population was exactly 350,000. As a result, more than four million people from central and western Poland had to be settled in the provinces in order to produce the present population figures. It is true that before the war Poland had much hidden rural unemployment,[172] the extent of which, however, must have been reduced by Nazi extermination of the Jews and some Polish elements. Thus the guided settlement of four million people from a densely populated but not overpopulated area must have resulted in adverse agricultural consequences.[173]

Industrially, only the oil fields of Drohobycz and the local industries of Lwów and Vilna were lost in the east. The production and potential of German Upper Silesia alone exceeds by several times the industrial worth of eastern Poland, and *Regierungsbezirk* Allenstein would have provided ample land for the resettlement of the repatriates if it were reactivated to the extent of 1939.

(3) A serious scholarly dispute rages about the role of the production of the provinces in the German diet. Professor Volz is cited by every Polish writer,[174] and statistics and marketing principles are thrown into the argument. Whatever the role the agricultural production of the provinces might have been, there is little dissension about the fact that Poland would not need their produce if she aban-

doned her forced-industrialization policies and concentrated her efforts on improving acreage yield and agricultural methods. As far as German needs are concerned, it is obvious that the detachment of extensive, highly developed agricultural regions and the simultaneous expulsion of their residents into the remaining overindustrialized provinces of the country will impair that country's economy, regardless of the financial profitability of the agricultural production in the detached provinces. Overindustrialization remains no panacea, and Poland herself is experiencing the disadvantages of her heavy-industry investments over consumer-goods production.

(4) The presence of 7.2 million residents and the organic, economic, and administrative connection of the provinces with Poland proper are unchangeable facts which outweigh any German ethnic or legal claims to the provinces. Radio Warsaw has broadcast:

> What is the real picture? In the nationalized industry of the Western territories, twenty-two per cent of all Polish industrial laborers work. The agricultural enterprises [both state owned and private] are cultivating all of the arable land. Great industrial projects were begun and constructed. . . .[175]

Recently, the same radio spoke of 7.5 million Poles living in the area, an obvious exaggeration in the view of Polish reports of the widespread decline of small towns and farms.[176] German sources, which probably minimized their number, put the population at 6.5 million. In view of other Polish sources, it seems probable that the population fluctuates between 6.8 and 7.1 million.[177] None of these figures compare favorably with the 9.2 million inhabitants in 1939, the natural increase of which would have been at least 1.2 million. With regard to economic and administrative integration, it must be noted that the Oder has declined as a waterway and that Polish rule cost Szczecin a considerable percentage of her flourishing sea trade. In Pomerania, Stolpmünde and many other small towns are declining and disappearing, and railway connections are left unreconstructed or have been dismantled. The plight of the province Olsztyn is openly admitted in many Polish reports describing ridiculously low acreage yields and the lack of settlers.[178] Only Upper Silesian industry, partitioned in 1921, benefited by the reunification in 1945.

(5) In a French-language broadcast, Radio Warsaw explained:

These ancient territories were returned to us in a devastated and almost depopulated condition. One should keep in mind the efforts which were necessary to have them again populated with 7.3 million people.[179]

Or in the words of Machrowitz:

Poland, extending to the West in accordance with the Potsdam Three Power decision, entered a desert. In 1945, the Territories East of the Oder-Neisse line presented a picture of ruin.[180]

It is true that considerable damage was wrought by the hostilities and by the Red Army occupation of the provinces. The work of the Polish administration in the reconstruction and the reorientation of the industries of Upper and Lower Silesia was commendable. Yet much of the ruin still remains, many of the farms are still deserted or operated at a low efficiency,[181] and, under present planning, the standards of 1939 are supposed to be regained only in 1970. The wrecking of untouched or slightly damaged houses and buildings for the rebuilding of cities in Poland, or often for individual pecuniary advantage, has been and remains common.[182]

(6) Both Polish writers and radio commentators argue that the "autochthons" are Poles. This argument has a kernel of truth when applied to the members of the former Polish minority in Germany, but Communist oppression and national discrimination seem to have succeeded in alienating from Poland many of the bilingual inhabitants of Upper Silesia who were willing to make their peace with the Polish state in 1945.[183]

The strongest arguments of the Poles remains that the new Polish settlements could not be eliminated without a new wave of expulsions. Whatever the final compromise might be, it should not duplicate the solutions of 1940 and 1945. Present Polish possession of the provinces would render complete restoration of all provinces to Germany possible only under conditions unusually favorable to Germany, despite her legal arguments, but some revision will be necessary to achieve a German-Polish detente and for the relaxation of tensions in Europe.

CHAPTER VIII

Germany and the Oder-Neisse Provinces

1. THE FATE OF THE PROVINCES AT POSTWAR CONFERENCES

WHEN Hitler's Reich collapsed and the problem of feeding the daily increasing population of the Western zones was faced squarely, the voices of revenge and Draconic peace in Great Britain and the United States yielded to a new policy based on humanitarian, economic, and political considerations and on the growing mistrust of the intentions of the Soviet Union. The Western Allies wanted to reconstruct a stable, democratic, and demilitarized Germany whose government would be able to live in peace and without economic misery. While the implementation of such an aim was compatible with a delay in the re-establishment of a national government and with some dismantling of industries, economic looting and political isolation of their zone by the Russians would wreck the Allies' plans if allowed to continue unchecked. Anglo-American policy was designed to promote the unification of the country by reopening the frontier question at the earliest opportunity in favor of a revision in order to exert pressure upon the U.S.S.R. and Poland.[1]

While the threat of permanent Russian domination of the Balkans and the Danubian basin was the primary concern of Western politicians in 1945, British Foreign Minister Ernest Bevin stated unequivocally that the Oder-Neisse Line was a problem yet to be solved rather than a question definitely settled at the Potsdam Conference.

One of the great problems which still faces us is that of Poland and I know there is some feeling about the extent of the area which has been included in the Polish zone. The question of the actual future area of Poland must be settled at the peace table and I admit personally taking the view expressed by . . . Mr. Churchill with regard to the danger of the Poles going far to [the] west.[2]

Churchill, now in charge of His Majesty's opposition, understood Russia's reason for establishing the Oder-Neisse Line and recognized the grievous repercussions on the plan of the Anglo-American powers to re-establish an economically viable and politically stable Germany and to guarantee future European peace, for any permanent European settlement must include a *modus vivendi* between Germany and Poland. Churchill courageously raised the question of the missing millions of Germans, though his position on the question would have stood up to the test of history better had he refused to advocate mass expulsions on a smaller scale eight months before his August 16, 1945 speech in the House of Commons.[3]

The increasingly defiant attitude of the Soviet Union in the Balkans and toward German economic unity and reparations wrought a progressive change in Western policies toward the U.S.S.R. In 1946, the United States, already shifting the bases of her German policy, still made a last effort to reach agreement with the Soviet Union. The policy was aimed at the restoration of a German national administration able to maintain a course independent of Moscow under the control of the Big Four, but as an alternative, Washington had already considered the creation of a West German state. The requirement for either course was American advocacy of the return of some of the Oder-Neisse provinces in order to strengthen the economy of a united Germany or to solicit German backing for a West German state by supporting their demands against the Poles and the Russians.

The result of the change in policy was the speech of Secretary of State James F. Byrnes at Stuttgart on September 6, 1946, describing the new American policy on German unity, economics, political affairs, and boundaries. Byrnes's interpretation of the Potsdam Protocol was as follows:

The Heads of Governments agreed that, preceding the final determination of Poland's western frontier, Silesia and other eastern German areas should be under the administration of the Polish state and for such purposes should not be considered as a part of the Soviet zone of occupation in Germany. However, as the Protocol of the Potsdam Conference makes clear, the Heads of Governments did not agree to support at the peace settlement the cession of this particular area. . . .

As a result of the agreement at Yalta, Poland ceded to the Soviet Union territory east of the Curzon line. Because of this, Poland asked for revision of her northern and western frontiers in Poland's favor. The United States will support a revision of these frontiers in Poland's favor. However, the extent of the area to be ceded to Poland must be determined when the final settlement is agreed upon.[4]

At the crucial Moscow Conference of Foreign Ministers on the German and Austrian problems, held between March 10 and April 24, 1947, the American position crystallized to an unexpected degree. Instead of accepting an ambiguous wording, like that of the Potsdam Protocol, or hiding behind generalized utterances on frontier revision, the American delegation, led by Secretary of State George C. Marshall, presented a program which still serves as a guideline of American policy in regard to the Oder-Neisse frontier. It included the following criteria:[5]

(1) The Teheran and Yalta decisions and Russian annexation of the Polish provinces (not the amount of damage wrought by the Germans in Poland or so-called historical arguments) require a "substantial revision of the pre-war German frontier in Poland's favor."

(2) The Polish-German frontier should not be considered entirely as a German-Polish problem. "We are dealing with the problem that touches closely on the political stability and economic health of much of Europe. . . . We should see to it that the new frontiers . . . do not create a continuing political problem and are not barriers to the accustomed and healthful flow of trade and commerce and human intercourse." "Let us start to apply the conception that European matters which are of general concern should be dealt with in the general interest."[6]

(3) Poland should receive sufficient territory and industrial resources "at least as great as she had before the war and capable of maintaining her people at a good standard of life."[7]

(4) However, Poland should only be awarded areas which she "needs and can effectively settle. We must avoid making a settlement which would only create difficulties for Poland and for Europe in future years."

(5) Germany should not lose one-fifth of her prewar food supply. The result would be overindustrialization beyond the prewar level, and "there is danger in requiring an eventual German population of over 66,000,000 to live within the confines of a smaller Germany" because of the inherent employment and economic problems.[8]

(6) The solution should not destroy the hope that in future years Polish-German relations may become genuinely peaceful and co-operative.

"It should not discredit the democratic forces in Germany"[9] and ". . . give militant nationalist groups the chance to gain a hold on another generation of German youth."[10]

At the subsequent Conference of the Foreign Ministers in London, Secretary Marshall elaborated on this criterion by adding: "We must take the broader view and establish a frontier which reduces irredentist sentiment to a minimum and promises to be lasting."[11]

(7) The limits of the investigation of the problem should be set as follows: Southern East Prussia should become Polish; Upper Silesia should be placed under Polish sovereignty, "but there should be provisions to assure that its coal and other resources will be available to help sustain the economy of Europe";[12] and "The division of the remaining territory, which is largely agricultural land, requires consideration of the needs of the Polish and German peoples and of Europe as a whole."[13]

This wording leaves no doubt that Secretary Marshall wanted the larger part of the remaining territories returned to Germany, since Poland obviously had no need for increased acreage over and beyond the lands of East Prussia and Upper Silesia in view of her small population increase. A further proof can be found in Marshall's interpretation at the London Conference:

We must bear in mind that much of the territory now under Polish administration has long been German and contains agricultural resources of vital importance to the German and European economy.[14]

The American position has not changed fundamentally since 1947. The old Stimson doctrine of nonrecognition of territorial changes effected by force has been continuously applied by the State Department, as in the denunciation of the Görlitz agreement of the Polish and German Communist regimes of June 6, 1950, and in the commentary thereon of United States High Commissioner John J. McCloy. Referring to the Byrnes speech and the Marshall statement of 1947, McCloy concluded

> . . . that the question of Germany's eastern boundaries is one to be settled in the peace treaty with Germany. . . . It cannot be settled for Germany by representatives of a regime that has no real support among the German people. The United States Government has not, therefore, recognized the Oder-Neisse boundary, nor the incorporation into the Polish state of those German territories placed under Polish administration at Potsdam.[15]

The two statements of 1950 added, therefore, a new criterion to the American position. Before the United States government would recognize any German-Polish frontier, the latter should have the sanction of the legal representatives of the German people. This paralleled Marshall's definition of the frontier's European significance, but added a new, additional dictum in view of the existence of the German Federal Republic.

Two years later, in replying to the Russian note of March 10, 1952, the United States, Britain, and France declared:

> The United States Government would recall that in fact no definite German frontiers were laid down by the Potsdam decisions, which clearly provided that the final determination of territorial questions must await the peace settlement.[16]

The State Department still issues passports to persons entering the provinces with the remark: "Germany—Under Polish Administration."

American initiative in the question has decreased in recent years. At the Berlin Conference of Foreign Ministers, January 25 to February 18, 1954, the United States took no additional stand on the boundaries. Only the British draft noted the necessity of giving the all-German government the right to reject or accept any international obligations of either the Federal Republic of Germany or the German Democratic Republic.[17]

The most recent official reiteration of the American position is contained in the New York Conference of the Western Foreign Ministers of September 28, 1955, which stated:

... the foreign ministers reaffirm the repeatedly expressed position of their governments that a final determination of the frontier of Germany must await a peace settlement for the whole of
Germany.[18]

The problem was not reopened at the Second Geneva Conference,
except for Molotov's query of November 3, 1955. Many Americans
of Polish origin, even if they are not so excited as to ask for protest
marches and strikes to induce the State Department to recognize the
Oder-Neisse Line,[19] at least hope that the absence of new statements
is a sign that American policy is shifting toward that of Poland and
the U.S.S.R. in the frontier question. Despite the fact that Gomulka
remains a loyal satellite of Moscow, his efforts to reduce his economic
and political commitments to the Kremlin and his changes in agricultural policy undoubtedly impress American policy-makers, who still
believe in the unrealistic policy of weaning Communist leaders away
from the U.S.S.R. The new loan of 1958 provides for the appropriation
of $25,000,000 for the purchase of machinery and spare parts, part of
which will be used in the Oder-Neisse provinces.[20] This, however, does
not mean that the Department of State is willing to abandon its demand for the revision of the frontiers, for official statements by State
Department spokesmen since 1955 reaffirm the former position.

Decreasing American initiative can be explained by the growing
realization of United States policy-makers that the restoration of the
sovereignty of the Federal Republic has placed the question in German hands. And final settlement of the frontier will be dependent
upon German unification and the creation of an all-German government. Consequently, it is the task of the successor of the Federal Republic, the all-German government, to reopen the question at a future
German peace conference and to enter into bilateral negotiations
with Poland on the subject. The role of the United States since 1955
has been restricted to advice, good offices, mediation, and other steps
of assistance in order to support the German government on the frontier issue.[21]

The British position has also undergone only minor changes since
1945. Foreign Minister Bevin seconded Secretary Marshall's initiative in 1947, since he believed that a large-scale reivsion was mandatory. The difference lay in the admission of Bevin that Lower Silesia
was already "filled up" with Poles, but the Foreign Minister also defined more clearly the area to be subject to revision as

the territory between Frankfurt and the Baltic which is a great agricultural area and I am not sure about its repopulation.[22]

Furthermore, Bevin, more than his American colleague, used the argument that Poland's own interests required the renunciation of some territories, while he underemphasized German interests in a future solution. At the London Conference, the Foreign Minister formally asked for the establishment of a "Territorial Commission" to decide upon the frontiers, but his request was blocked by Molotov's veto on November 28, 1947.[23]

In 1950, the statement of the Foreign Office deviated slightly from Bevin's position. In denouncing the Görlitz Agreement and in repeating its position, the Foreign Office added:

The British Government regarded the Oder-Neisse line laid down at Potsdam in July, 1945, as the provisional frontier between East Germany and Poland as long as the frontier had not been determined by the Peace Conference.[24]

A month later, however, a spokesman of the Foreign Office declared that

the proposed termination of the war with Germany would embrace not only the Federal Republic but also the Soviet Zone and the territory beyond the Oder-Neisse line. The area east of the Oder-Neisse line had been included because the three Western Powers had never recognized the cession of that area to Poland. . . .[25]

In 1955, the British Foreign Office commented on the Russian answer to the West German Federal Republic Chancellor's reservations on the occasion of resuming relations between the U.S.S.R. and Germany and reaffirmed its opposition to the Oder-Neisse Line as a permanent frontier.[26]

Since Great Britain also participated in the New York Conference of Foreign Ministers on September 28, 1955, and signed the Three Power Declaration,[27] there is no reason to believe that she is at present willing to renounce her position in favor of a revision of the Oder-Neisse frontier. She also agrees with the American attitude toward the necessity of reopening of the question at a future peace conference and about the primary responsibility of the West German government and its successor *in re* German frontiers.

The French position on the German-Polish frontier differed from those of the United States and Great Britain. Besides the traditional French-Polish friendship, both countries were convinced of the necessity of permanently weakening Germany by detaching her industrial regions. French *de facto* separation of the Saar from Germany, with the corresponding creation of a Franco-Saar customs union, and French insistence on the internationalization of the Ruhr and the Rhineland were official aims which could be synchronized with Polish demands. Therefore, France could not adopt a no-annexation policy, and she could not deny Polish claims to eastern German territories without compromising her demands to the Saar and the Rhineland. Still, France had two objections to the Potsdam Protocol. First, she was not invited to the Potsdam Conference and had no part in the decisions. She felt slighted because Polish claims were given obvious priority over considerably more modest French demands. Second, she became increasingly alarmed about the heavy influx into Germany of destitute, ill-nourished expellees, since she realized both their potential political explosiveness and the rise in Allied financial assistance that would be needed by any new German state if expulsion were allowed to proceed without restriction.[28]

At the London and Moscow conferences, the French position therefore contained some arguments used by the Western powers and others employed by the U.S.S.R. Foreign Minister Bidault maintained that the Potsdam Protocol provided only for a provisional settlement subject to change by the peace conference. However, he considered the Polish settlement of the provinces an accomplished fact that could not well be upset by the peace conference.[29] Bidault demanded an immediate halt to all expulsion in order to permit a stabilization of political and economic conditions in Germany. He remarked that if expulsions should continue, Germany's population density would soon reach 300 per cent of that of France.[30]

The Quai d'Orsay published almost no statements on the subject between December, 1947, and June 8, 1950. In the meantime, the political situation changed. The acceptance of Marshall Plan aid and the signing of the Western Union and NATO treaties by the French government effected a synchronization of American and French policies in Germany. A federal government and a West German state was created, the full sovereignty of the military governments was replaced by the Occupation Statute, and Germany was entreated as a future ally. France, while consolidating her hold on the Saar, has abandoned all claims to the Rhineland and gave her consent to the new Ruhr Statute, leaving German political sovereignty in this industrial region untouched. The Berlin Blockade and the creation of the so-called German Democratic Republic in the Russian Zone widened the rift between the East and West. The Quai d'Orsay reconsidered the wisdom of recognizing the Oder-Neisse Line as a *de facto,* but not as a *de iure,* frontier, and High Commissioner François-Poncet commented on the Görlitz Agreement by stating that "France explicitly recognizes the territory of the German state within the frontiers of 1937 and the Federal Republic as the only government to speak for the whole of Germany."[31] Similar statements were made by the Quai d'Orsay on October 10, 1951. The return of the Saar to Germany removed the last reason for French reservations, and her position now coincides with that of the United States and Britain. However, recently, President de Gaulle seems to believe that German unification would have to stop at the Oder and Neisse.

The Russian position at the Potsdam Conference has been discussed before. After Potsdam, Moscow felt sufficiently strong to repel Western overtures for a revision, since the Western powers had compromised their position by provisional acceptance of a Polish administration in the provinces. The Russian argument was reinforced by the accelerated expulsion process of the Polish authorities and by the rising tide of Polish settlers. After an interview with Stalin, *Pravda,* on March 4, 1946,[32] quoted the Russian dictator's statement, with emphasis on the permanent character of the frontier, denouncing Churchill's remark to the contrary at Fulton, Missouri. In that speech, the former British Premier declared:

> The Russian-dominated Polish government has been encouraged to make enormous and grievous inroads upon Germany, and mass expulsions of millions of Germans on a scale grievous and undreamed of are now taking place.[33]

The first detailed statement was made by Foreign Minister Molotov in answer to Secretary Byrnes's Stuttgart speech. Interviewed by the Polish News Agency on September 16, 1946, Molotov reaffirmed the Russian position that Poland's western frontiers had been laid down at the Potsdam Conference and now only required formal acknowledgment at the peace conference.[34]

At the Moscow Conference, Molotov refused to accept the provisional character of the Potsdam frontiers[35] and blatantly denied that Poland received the eastern German territories as well-deserved "compensation" for the loss of the eastern Polish provinces. This change in Russian policy rendered the Western argument of "adequate compensation" unacceptable to Moscow, and the Russian counterargument, based on Polish historical rights, was rejected by Britain and the United States.[36] As a result, Molotov, after Secretary Marshall had insisted upon inclusion of the distribution of Upper Silesian coal in the discussions over German reparations,[37] vetoed the creation of a frontier commission and reprimanded the American delegates for "intervening in the internal affairs of an Allied state." At the London Conference, Molotov went further by maintaining that the heads of governments had fixed the boundary at the Potsdam Conference and that their resolution was later approved by France, an obvious misrepresentation.[38] He again vetoed the establishment of a frontier commission.[39]

The position of Moscow has never wavered, although, according to recurring rumors, a possible change was threatened by Party Secretary Khrushchev during his fateful visit to Warsaw in October, 1956.[40] In 1952, the Russian proposal on unification included Molotov's interpretation of the Potsdam Protocol at the London Conference,[41] and at the Berlin Conference, Molotov submitted a draft peace treaty which included the provision: "The territory of Germany is determined by the frontiers laid down by the resolution of the Great Powers at the Potsdam Conference."[42]

In 1955, Molotov again changed his justification for the existence of the Oder-Neisse frontier by maintaining that events had outstripped many of the paragraphs of the Yalta Agreement and the Potsdam Protocol. A certain restraint was exercised *in re* Polish frontiers between Molotov's speech and Premier Bulganin's reiteration of Russian guarantees in Silesia in the summer of 1956.[43] The reservation was probably due to Russian efforts to allay Western distrust at the Geneva Conference and to avoid Western insistence to put the issue on the agenda of the summit meeting. The present position of the Soviet Union is clear: she wants to preserve the Oder-Neisse frontier but would insist upon a revision in favor of her central German

satellite if Warsaw attempted to leave the Warsaw Pact and/or to conduct an independent foreign policy.

2. THE POPULATION OF THE ODER-NEISSE PROVINCES IN GERMANY

Before the official German position on the Oder-Neisse frontier is
described, the problems of integration of the refugees and expellees
from the Oder-Neisse provinces into the economic, political, and social
life of the Federal Republic and the "German Democratic Republic"
and their influence upon the foreign policy of the German states
should be discussed.

The refugees and expellees from the Oder-Neisse provinces were
not the only group to enter Germany proper after World War II.
Although the Oder-Neisse group was the largest one, there were many
other influential expellee groups of German and non-German origin
in the territory of the Federal Republic between 1945-49. The two
and a half million Sudeten Germans, the 185,000 Germans expelled
from Hungary, the several hundred thousand German and non-German refugees, and the remainder of displaced Poles, Ukrainians, and
Balts were all crowded into what was left of the Reich. This subproletarian "have not" mass comprised 8,024,000 persons in West
Germany and West Berlin alone, of which 4,541,000 were from the
Oder-Neisse area.[44] The last census taken in the Soviet Russian Zone
gave, on October 20, 1946, the number of refugees and expellees as
2,273,000 persons from the Oder-Neisse provinces out of a total of
3,605,000 refugees and expellees.[45] Since the victims of the 1947 expulsions were settled in the Russian Zone and since individual expulsions constantly augment their number, it is probable that despite the
subsequent flight of many expellees, about 2,750,000 to 2,850,000
refugees and expellees from the Oder-Neisse provinces still live in the
Russian Zone. In the Federal Republic, the birth rate of all the German expellee groups in 1951 was 18.9 per thousand, as compared to
15.8 per thousand for the West German population, showing the
virility of the East German race.[46] The natural and immigration increase of refugees and expellees in West Germany between 1950 and
1953 was 9.2 per cent, increasing their number to roughly 5,000,000,
or 10 per cent, in the Federal Republic and to 16 per cent of the
population of the so-called German Democratic Republic.[47] Besides
the expellees, many residents formerly domiciled in the Russian Zone
live in West Germany, and, together with some non-German refugees,

the refugee and expellee population in West Germany amounts to 25 per cent of the total population. As a result, Germany has a population density of 201 persons per square kilometer, as compared to 160 in 1939.[48]

The resettlement of the refugees and expellees in Germany occurred without any comprehensive planning or adequate financial, housing, or food resources. Without respect to professional or social background, expellees were settled in emergency accommodations ranging from a one-room apartment with a common kitchen to a straw-sack in overcrowded wooden barracks or other camp facilities. The French occupation zone refused to admit any expellees, and since the Sudeten Germans were geographically nearest the American Zone, most of the Oder-Neisse group landed in the British Zone, in Lower Saxony and in Schleswig-Holstein.[49] Only the Silesians were scattered over the American and British zones.[50]

The consequences of such haphazard distribution were that Silesian factory and mine workers were often compelled to live in some isolated rural area, while Pomeranian and East Prussian farmers had to find a meager livelihood amidst the ruins of West German cities. Unemployment among expellees was long a chronic condition in the West Germany economy, even after its recovery had captured the attention of the Western world. At the end of March, 1950, after two years of generous European Recovery Program (ERP) aid, 35.6 per cent of all unemployed were refugees and expellees, though they comprised only about 20 per cent of the population.[51] The real situation was even more serious because in the three *Länder* with the highest number of expellees and refugees, these groups formed: Schleswig-Holstein, 58.5 per cent of all unemployed; Lower Saxony, 42.4 per cent of all unemployed; Bavaria, 40.4 per cent of all unemployed.[52] The hardest fate was experienced by East German farmers. Even in 1953, some 59 per cent of them were unemployed.[53]

It is maintained that the Soviet Union, in abetting Polish administration of the Oder-Neisse provinces and the expulsion of the German population, planned not only to perpetuate the political allegiance of Poland to the Soviet Union but also to promote the conquest of West Germany by political means, that is, by using the subproletarian masses of refugees and expellees in poverty-stricken Germany as a social-revolutionary element to help Communism to power. The surface evidence supports such a reasoning. Here, however, Communist thinking, which explains all political and social phenomena in economic terms, collided with the facts of political reality, for popular political actions and reactions are rightly described as a conglomerate of economic, religious, and ethnic constituents in which irrational forces exercise a wide influence. The strength of German-expellee patriotism and nationalism, their horrible experiences with the Red Army, and continued Russian advocacy of the Oder-Neisse frontier evoked in the expellees and refugees a political attitude which united them against the *spiritus rector* of their sufferings, regardless of the economic misery of the years 1945-49 in West Germany. Western demands for frontier revision and relief packages sent by private organizations in Western countries were also good political investments.[54] Soon the expellee groups became interested in democratic policies, which they embraced in order to secure Western support in their quest for return to their homeland.

It was not only this consideration of political tactics and economic and social adaptation to the new democratic state but also their war and postwar experiences which induced the expellees to rethink their political ideology. All of them were residents of frontier districts, and while many of them had in the past been untouched by the vicissitudes of nationality struggle, they also understood, after the individual catastrophes of 1945-47, that the Reich's former oppressive policy and the immorality of Polish rule were rooted in the nation-state, with unlimited sovereignty, which insists upon linguistic-cultural assimilation of its ethnic minorities. Despite the practice of parliamentary elections, the ethnic minorities were no longer protected against the majority in the new, undemocratic nation-states of the interwar period. No chance was given to the minority to become a majority party, no matter how free the elections were. The German and Polish examples of the past and present were and are obvious enough.

Despite this insight, the East German refugees and expellees still cling to the idea of the nation-state as the greatest political achievement of the past century which should be reformed instead of abolished. They want no cosmopolitanism or denationalization; they want the survival of the properly restricted nation-state as the carrier of the cultural and political development of the nation. It is out of this contradiction that the present European concept of the expellees arose.[55] Some foreign authors remain skeptical. They describe the European orientation of these groups as a devious plot to inveigle themselves into the good graces of the unsuspecting West and believe that the *Drang nach Osten,* although not publicly emphasized, is very much alive in many refugee circles.[56] Yet the fact remains that the different social, economic, and cultural environment of West Germany and of refugee life, together with the failure of the old political order, could not help but influence the thinking of this group, rendering them receptive to ideas which they considered unattractive a decade ago.

German refugee and expellee preoccupation with Europe is very different from the Carolingian outlook, often found in West Germany and France, on a united Europe, which is considered as a new state with unlimited sovereignty. The distinctly confederative expellee concept of Europe is based on common European culture and economic needs.[57] The political *raison d'être* of such a European union would be the creation of an authority with limited powers to prevent economic and cultural oppression of European nations by one another and by outside powers.[58] It remains to be seen whether the realization of such a concept is at all practicable in the grandiose dimensions postulated by the expellees or whether it is only the protective self-deception of expellee thinkers. If so, the concept will evaporate with German unification when the thinkers will still find themselves living in a Europe influenced by Russian imperialism and Western supranational interests.

Whether truth or illusion, the European orientation has left a great impact on the political aims and tactics of the German refugees and expellees. It has enabled them to accept the principles of a peaceful solution of their right to the homeland and to the Oder-Neisse provinces and to renounce revenge as a means of policy while maintaining the right to the homeland as a human, instead of only a civil, right. It has also given them the opportunity to assist in the constructive task of building a united Europe in "which peoples can live without fear and compulsion," even though the day of its realization is still in the future. The Charter of Expellees, signed by their responsible leaders at Stuttgart in 1950, forms an eloquent document which reflects the changing ideological and political position of group thinking, a good omen for the future of Europe.[59]

The experience with the Red Army and the Communist-dominated Polish militia created in the minds of the refugees an almost traumatic rejection of a return to a Communist country. The expellees have actually become great supporters of the democratic Federal Republic and of her adherence to Western political and military pacts.[60] With the exception of the repudiated Dr. Gerecke of Lower Saxony, no expellee politician has ever proposed co-operation with the Russians or the Polish Communists or has become a partisan of "peaceful co-existence," as preached by the Russian Communist Premier.

These experiences and ideological principles failed, however, to render the expellee masses docile. Their quest for organization was originally feared by the Allied military governments but could not be suppressed. On April 9, 1949, the *Zentralverband vertriebener Deutschen* was founded, although Allied decrees prevented the creation of a refugee political party in time for the 1949 elections.[61]

Besides organizational and political activities, the years from 1950 to 1958 had a great economic and professional impact on the expellee population. The Law of Equalization of Burdens was passed by the West German Parliament in 1952 on behalf of all refugees and expellees, and a *Flüchtlingsgesetz* cleared up their position under domestic public and international law. The Equalization of Burdens Law provides for indemnification of lost property by annuities and grants-in-aid, primarily to repurchase the most necessary household equipment. Credits were awarded to expellee and refugee industries and scholarships to students. This program was financed by levying a tax on the real estate and corporate income of the native population for more than a decade. More than $9,000,000,000 was paid out of the Equalization of Burdens fund by 1956, one-fourth of which was provided for industrial credits and mortgages for the purchase and reconstruction of buildings, homes, and farms.[62] Some 10,621 industrial enterprises were established by refugees and expellees (about 60 per cent of the enterprises by those of the Oder-Neisse group).[63] They employ 330,000 workers. And 84,999 farms were distributed to farmers, mostly from the Oder-Neisse provinces, awaiting resettlement on West German farms.[64] But the percentage of expellee enterprises is below that of the native population (11 per cent of all the refugees and expellees are in this field, while the corresponding number of natives is 25 per cent).[65] Former state employees, including public-school teachers, again receive pensions and/or were reinstated in their former positions in the West German bureaucracy. According to 1958 figures, more than 80 per cent of this group is fully integrated, while only 50 per cent of all the refugees and expellees can be regarded as integrated in the Federal Republic's economy.[66] This latter group includes chiefly the bureaucracy and industrial workers. The other 50 per cent is only partially integrated (they are unemployed or work outside their former professions). The self-employed suffered most;

the percentage of professionals among expellees fell from 18.3 per cent in 1939 in their homeland to 6.3 per cent in 1957 in West Germany.[67]

The integration, however incomplete, was a major accomplishment of the West German government and the mutual assistance of the expellee population. The Polish press sees in the success of economic integration an added proof that Germany does not need the provinces for food supply and that the expellee population would not return even if the territories were to become German again.[68]

An objective analysis would, however, have to take into consideration the many drastic sociological and economic changes the arrival of the expellees and refugees wrought in the Federal Republic's political and economic life, which have both their favorable and unfavorable effects on the latter. The so-called German "economic wonder" would not have been possible without the hard work of the expellees and refugees, often for wages lower than those of the native group, and without the creative and business skills they brought from the east. However, German economy at the present is more vulnerable to economic recession or depression than at any time before. This vulnerability is due in part to the presence of the expellees and refugees and in part to the loss of the agricultural provinces east of the Oder and Neisse rivers. In 1956, the Federal Republic (half of the territory and 75 per cent of the population of the Reich) exported more than DM 30,000,000,000 worth of goods, the equivalent of $7,200,000,000.[69] In 1937, the German Reich exported only RM 5,900,000,000, the equivalent of $1,700,000,000.[70] Even if cost and price increases are taken into account, the exports of the West German state were 220 per cent of the Reich's exports in 1937. The industrial-production index of the Federal Republic also spiraled, outdistancing even that of the Soviet Union.[71]

The vulnerability of such an artificially increased production is augmented by the contraction of the food supply and by the absence of preferential markets in the countries of the Coal and Steel Community. The Common Market plan will need fifteen years for implementation, and its success is still in doubt because of the revival of economic nationalism in France. Any contraction of the world market, even if only moderate, would hamper the import of raw materials and food by Germany, restricting both industrial production for export and the German diet. Although these facts are not prominently discussed by German and Western politicians, the recent contraction of American business should have been a warning in regard to the extremely small margin of maneuverability of the German economy in the face of any world-wide recession.[72]

The second problem has more of a sociological character. Would the Oder-Neisse expellees return to the provinces if the area were to be returned to Germany or at least detached from Poland? It is undeniable that the creation of a secure economic existence by individual expellees in the West would render some of them unwilling to return, that the percentage of intermarriage between expellee youth and the West German population is on the increase, and that, in many cases, the intermarried youth would not want to return. Finally, many other factors would also influence the decision of the individual expellee. These include the conditions prevailing in the provinces at the time of the proposed return and its political belonging to Germany, to Poland, or to some temporary international administration. The best, yet hazardous, guess is contained in the EMNID Bureau's poll made in the fall of 1956.[73]

The result of the poll has been somewhat different from that of the *Institut für Demiskopie* in 1953.[74] According to the EMNID poll, 57 per cent of all refugees and expellees were willing to live in the Oder-Neisse provinces if given the opportunity. Since the group also included other expellees, the percentage of Oder-Neisse expellees would be as high as 60 per cent. Thus from West Germany alone, more than 3,000,000 former residents of the provinces would return, given a solution favorable to their re-immigration. If the same proportion is correct in regard to those in the Russian Zone, another 1,500,000 would join the drive, and altogether, 4,500,000 people would be available for the repopulation of the provinces, a number sufficient to populate Lower Silesia and Pomerania to the 1939 level.[75] These results agree with the figures published on the economic and social integration of expellees and refugees, which is given as 50 per cent.

The EMNID poll also showed some unexpected results. Among the refugees formerly domiciled in the Russian Zone, about 22 per cent would prefer resettlement in the Oder-Neisse provinces. They alone would provide settlers to repopulate eastern Brandenburg,[76] without considering the wish of the West German population, 1.6 million of whom expressed willingness to move to the Oder-Neisse region.[77] Thus even after a wholesale removal of the new Polish settlers, which is not contemplated in any event, there should be sufficient number of German settlers to repopulate the area west of the Stettinius-Eden Line, drawn at Malta.

The next question is whether this percentage would remain constant if the next five years did not bring about a solution enabling them to return. It is undeniable that as late as 1948 the overwhelming majority of the Oder-Neisse group wanted and hoped to return. Regardless of whether 57 per cent or 60 per cent is considered correct, a significant decrease of those willing to return has occurred. Yet the decrease took place between 1949 and 1952, rather than afterwards, for the figures of the *Institut* and EMNID are almost the same, and the latter's, taken in 1956, are even slightly higher. It can be assumed that as long as the *Landsmannschaften* remain active in the cultural and political education of the expellee youth, no further significant decrease would occur in the next few years.

If the majority of the expellees are still attached to their homeland, the next problem becomes that of their political and economic strength and the amount of influence they exercise over West German foreign policy and in which direction any such influence is exerted. The political strength of the group consists of their influence on the federal and state governments, on opinion-forming groups and media, and on their involvement in the forming of public opinion as a political movement.

Between 1949 and 1959, every Adenauer cabinet had a member who came from the provinces east of the Oder and Neisse rivers. In the first cabinet, the Minister for Refugees and Expellees was the first president of the *Zentralverband vertriebener Deutschen* (Central Association of Expelled Germans) and former *Regierungspräsident* of Upper Silesia, Dr. Hans Lukaschek, a moderate Catholic gentleman. He preferred to select his advisors from the Catholic groups of the southern parts of the provinces and came increasingly under attack from refugee groups.

In the second Adenauer cabinet, the same ministry was awarded to Professor Dr. Theodor Oberländer, who at first served as a deputy of the *Block der Heimatvertriebenen und Entrechteten* (BHE), known in English as the Refugee Party, and, after 1955, as a member of the CDU/CSU. There are many divergent statements concerning the personage and past of the German Minister of Expellees and Refugees, who, by adroit political maneuvering, not only survived the split in the BHE but also succeeded in securing reappointment in the third

Adenauer cabinet in 1957.[78] One source considers him a Nazi fellow-traveler, and in 1954, he had some opposition from the left-of-center parties and circles in West Germany because of his personnel policies within his department. His successfully executed policy plans (Two Year Plan), his moderation on foreign policy (voted for the Paris Agreements, Germany's participation in NATO, and the Saar Agreement),[79] and his talented defense of German rights to the eastern provinces seem to refute the accusation that he is an intransigent "revisionist." His past hardly qualifies him as an enemy of the Poles or as a Nazi ideologist.

Professor Oberländer was originally an agricultural scientist who held a chair at several East German universities and, later, at the University of Prague. In the thirties, he was director of the *Institut für osteuropäische Wirtschaft* (Institute for East German Economy) at the University of Königsberg, East Prussia.[80] During the war, he experienced the dilemma common to many sober-thinking Germans caught between Hitler's policies and their innate feeling of nationalism. His conscience decided against approving and executing Hitler's oppressive policy in Poland and the U.S.S.R., and he was arrested in 1942. Oberländer was released in 1944, and sent to the Vlassov army formations as Hitler finally realized his monstrous mistake in not using anti-Communist Russian and Ukrainian POW's against their Communist masters.[81] The demotion during the Third Reich enabled him to re-enter political life in Germany, and in 1950, he was elected to the Bavarian Parliament as a member of the BHE. Soon he became *Land* Chairman of the BHE, and in 1953, he became its national vice-chairman. More experienced, moderate, and able than Waldemar Kraft, Professor Oberländer was selected by the Chancellor as Minister of Expellees and Refugees. His support of Adenauer's policies and the unavoidable shortcomings of refugee and expellee integration by the means available to him led to an open conflict in the BHE between Professor Oberländer and Waldemar Kraft. Because he insisted upon an independent line in 1954 toward the Western treaties and upon the return of the Saar, he succeeded Mr. Kraft as national chairman of the BHE but was defeated in the following year when his prognostication of the outcome of the Saar elections made him reconsider his opposition to the 1955 Saar Agreement.

The second important leader of the BHE was Mr. Waldemar Kraft, who participated in the federal cabinet as a minister-without-portfolio between 1953 and 1957. After an almost spectacular rise in West

German politics—from an unknown organizer of Silesian and East Prussian expellees in Schleswig-Holstein to the position of Minister of Justice in the same state and to the national chairmanship of the BHE—Kraft's fortunes soon declined. It should be noted, however, that it was Mr. Kraft who transformed the BHE into a strong, nationally recognized party included as the fourth member of the government coalition and represented in the *Bundestag* with twenty-seven deputies. Mr. Kraft was more of an emotional speaker and a more magnetic personality than Professor Oberländer or Frank Seiboth, the leader of the rump party after 1955. He had, however, a more questionable political past because he had co-operated with the Hitler regime as the leader of the German farmers in Pomorze (West Prussia) during World War II.[82] He was also regarded as an unreconstructed German chauvinist of Prussian persuasion.[83]

In order to gauge the strength of the expellee and refugee groups in the political arena, it is not sufficient to consider their BHE representation in the federal and state governments. The presence of the BHE in the federal and state parliaments and the presence of expellee and refugee deputies in the two major parties also has to be considered.

In recent years, the BHE has undergone a meteoric rise followed by a relapse that has rendered the future of the party uncertain, though not necessarily hopeless. The concept of the BHE arose from the misery and political frustration of these groups in the late forties.[84] Yet these motivating forces offered a poor foundation for any political movement, and Western circles were genuinely afraid that Nazism or some other type of Rightist radicalism might exploit this party as its vanguard. To quote the *London Times*: "To a demagogue, refugees are what blood is to a shark and the refugee problem is large enough to create a revolutionary situation."[85]

It is to the credit of the expellee politicians and of the often-slandered Waldemar Kraft that the passionate emotions of hatred, envy and bitterness in which the victims of the expulsions and flight were engulfed were channeled into a constructive political and economic reform program. One may disagree with some of its points, or even question their relevancy, but it must be recognized that the platform of the BHE remained within the bounds of democratic fair play. The greatest successes of the Refugee Party were attained in the 1950-51 state elections in Schleswig-Holstein, Lower Saxony, and Bavaria.[86] The federal elections of 1953 showed that despite the greatly fluctuating strength of the expellee and refugee population in the various states, the BHE could attract approximately one-third of the refugee vote and elect twenty-seven deputies to the Lower House.[87]

Since the BHE was admitted to the coalition and could no longer afford to display the irresponsible features of the opposition, its heterogeneous character was proved. Dissensions, expulsions, and change of leadership soon occurred. The question of priority given to the Oder-Neisse question by the Adenauer government and the adequacy or inadequacy of the measures taken in order to improve the economic and social conditions of the expellees soon became instrumental in breaking up party unity, with corresponding results in state elections and in the 1957 federal elections.[88] In the latter, the BHE lost its representation in the national legislative body by failing to win 5 per cent of the votes nationally. It attained only 4.6 per cent, as compared to 6.5 per cent in 1953.[89] This did not, however, interfere with the representation of the BHE in state parliaments, where it retained some of the ministries for expellees.

The absence of the BHE from the third *Bundestag* fails to deprive the Oder-Neisse group or other expellees of direct representation in that body. In the first two *Bundestag*s, about one hundred of all deputies were either expellees and refugees or had lived for a considerable time in the Oder-Neisse provinces.[90] In the new Lower House, there are forty-four deputies who, coming from areas east of the Oder and Neisse or from non-German territories, were given committee assignments in the West German Parliament.[91] About two-thirds of them belong to the Oder-Neisse group. On the Committee on Foreign Affairs, there are three members of this group (two from the CDU/CSU and one from the SPD), and among the alternates there are another three expellees and refugees, two of them Sudeten Germans.[92] The CDU/CSU sends such deputies to nine different committees, the SPD to eight. There are no committees in the Lower House without expellee and refugee representation as members or alternates.[93]

Besides parliamentary and government representation, the reunited expellee federation, the *Bund der Vertriebenen,* with a composite membership of six and one-half million, serves as a major pressure group which looks out for the rights and interests of the expellee minority, despite continuing internal rivalries of the two federations comprising it. The *Bund* is now headed by the able and talented deputy, Hans Krüger, from the Pomeranian *Landsmannschaft*. It consists of the federation of the former *Zentralverband vertriebener Deutschen* (Central Association of Expelled Germans) and the *Ver-*

band der Landsmannschaften, which were under the leadership of Mr. Linus Kather and Baron von Manteuffel-Szoege, respectively. The disappearance of the BHE from the Lower House and renewed Polish propaganda and diplomatic efforts to induce the Western powers to accept the Oder-Neisse frontier contributed greatly to the union of the two organizations in the fall of 1958.

The *Zentralverband* was created of the local and district expellee and refugee representatives, regardless of their former abodes. It was primarily a horizontal, geographic organization devoted to the improvement of the economic and political lot of its members. Although only indirectly active in matters of foreign policy, the *Zentralverband* also demanded the restoration of the frontiers of 1937 and regarded the Oder-Neisse provinces as German.[94]

The vertical and cultural organization of the Oder-Neisse group and of other expellees were the *Landsmannschaften* (a term untranslatable into English), organized originally as a part of the *Zentralverband.* The purpose of the *Landsmannschaften* was to direct[95] the organization of the groups on the basis of their former domicile, namely, Upper Silesia, Silesia, eastern Brandenburg, Pomerania, Danzig, and East Prussia within the Oder-Neisse territories. Originally, an agreement was signed with the *Zentralverband* for an appropriate division of labor, but it was not honored after 1951, and six years passed before the re-establishment of co-operation between the two organizations.

The task of the *Landsmannschaften* is to keep the attachment of the group to the homeland alive, to teach the history of the provinces to the youth and the native population, and to serve as a direct outlet for the cultural activities and talents of the group. Annual meetings, held in a particular city and attended by hundreds of thousands of the group, as well as recreational or lecture-type get-togethers, held in West German towns and villages with audiences hardly in excess of fifty people, are both serving this purpose.[96] The *Landsmannschaften* have the advantage of an eager and talented leadership, and many of the leading spokesmen of the Oder-Neisse group, including Dr. Herbert Hupka, Dr. Oskar Eggert, and Mr. Linus Kather, rose from their ranks.

Since Heinrich von Brentano became German Foreign Minister, the Foreign Office, too, has paid more attention to the *Landsmannschaften* and to the various research and informational organizations of the Oder-Neisse group. Their great reservoir of area knowledge and their selfless enthusiasm and personal experiences were all considered great assets by the CDU and SPD in the formulation of the principles of German foreign policy. The major scholarly and literary organizations, such as the *Göttinger Arbeitskreis*,[97] whose chairman, Professor Dr. Herbert Kraus, has recently received the *Grosser Verdienstkreuz der Bundesrepublik,* the Johann Gottfried Herder Institute, under the able direction of Professor Erich Keyser, and the *Arbeitskreis für Ostfragen,* headed by Professor Georg Stadtmüller at Munich, continue to exercise a great influence on the policy-making organs. If any western or eastern European politician is searching for the beginnings of a new German *Ostpolitik* with a more European accent, the expellee politicians and scholars can provide the most accurate answers.

3. THE OFFICIAL GERMAN POSITION ON THE ODER-NEISSE FRONTIER

In the preceding chapters, the position assumed by the federal government, the Oder-Neisse expellees, and the Russian-dominated central German government toward the eastern frontiers of Germany was mentioned only in passing. Their central importance to any solution of the problem makes consideration of their claims and proposals necessary, and in analyzing them, a small distinction must be made between those of the federal government and those of the expellee and refugee groups. The difference is based on the following three elements:

(1) The government wants to retain its flexibility in regard to a future solution to the question within the limits of nonrecognition of the present line. It insists, however, that at the outset of negotiations, the provinces should be considered German instead of Polish, according to their status in international law.

(2) The government considers the frontier problem as one for the future, rather than the present, since any practical solution could be implemented only after the disappearance of the Russian-supported German Democratic Republic and the reunification of Germany.

(3) The government relies on the expellee groups to devise practical solutions to the question because it has no clear-cut *ad hoc* proposals to the problem. Unity of purpose and expert knowledge, in turn, enable the Oder-Neisse group to formulate the ideas of the government on the subject without necessarily dictating them.

In regard to the legality[98] of the Oder-Neisse Line, the position of the Oder-Neisse groups and the federal government can be summarized as follows:

(1) There are no international agreements binding upon either the Federal Republic or the great powers which establish the Line as the German-Polish frontier. The German position emphasizes the provisional character of the Line in the Potsdam Protocol and introduces subsidiary arguments to demonstrate the real intentions of the great powers as of 1945-1947.

It is argued that only one four-power agreement, that of June 5, 1945, has remained in force since the abrogation of the Potsdam Protocol by Russian violations. Although formal abrogation was never completed, the initial breaches of the agreement by the U.S.S.R. in regard to reparations, free elections, and economic unity and the Allied creation of a West German state are considered as fulfilling the criteria of nullification in the German view. They call attention to Molotov's speech before the Supreme Soviet in 1955:[99] that many of the provisions of the Protocol were rendered obsolete by the progress of events and should be disregarded. Khrushchev's abrogation of the agreement on November 24, 1958, completes the circle. Furthermore, American policy-makers consider only the Berlin occupation provisions of the Protocol to be valid, despite the defeat of the bill in 1953 in the United States Congress to abrogate the treaty.

Consequently, the Germans maintain that the June 5, 1945 agreement, which provided for the assumption of sovereignty by the four Allied powers in Germany, remains the only document on which East and West agree. The document, the Germans point out, provides for the assumption of sovereignty in Germany, the territory of which is defined for occupation purposes "as of December 31, 1957," and the Oder-Neisse provinces are therefore considered German territory by the great powers.

(2) German sources[100] maintain that international morality, if not customary international law,[101] forbids any detachment of territories from any state without the permission of that state. They add that the June 5, 1945 agreement expressly stated that the assumption of sovereign powers in Germany by the four powers did not mean an annexation of Germany.[102] For evidence of the no-annexation rule, German sources refer to the Atlantic Charter, which forbade territorial changes without the express will of the inhabitants. Robert E. Sherwood's opinion,[103] that the Charter was only a disguised means of Anglo-

American psychological warfare, as underlined by Prime Minister Churchill's statement in the House of Commons on February 22, 1944, that there should be "no question of the Atlantic Charter applying to Germany as a matter of right and barring territorial transferences and adjustments in enemy countries,"[104] is not denied by German sources. Professor Herbert Kraus emphasizes, however, that the Atlantic Charter was later formalized into a multilateral treaty signed by Poland and the U.S.S.R., thereby creating obligations for the participants which could not be abrogated by a unilateral action by the British or Polish Prime Ministers.[105] Churchill himself must have undergone a substantial change of mind insofar as his interpretation of the binding character of the Charter is concerned, for as late as January 8, 1942, he wrote to Foreign Minister Eden:

> ... in my opinion, if we deviate from the principles of the Atlantic Charter to which Stalin himself adhered, we would put our political reliability at stake. No British Government headed by me should leave the slightest doubt about its determination to be bound by the principles of freedom and democracy as laid down in the Atlantic Charter, or about its opinion that these principles assume a special importance when territorial changes are discussed.[106]

It is also pointed out that the term "Germany as of December 31, 1937," which was used in the September 20, 1945 "Agreement on Additional Demands on Germany" by the four powers, is quoted and that the Russian-Polish frontier treaty of August 16, 1945, also recognized the provisional character of the Oder-Neisse Line.[107]

(3) Not content to show the grave breach of international law involved in considering the present Oder-Neisse Line as the Polish-German frontier, German scholars also attempt to prove that annexations as such are outlawed by international law and that therefore even a peace conference would lack the authority under international law to transfer these territories to Poland without the consent of the German government. Professor Herbert Kraus defines annexation as follows:

> Vorgang gewaltsamer, gegen den Willen des Gebietsherrn erfolgender Aneignung fremden Staatsgebietes. Mit Gewalt erzwungene Abtretungsverträge stehen ihnen rechtlich gleich.[108]

He also remarks that the fact of annexation fulfills the requirements of an act of aggression under present international law, so that the conditions created by annexation are legally null and void. Any administration erected as a result of an act of agression will represent only *de facto* occupation, and the state whose nationals were expelled may, in accordance with international law, demand the restoration of the *status quo ante*.

Many instances in regional international law are cited as evidence for the contention of the no-annexation rule. The evidence starts with the declaration of the Washington Conference of the Pan-American States[109] in 1889-90 and climaxes in Article II, Section 4, of the United Nations Charter.[110] The Germans are quick to remark that the transfer of adminstration of the Oder-Neisse provinces occurred after the signing of the Charter by the U.S.S.R. and represented a breach of her obligations under the Charter. To the consolation of the Germans, it should be remarked that between 1917 and 1959, the Soviet Union has unilaterally violated about 80 per cent of all treaties concluded by her with other powers.

(4) Besides the no-annexation rule, the German position on the right to national self-determination has also crystallized. In the long run, this German argument could acquire greater significance than the contention that the no-annexation rule already forms an integral part of international law instead of representing a *desideratum* of international morality only.

The German concept of self-determination is a concept based less on a nation than on the people inhabiting the contested territory. In case of cession of territory, therefore, German experts demand plebiscites in order to ascertain the wishes of the resident population.[111] Basically, in regard to ethnic minorities, the German position is identical with that of Premiers Churchill and Mikolajczyk, who both believed that the presence of large German minorities would produce new factors of instability. One eminent German international lawyer, however, sees in the popular self-determination concept an epoch-making element of the nineteenth and twentieth centuries and maintains that in regional international law, it is rapidly becoming a binding precept.[112] He produces several examples in support of his hypothesis.

First, he cites the Soviet Russian concept of self-determination contained in the "Declaration of Rights of the Peoples of Russia," adopted by the Second All-Russian Congress of November 15, 1917.

The document called for plebiscites to be held "with absolute freedom of all inhabitants of the said areas, including emigrants and refugees."[113] Of course, German international lawyers are aware of the Soviet Union's countless violations of the right to self-determination in the Ukraine, the Baltic States, central Asia, and Byelorussia, but they remark that these actions were originally denounced by the Communists themselves.

Second, German sources quote the American Ambassador at Copenhagen, who, in a note to Denmark on June 17, 1867, remarked:

> The modern practice in Europe in regard to this subject [i.e., plebiscites by cessions of territory] is so regular as to almost become a rule of public law.[114]

Third, German sources again refer to the Atlantic Charter, which, in this case, is unequivocal in recognizing the rights of people to live under a governmental order of their own choosing and includes the confirmation of the signatory powers that they do not desire any territorial changes which are not in accordance with the will of the people.

Finally, reference is made to the two drafts of the Convention on Human Rights, which include this passage: "All peoples and nations shall have the right of self-determination, namely, the right to determine freely their political, economic, social and cultural status."[115]

(5) Naturally, the German sources deal in detailed manner with the illegality of the mass expulsion. While there is no reasonable doubt that both President Roosevelt and Prime Minister Churchill subscribed, in 1944-45, to the theory of an exchange of populations, there is considerable question as to whether mass expulsions as an instrument of national policy could be recognized under international law. All population exchanges in the past, with the exception of the expulsion of the German population from the Oder-Neisse provinces and that of the German population from Poland and other states of east central Europe, were based on real or sham reciprocity (Greek-Turkish, Hungarian-Czechoslovak) or were denounced as violations of international law. If, however, mass expulsion is inadmissible under international law, then the state whose citizens were expelled would acquire the right to adequate material restitution when unilateral expulsions had taken place without the consent of the injured state. This

stipulation would be valid for the German expulsion of Polish citizens from Poznań and Lodz in 1939-40, too. If the counterclaims are duly considered, however, the amount of compensation payable to German citizens by Poland would still be so staggeringly high that it could never be solved by financial restitution but only by territorial compensation.

There are several documents which prove the illegality of expulsions. The resolution of the *Institut de Droit International* on September 20, 1896, stated: "Denationalization can never be imposed as a punishment."[116] The Hague Rules of Land Warfare of 1907 deprive the occupant of the right to expel at will the inhabitants of the area of occupation, with the exception of individual deportation of undesirable elements. This rule has been tightened by Article 48 of the 1949 Geneva Agreement, also signed by the U.S.S.R., so that at present all mass expulsions are interdicted by international law, no matter what the cause.[117]

Conclusively, the Germans argue that the expulsion of the population of the Oder-Neisse provinces occurred in violation of international law because:

(1) The expulsion took place in an area under *de iure* German sovereignty, under Soviet Russian occupation, and only provisionally under Polish administration and, therefore, violated the Hague Rules of 1907.[118]

(2) The expulsion could not have been justified as a "collective punishment" of the citizens of the German Reich because of the criminal activities of the Hitler government or the crimes perpetrated by individuals from inside or outside the provinces. According to the verdict of the International Court at Nuremberg against Hermann Göring: "One of the most important legal principles consists of the individual character of criminal responsibility and mass punishment should be avoided.[119]

(3) The possible future aversion or disloyalty of the German population in the provinces to be allotted to Poland fails to justify the expulsion because, in the words of the Italian international lawyer, Pallieri:

It is sufficient to consider the fact that a state is never compelled to acquire this or that territory. If it possesses the territory, this serves as a proof that it had wanted the territory, and often also, that it had fought in order to possess it. The responsibility of making the inhabitants of the territory into good citizens rests with the state and it has to exert itself to this end.[120]

Legal claims are not the only argument of the federal government and the Oder-Neisse expellee group. Historically, they can prove that all of the area has belonged, for five to six hundred years, to the Holy Roman Empire, Prussia, or Germany, and that the provinces belonged to Poland for a much shorter time, even during the early Middle Ages. The relevance of the German argument has been discussed before, and here it need only be remarked that even President Roosevelt and Prime Minister Churchill ridiculed Russian Foreign Commissar Molotov at the Yalta Conference for his proposal to regard the westward shift of Poland as her return to her historical frontiers.[121]

German arguments also emphasize the almost absolute German ethnic character of the population as of 1939 and 1944. As an expellee newspaper remarks, there were only 645 Polish votes in Pomerania at the time of the last free elections in Germany in 1933. With the exception of Upper Silesia, no ethnic problem has ever existed, and the Germans point out that the inhabitants of the western part of the province voted overwhelmingly for Germany in the plebiscite of 1921.

Germans also use economic arguments relating to the importance of the provinces to the German, Polish, and European economy and to their present role in the economy of the Communist bloc. The utmost indispensability of the provinces to a balanced German economy is well documented by the 1939 population figures, which show that several million Germans have been fed by the agricultural surplus of the provinces.[122] The Germans point out that the 220 per cent increase in German exports (excluding the exports of the German Democratic Republic) and the corresponding increase of the percentage of imported agricultural products will have an unfavorable effect upon German economy in case of a world-market contraction. As a result, Germans consider the return of the agricultural provinces to Germany as an absolute necessity for the preservation of peace and prosperity in their country in particular and Europe in general.

There are many German arguments denying the availability of Polish means to restore and revitalize the provinces. Polish sources, also, often recognize the serious shortcomings of Polish administration, especially in the voivodships of Szczecin (Stettin), Koszalin

(Köslin), Olsztyn (Allenstein), and Gdańsk (Danzig), the decline of Oder shipping, and the demise of small towns everywhere in the region, with the exception of Upper Silesia east of the Oder, and they are frequently cited by the Germans.[123] The Germans argue that the few spectacular successes of Polish administration, such as reorientation and expansion of Upper Silesian industry and the building of cement and fertilizer plants, were made possible only by the following three factors: (1) the presence of large-scale heavy industry before 1945; (2) the provisions of credits, raw materials, and technical personnel by the U.S.S.R. (she wanted to build a western *Kombinat* between 1950 and 1956); and (3) the utter neglect of industrial expansion of Poland proper with the exception of Polish Upper Silesia (Śląsk).

Silesian coal has played a substantial role in the Scandinavian, German, Polish, Czech, Hungarian, Austrian, and Rumanian economies alike. Its reorientation toward the East and to economically unprofitable Polish plants is the major cause of the until recently continued high-priced American coal imports to Europe, which, in turn, contribute toward a gap in the trade balances of the western European countries *vis-à-vis* the dollar bloc. Furthermore, overindustrialization of West Germany influences the growth of other western European industries unfavorably and has major effects on the British economy.

The major German argument, however, continues to be the role played by the Silesian coal mines and steel plants in the economy of the Communist bloc. The Upper Silesian Triangle and the adjacent Morawska-Ostrawa area form the industrial backbone of the satellite empire of the Soviet Union.[124] Control of this area enables the U.S.S.R. to exercise economic supremacy over the Balkans and eastern Europe, for the Silesian and northern Czech industries provide the capital goods necessary to maintain and expand the level of industrialization in the other satellite states and produce the needed military equipment. If Upper Silesia is returned to Germany, the Soviet Union will have the choice of either relinquishing its hold on the satellites or increasing substantially the amount of machinery, engineers, and credits flowing to the area, thereby weakening its economy.

Many of the expellees and refugees point to the tremendous contributions of the eastern Germans to European culture in past centuries. While cultural accomplishments and a high standard of material and intellectual civilization form a very ineffective argument in power politics, the impressive scientific, literary, and architectural accomplishments of German talent in the provinces, especially Silesia, that transformed them through the centuries into one of the most cultured and civilized areas in central Europe, with a high living standard, greatly reinforces the moral side of the German argument for a return of the homeland of the expellees and refugees to Germany.

4. THE SOLUTION PROPOSED BY GERMAN EXPELLEES

Since the German-Polish problem is not only a juridical and historical dispute and involves, besides the rights and wrongs of the case, the search for an equitable political solution, the Germans must devise a plan which can be proposed to the Poles without further violating international law or weakening Western unity. The federal government has expressed its adherence to the nonrecognition of the frontier, as based on the provisional character of the Potsdam Protocol, and has proposed avenues and methods to solve the problem after the liquidation of the German Democratic Republic. The official position has evolved as follows.

On May 29, 1953, the West German Chancellor submitted to President Eisenhower an eight-point memorandum containing the following provisions:

6. In this Peace Treaty the right of all people to their homeland should be considered, in accordance with Christian and ethical principles.

7. The German Government will never be able to recognize the Oder-Neisse line. Germany will, however, endeavor to settle the territorial question bound up there with a new spirit of peaceful international cooperation."[125]

This statement was elaborated upon by the Chancellor in September, 1953, when he expressed his view that the Oder-Neisse provinces could be administered by a Polish-German condominium or by the United Nations. This statement resulted in protests from the *Landsmannschaften* and Mr. Linus Kather from the *Zentralverband*, and the condominium concept, also opposed by Communist Poland, was never again mentioned publicly. On October 23, 1953, the Chancellor officially denied the idea by taking refuge in the explanation that the problem would be solved only in a Peace Treaty and expressed the hope that the European idea—and Poland belongs to Europe, too—will have made further progress by then and that by then also the spirit of nationalism will have dwindled further and that it will then be possible to come to an understanding.[126]

In Dr. Adenauer's mind, the Europeanization concept was not to be used as a subterfuge or the renunciation of Germany claims but, rather, as a common denominator enabling the contending parties to start negotiations by referring to the common interest.

The 1953 discussion evoked new assurances by the federal government that the Oder-Neisse problem would not be solved by force but exclusively by peaceful means.[127] These reassurances were then formalized in Section V of the Final Act of the London Conference in September and October, 1954:

In particular, the German Federal Republic undertakes never to have recourse to force to achieve the reunification of Germany or the modification of the present boundaries of the Federal Republic, and to resolve by peaceful means any disputes which may arise between the Federal Republic and other states."[128]

Between the London Conference and May, 1956, government declarations by members of the second Adenauer cabinet—Vice-Chancellor Blücher, Minister for All-German Affairs Kaiser, and Under-Secretary of State Hallstein—occurred with increasing frequency.[129] The Chancellor himself inserted clearly defined reservations in his note to Russian Prime Minister Bulganin in September, 1955, when diplomatic relations between the U.S.S.R. and the Federal Republic were re-established.[130]

The only statement critical of German insistence upon the revision of the Oder-Neisse Line came from the new German Foreign Minister, Dr. Heinrich von Brentano, when, probably reflecting upon personal priorities rather than on official opinion, he told the press on May 1, 1956, at London that

I personally regard this question in conjunction with the reunification, and I consider it very well possible that the German people may one day be confronted with the question whether it is prepared to renounce these territories in order thereby to liberate the 17 million Germans in the Soviet Zone or whether it will not be prepared to do this, merely to uphold a somewhat problematic claim to the Eastern territories."[131]

On May 2, 1956, von Brentano elaborated on his statement in the *Südwestfunk* (Southwest German Radio) at Baden-Baden as follows:

The problematic nature of the question does not lie in the validity of the legal claim, which is undenied and undeniable, but rather in the realization of that legal claim. And I believe that no one will fail to agree with this."[132]

On May 3, 1956, as a consequence of the mounting protest of public opinion and expellee and refugee organizations, Herr von Brentano revised his position by redefining it and explaining that all he meant was

. . . that the solution of the problem of reunification . . . must precede the solution of the frontier question for the whole of Germany. . . . The Federal Government will never recognize the Oder-Neisse frontier, nor will it ever permit the German Eastern Territories to become the object of barter.[133]

At the same time, in contrast to his equivocal position on the territorial question, Herr von Brentano was very emphatic on the right of the East Germans to their homeland. In describing the reasons for non-recognition of the frontier, the German Foreign Minister stated that the

Government will not do so, because it is not entitled to do so towards the people, the German people, who have lived in that territory for centuries. I said yesterday and I say it to-day: this right to their native soil is an expression of the right of self-determination for others and shall always claim it passionately for ourselves.[134]

In the following weeks, under the continuing criticism of the expellee and refugee organizations,[135] Herr von Brentano retreated to the former governmental position. In his letter to the President of the *Verband der Landsmannschaften,* Baron von Manteuffel-Szoege, the German Foreign Minister stated:

I myself am, needless to say, of the opinion—and I know that in this I agree with all Germans, irrespective of the region from which they hail—that the German territories beyond the Oder-Neisse are integral parts of Germany.[136]

On May 29, 1956, Herr von Brentano declared at Oslo, Norway:

We firmly believe, together with all free nations, that no German government and no German citizen will ever voluntarily renounce any parts of German territory held according to the position of 1937. But we solemnly declare that we shall never use force to regain the lost territories.[137]

This ended the official controversy over the question within the federal government. In September, 1957, shortly after his re-election, Chancellor Adenauer granted a television interview to the CBS network. During the interview, reporters asked him about the question of the Oder-Neisse provinces.[138] Dr. Adenauer explained that German opposition to the frontier is based upon the denial to the original German residents of their right to their homeland and that no solution can be devised before the wishes of these people are taken into consideration and their rights to their homes restored. Chancellor Adenauer's statement is very important because it was given shortly after the 1957 elections, when, after the disappearance of the BHE from the Lower House, the restoration of relations between Warsaw and Bonn was widely discussed. The position was stated as follows:

(1) Nonrecognition of the Oder-Neisse frontier;

(2) Emphasis on the return of the expelled German population to the provinces;

(3) A yet undefined agreement of co-existence between the returning Germans and the new Polish settlers who do not prefer to return to Poland; and

(4) A final decision of the territorial issue to await the peace conference.

In contrast to the position taken by the federal government, the German Democratic Republic, upon direct orders of Moscow, has recognized the Oder-Neisse Line. This was done in the infamous Görlitz Agreement of June 6, 1950, but since the German Democratic Republic has no right to represent the German Reich, it was not entitled to such a step under international law. Consequently, even Eastern-

bloc countries consider the Görlitz Agreement as only a partial solution of the problem because they act on the assumption of the existence
of two sovereign German states.

More precise than the plans of the federal government are the
proposals of the expellees on the frontiers and resettlement. These
groups were not surprised by the intensification, rather than decrease,
in anti-German propaganda after the political liberalization in Poland,
for they were only too familiar with the activities of Wladyslaw
Gomulka as Minister for the "Recovered Territories" in 1945-47.

Most Germans, whether expellees or native residents of the Federal
Republic, reject the Polish view of Polish-German relations as a cen-
tury-old struggle between the two nations. In the view of many Polish
historians, alleged injustice was "avenged" by the injured party as
soon as circumstances allowed. The evil spiral of injustices and revenge, beginning with Chancellor Bismarck's expulsion of Poles who
did not possess Prussian citizenship, winding through the Polish
method of encouraging the German minority by economic and social
boycott to return to the Reich, and rising to the Hitlerian and postwar expulsions, which have snowballed from thousands to several millions, is described as a relationship of cause and effect by Polish
writers.[139] If, however, the vicious circle is not broken, the next German move, whether in ten or thirty years, does not augur well for the
existence of the Polish nation. To some pro-Polish authors, the swing
of the pendulum can be stopped by arbitrary outside force, i.e., by a
Western and German recognition of the Oder-Neisse Line, a frontier
unilaterally imposed both upon Poland and Germany by the U.S.S.R.,
whose interest is to keep Poles and Germans permanently hostile.[140]
The precariousness of this position becomes clear when it is realized
that Germany, a state with a population of seventy million and a highly
developed industry, will finally prevail over the Polish state, with its
population of twenty-eight million, unless the latter remains utterly
subservient to Russia, a sad fate for the courageous Polish people.
Therefore, to attempt a perpetuation of the Oder-Neisse frontier
means:

(1) To promote stabilization of Russian influence in Poland;

(2) To pave the way for a new political and military conflict between Poland and Germany in the future, resuscitating all of the feelings of past injustices and revenge; and

(3) To prevent any equilibrium in the area unless the hegemony of
the U.S.S.R. in central Europe is to be recognized, with all its power

political and ideological repercussions for the fate of Europe and the free world.

The contemplated result shows that such a course would not be in the interest of either world peace or of the German and Polish peoples.

A basic assumption of the German refugee plan to escape from the vicious circle is that no mass expulsion of Poles from the provinces would be admissible, even if all the provinces were to return to Germany.[141] They, of course, assume a complete restoration of the 1937 frontiers, including Russian-annexed northern East Prussia, which has now become the westernmost Russian rocket-launching base against the free world. One has neither to endorse all details of plan nor to assume the premise of the return of all of the provinces, a very hypothetical assumption, in order to admit that this plan is a fairly reasonable proposal concerning the problem of population exchanges involved in the revision of the Oder-Neisse Line and the assurance of tranquillity in central Europe in case of a German reunification.

The German-expellee proposal divides the Polish population of the Oder-Neisse provinces into five categories:[142]

(1) Native residents (Polish "autochthons"), 1,300,000, whom the proposal considers German citizens and, for the most part, German nationals.

(2) Ukrainians, 200,000, who would immediately leave the provinces. They are even at the present leaving in small numbers, and many of them continue to petition the Warsaw regime for permission to return to western Galicia.

(3) Polish expellees, 1,600,000, from the areas east of the Bug and San rivers. The Germans would not require their return to Poland:

The Polish expellees, German sources emphasize, have shown such an understanding and often helpful attitude toward the German population still in the provinces, that on the basis of this attitude a good-neighbor relationship between the new settlers and the returning German administration promises to be ensured."[143]

(4) Officials, party leaders, and other bureaucrats, whose number, according to the Germans, is close to 1,000,000 in the provinces.[144] They would, of course, move to Poland as fast as the less-compromised German administrators and officials who disappeared from Pomorze and Poznańia in 1919-21.

(5) Close to 3,000,000 other Polish settlers from western and central Poland. According to the German proposal, they should not be expelled, but a part of them would probably leave voluntarily for Poland if large-scale German economic aid were granted to Poland for the purpose of creating homes and jobs for the repatriates. Although it may be questionable whether Germany herself would be willing to undertake such a one-country ERP program, the offer, coming from expellees and refugees who were robbed of their last property and personal goods, shows a new spirit which is badly needed in central Europe. German insistence upon United Nations control of the region for the period of population readjustment also shows German recognition of the need for internationalizing the problem in order to achieve an equitable solution.

According to the German-expellee proposal, about 2,000,000 Poles would remain in the provinces even after a five-year voluntary resettlement program. The proposal calls for an internationally protected minority-rights convention granting all civil rights to these Poles under German administration.[145] The question could be raised whether it would not be more practicable to leave Poland in possession of part of the provinces, thereby reducing the number of people to be transferred and avoiding large minorities on either side of the new frontier, for it is to be assumed that the Germans from Poland and from East German areas which eventually would remain Polish would also want to return to their homeland, regardless of the absence of German political sovereignty. An interesting sequel to the German-expellee proposal is the readiness to accept the status of a noncommitted nation for Germany, should reunification and frontier revision occur with the acquiescence of the U.S.S.R.[146] The proposal also argues that the reconstruction of the eastern territories would necessitate the reduction of German exports, thereby enabling a more equal distribution of the export volume among western European countries.

The unrealistic aspect of the German-expellee proposals consists of the fact that the U.S.S.R. is unwilling to agree to free elections in the German Democratic Republic, which she considers the main bastion of her control of Poland and the other satellites. And the solution of the problem of German unity is a geographic *conditio sine qua non* for the *modus vivendi* in the Oder-Neisse question. Yet it is also true that Russian positions have been drastically influenced by changing events, and the perseverance of the peoples opposing them, as the examples of Finland and Austria have demonstrated, was sometimes crowned by success. The sense for reality causes the German expellees to insist that any negotiations about unity and frontier revision should be started in Moscow and to refuse to consider a pro-Polish orientation of West German foreign policy. At the same time, however, German-expellee writers also maintain that contracts with the Polish people, as distinguished from the present government, should be promoted, including travel into the provinces, and the new federation also proposed such steps in January, 1959. The choice now rests with the Western governments, whether the expellee group and, later, also the successor to the present West German government will turn toward neutralism in order to improve her position in central Europe or whether the U.S.S.R. will ultimately be compelled to release her hold on Pankow and Warsaw, enabling an equitable solution of the Oder-Neisse problem. History will judge Western peoples and diplomats according to the extent they show their understanding of the areas of conflict and according to the resolution they show in preventing conflicts from becoming new dangers to world peace in the hands of rulers bent on world revolution.

NOTES

CHAPTER I

1. Göttinger Arbeitskreis, *Ostdeutchland: Ein Hand- und Nachschlagebuch für die Gebiete ostwärts von Oder und Neisse* (cited hereafter as *Ostdeutschland*), p. 9.

2. On climate and precipitation, see Gotthold Rhode (ed.), *Die Ostgebiete des Deutschen Reiches*, pp. 4-5.

3. *Ibid.*, pp. 6-7.

4. *Ibid.*, p. 7.

5. *Ibid.*, pp. 8-10.

6. *Ostdeutschland*, pp. 119-20.

7. Peter Heinz Seraphim, *Die Wirtschaft Ostdeutschlands vor und nach dem Zweiten Weltkriege* (cited hereafter as *Wirtschaft Ostdeutschlands*) (Vol. I of Herbert Schlenger [ed.], *Handbuch der Deutschen Ostgebiete*), pp. 38f. Development of Silesian coal production (in thousands of metric tons), 1914-44:

	German Part	Polish Part
1914	9,398	27,598
1920	7,859	23,831
1925	14,274	21,433
1938	25,983	28,749
1944	28,367	39,869

8. Rhode, *op. cit.*, pp. 11-14 and 169f.

9. *Ibid.*, p. 168. Cf. *Ostdeutschland*, p. 134.

10. Population figures for all Oder-Neisse cities are as of 1939.

11. Rhode, *op. cit.*, pp. 258ff. Figures are as of 1939.

12. *Ostdeutschland*, pp. 13-14.

13. *Ibid.* Pp. 17-21 give a breakdown of the population of 1939.

14. The briefing book of the U.S. Department of State gave the following percentages in 1945: Lower Silesia, eastern Brandenburg, and Pomerania west of Kolberg, 100 per cent German; Pomerania east of Kolberg, 99 per cent; and southern East Prussia, 93.8 per cent. U.S. Department of State, *Foreign Relations of the United States. Diplomatic Papers. The Conferences of Malta and Yalta 1945.* (cited hereafter as *Malta and Yalta*), pp. 231ff.

15. Rhode, *op. cit.*, pp. 71-80.

16. W. Parker Mauldin *et al.*, *The Population of Poland*, pp. 32-35. This source gives the number of Germans in Poland as 120,000 and those Germans reclassified as Poles as 1,040,000.

17. For the result of the plebiscites, see M. Worgitski, *Geschichte der Abstimmung in Ostpreussen*, p. 142; Paul Hoffman, *Die Volksabstimmung in Westpreussen am 11. Juni 1920*, p. 7; and *Journal Officiel de la Haute Silèsie*, No. 5 (May 7, 1921).

18. Rhode, *op. cit.*, pp. 70ff.

19. Zigmunt Jordan (ed.), *The Oder-Neisse Line: A Study of the Political, Economic and European Significance of Poland's Western Frontier*, pp. 5 and 58ff.

20. For an excellent description on the question of migratory trends in the provinces, see Rhode, *op. cit.*, pp. 55-65.

21. Hermann Rauschning, *Die Entdeutschung Westpreussens und Posens*, pp. 340-41.

22. Rhode, *op. cit.*, pp. 60ff. Cf. Jordan, *op. cit.*, p. 5, quoting exaggerated and unreliable figures without any statistical evidence.

23. Rhode, *op. cit.*, pp. 60ff.

24. Comparative density of population (number of persons per square mile):

Oppeln	152	Katowice	307
Schneidemühl	57	Poznań	83
Köslin-Allenstein	49	Pomorze	73

25. Kurt Groba, "Wirtschaftwende im schlesischen Raum," *Schlesisches Jahrbuch* (1940), p. 61.

26. Emil von Lucadou, *Strukturwandel Schlesiens* (Vol. XVIII of Walter Geisler [ed.], *Zur Wirtschaftsgeographie des deutschen Ostens*).

27. *Ibid.,* p. 19.

28. *Ibid.,* pp. 20-21. These are 1938 figures: Upper Silesia, 1,859 kilograms per day per miner; Ruhr, 1,547 kilograms; and Aix-la-Chapelle, 1,090 kilograms.

29. Alfred Pott in *Deutsche Bergwerkszeitung,* June 16, 1940.

30. Peter H. Seraphim, *Wirtschaft Ostdeutschlands,* p. 34.

31. *Ibid.,* p. 147.

32. Lucadou, *op. cit.,* pp. 24-26.

33. *Ibid.,* pp. 27-28 and 33-34.

34. *Ibid.,* pp. 23-24.

35. *Ostdeutschland,* p. 147.

36. Peter H. Seraphim, *Wirtschaft Ostdeutschlands,* p. 34.

37. *Statistical Yearbook of Poland 1938,* p. 20.

38. Georges S. F. C. Kaeckenbeeck, *The International Experiment of Upper Silesia,* pp. 415-47.

39. For the first allegation, see Peter H. Seraphim, *Wirtschaft Ostdeutschlands,* pp. 58-60, and *Ostdeutschland,* pp. 119ff. For the second, see Jordan, *op. cit.,* pp. 38-58, and Elizabeth Wiskemann, *Germany's Eastern Neighbors,* pp. 169-81.

40. Karl Pagel (ed.), *The German East,* p. 123.

41. *Ibid.,* p. 123. Cf. *Ostdeutschland,* p. 21.

42. *Ostdeutschland,* p. 21.

43. Rhode, *op. cit.,* pp. 169-70.

44. *Ibid.,* pp. 151-52.

45. Pagel, *op. cit.,* p. 124.

46. *Ostdeutschland,* p. 121.

47. Rhode, *op. cit.,* p. 156. The following figures are in thousands of metric tons: bread grains, 9,280 west of the Oder and Neisse rivers and 3,205 east of the rivers; fodder grains, 7,286 and 2,668; totals, 17,106 and 5,873, or 25.6 per cent. Potatoes, 33,434 and 14,560; sugar beets, 9,584 and 3,277; other crops, 35,947 and 10,145.

48. *Ibid.,* pp. 176-78.

49. Wiskemann, *op. cit.,* pp. 169-79, and Jordan, *op. cit.,* pp. 45-48.

50. Wilhelm Volz, *Die ostdeutsche Wirtschaft: Eine wirtschaftsgeographische Untersuchung über die natürlichen Grundlagen des deutschen Ostens und seine Stellung in der gesamtdeutschen Wirtschaft.*

51. *Ibid.,* pp. 46-47.

52. Pagel, *op. cit.,* p. 125: "In a lively exchange of goods during the years 1938/39 a daily average of 16.3 goods-trains [*sic!*] (50 waggons each) rolled over the Oder-Neisse to Germany. That made 5,875 trains yearly, laden with potatoes, spirit and starch (2,159), with slaughtering stock (1,305), with grain and seed (1,906), with sugar (284), with butter, cheese and fat (93), with carp, eggs, honey (8) ... for a total value of 1,084,000,000 RM."

53. Rhode, *op. cit.,* pp. 179-80.

54. Pagel, *op. cit.,* p. 124.

55. *Ibid.,* p. 127.

56. *Ibid.,* pp. 127-28. Cf. Rhode, *op. cit.,* p. 176.

57. Rhode, *op. cit.,* p. 192. Cf. *Ostdeutschland,* pp. 129-31.

58. The figure five and one-half million is given in Pagel, *op. cit.*, p. 124. I have used the figures three and four million on the basis of the figures of Volz and the difference in German import level of grains between 1928 and 1938 and not the 1935-39 production figures alone.

CHAPTER II   •

1. Ernest Birke, "Geschichte der Schlesier," in Karl Hausdorff (ed.), *Unser Schlesien*, p. 28.

2. Birke, *loc. cit.*, p. 32. Cf. Kazimierz Tymieniecki, "Kolonizacja a germanizacja Śląska w wiekach srednich," *Polski Śląsk*, No. 27 (1937), pp. 12-18.

3. Pagel, *op. cit.*, pp. 46-47.

4. Birke, *loc. cit.*, pp. 33-34.

5. For the change in the language used by the cities, see Walter Kuhn, *Siedlungsgeschichte Oberschlesiens*, pp. 146-49. In Beuthen, the percentage of Germans fell from 100 per cent to 53 per cent between 1315 and 1500.

6. Birke, *loc. cit.*, pp. 33-34.

7. Bartel Stein (ed.), *Descriptio totius Silesiae, Scriptores rerum Silesiacarum* (Breslau; 1902), Vol. XII, p. 8: "Two peoples occupy Silesia, different not only in regions they inhabit, but also in their way of living. In the areas lying south and west, which are better tilled, live Germans; in the heavily wooded and less cultivated tracts to the east and north live Poles. The two people are separated, as by a definite boundary, by the Oder River from the point where the Neisse joins it and upward. Even in the cities German is the speech on one side, but Polish on the other." See also Walter Kuhn, *Geschichte der deutschen Ostsiedlung der Neuzeit* (cited hereafter as *Geschichte Neuzeit*), Vol. I, *passim*.

8. Birke, *loc. cit.*, pp. 44-55.

9. Pagel, *op. cit.*, p. 50: ". . . there was now an Austrian Silesia whose northeasterly boundary running through the old principalities Troppau and Jägerndorf was a 'bleeding frontier.' "

10. Birke, *loc. cit.*, pp. 49-50.

11. William J. Rose, *The Drama of Upper Silesia*, pp. 37-38.

12. Sarah Wambaugh, *Plebiscites Since the World War* (cited hereafter as *Plebiscites*), Vol. I, p. 209.

13. Compiled on the basis of Rose, *op. cit.*, pp. 23-24, and Kuhn, *Geschichte Neuzeit*, Vol. I, p. 252.

14. Kuhn, *Geschichte Neuzeit*, Vol. I, p. 253.

15. For a description, see Rose, *op. cit.*, pp. 75-96 (the land question), and Birke, *loc. cit.*, pp. 51-52 (the textile industry, the weavers).

16. Short histories of Pomerania are: *Der deutsche Osten*, pp. 57ff.; Oskar Eggert, *Geschichte Pommerns;* and Antony Plutynski, *Śląsk i Pomorze*, pp. 40-46.

17. Eggert, *op. cit.*, pp. 8-9. Cf. E. Murawski, "Die Provinz Pommern," in Karl C. Thalheim and A. Hillen Ziegfield (eds.), *Der deutsche Osten: Seine Geschichte, sein Wesen und seine Aufgabe*, pp. 98-116

18. Eggert, *op. cit.*, p. 9.

19. *Ibid.*, p. 11.

20. *Ibid.*, p. 10.

21. *Ibid.*, pp. 12-13.

22. *Ibid.*, p. 15.

23. *Der deutsche Osten*, p. 60.

24. *Ibid.*, pp. 60-61.

25. *Ibid.*, p. 62.

26. *Ibid.*
27. Eggert, *op. cit.,* p. 25.
28. *Ibid.,* pp. 25-26.
29. Bruno Schumacher, *Die Geschichte West- und Ostpreussens* (1st ed.), p. 33. Cf. O. Weber-Krohse, "Ostpreussen," in Thalheim and Ziegfield, *op. cit.,* pp. 55-81.
30. Plutynski, *op. cit.,* pp. 24-25.
31. Kazimierz Tymieniecki, *History of Polish Pomerania,* pp. 28-29 and 35-36.
32. Plutynski, *op. cit.,* p. 17.
33. Schumacher, *op. cit.,* pp. 18-20.
34. Schumacher, *op. cit.,* pp. 26-36, and Tymieniecki, *op. cit.,* pp. 21-29.
35. Tymieniecki, *op. cit.,* p. 35.
36. Schumacher, *op. cit.,* p. 49.
37. *Ibid.,* pp. 72-76.
38. *Ibid.,* pp. 64-65.
39. Tymieniecki, *op. cit.,* pp. 41-44.
40. *Ibid.,* pp. 43-44.
41. Schumacher, *op. cit.,* p. 77.
42. Tymieniecki, *op. cit.,* p. 77.
43. *Ibid.,* p. 58.
44. Schumacher, *op. cit.,* pp. 152-54.
45. *Ibid.,* pp. 163ff.
46. *Ibid.,* pp. 141-42. Cf. Tymieniecki, *op. cit.,* p. 62.
47. Schumacher, *op. cit.,* pp. 150-54.
48. Tymieniecki, *op. cit.,* pp. 53-58.
49. Schumacher, *op. cit.,* p. 174.
50. Tymieniecki, *op. cit.,* pp. 77-78.
51. This was recognized by Wiskemann, *op. cit.,* p. 92.
52. Tymieniecki, *op. cit.,* pp. 121ff.
53. *Ibid.,* pp. 133-35.
54. *Ibid.,* pp. 136ff.

CHAPTER III

1. Some of the best works include Sidney Osborne, *The Upper Silesian Question and Germany's Coal Problem;* Rose, *op. cit.;* Graham S. Hutchison, *Silesia Revisited 1929;* Kaeckenbeeck, *op. cit.;* Kazimierz M. Smogorzewski, *La Silèsie polonaise;* Günter H. Hahn, *Die deutsche Publizistik im Kampf um Oberschlesien;* Kazimicrz M. Smogorzewski, *Sprawa Śląska na konferencji pokojowej 1919 roku* (cited hereafter as *Sprawa Śląska);* and Gerhard Wende, *Die Auswirkungen der Grenzziehung auf die oberschlesische Montanindustrie, passim.*
2. Kaeckenbeeck, *op. cit.,* pp. 6-30.
3. Rose, *op. cit.,* pp. 137ff.
4. On Miarka, see *ibid.,* pp. 106-10.
5. Rose, *op. cit.,* p. 119. Napiarelski's program: "Polish state sovereignty is in theory unnecessary and in practice useless. The concept of 'ethnographical' Poles need not offend anyone and is for the time being quite adequate. A close alliance with the German Catholics, then, in keeping with this, the maintenance of Catholic faith, to which comes as a secondary issue the defense of the Polish language—these are the broad programs of the Poles of Upper Silesia."
6. Rudolf Küster, *Die polnische Irredenta in Westoberschlesien,* pp. 34-35.
7. Osborne, *op. cit.,* pp. 62-63.
8. Rose, *op. cit.,* pp. 140ff. Cf. Osborne, *op. cit.,* p. 49, quoting Archbishop Stablewski's

statement: "It appears unfit and unjustified to drag Silesia into the sphere of the political activity—the aspirations of the Poles, so to speak, joined to Prussia after 1772."

9. Osborne, *op. cit.*, pp. 62ff.

10. *Ibid.*, pp. 45ff.

11. Breslau, Osteuropa-Institut, *Oberschlesien und der Genfer Schiedsspruch*, p. 47. Cf. Hahn, *op. cit.*, p. 12.

12. Rose, *op. cit.*, pp. 151-54.

13. Rose, *op. cit.*, pp. 118-20, and Wambaugh, *Plebiscites*, Vol. I, p. 210.

14. Wambaugh, *Plebiscites*, Vol. I, p. 211. Cf. August Scholtis, *Ostwind*, p. 234: "In Sch . . . whither the last of the combattants returned with ragged and bloody bodies and with ranks sadly thinned, popular sentiment was aroused now, not against the Director, but against Germany. On the barricades, Wojtiech's helper D. was speaking: 'Know that ye are landless. . . . To be landless in Upper Silesia means to be a Pole. To possess land here means to be German. . . . "

15. Osborne, *op. cit.*, pp. 62-66.

16. Gainborough Commission, *Report of the Gainborough Commission on Life and Labour in Germany*, in Rose, *op. cit.*, p. 155.

17. Rose, *op. cit.*, pp. 159-60. Cf. Eugen Schohl, *Die Polenfrage in Oberschlesien*, pp. 7-14.

18. Schohl, *op. cit.*, p. 160. Cf. Professor Laubert's statement: "This organized German offensive revealed that the National Polish ideas of the common people had not yet become flesh and blood, but that a clever social welfare policy could win back large territory. The system of cultural service connected with the names of von Schwerin and Kuester made itself felt, having its roots in a right understanding of the idea how to nourish and promote Germandom." Friedrich Kampers *et al.*, *Schlesische Landeskunde*, p. 172.

19. The show of German-Polish unity in the province in 1914 was also conceded by Rose, *op. cit.*, p. 165.

20. Wambaugh, *Plebiscites*, Vol. I, p. 211.

21. Hahn, *op. cit.*, pp. 16-17, gives names and dates of purchase of German newspapers bought by Korfanty.

22. Rose, *op. cit.*, p. 169.

23. On protests in Silesia, see Karl Schodrok, "*Der Abstimmungskampf in Oberschlesien*," in Karl Schodrok (ed.), *Das Erlebnis der oberschlesischen Volksabstimmung*, pp. 13-14.

24. On Lloyd George, see Mermeix, *Le combat de Trois; Notes et Documents sur la Conférence de la Paix*, pp. 233ff. Cf. Smogorzewski, *Sprawa Śląska*, pp. 19-31.

25. Lloyd George to Paderewski, Mermeix, *op. cit.*, pp. 245f.

26. Provisions of the treaty, proclamation of the IK, and Plebiscite Commission are given in Wambaugh, *Plebiscites*, Vol. II, pp. 163-69.

27. Schodrok, *op. cit.*, pp. 14-16.

28. Osborne, *op. cit.*, pp. 91-93.

29. On the communal elections, see Rose, *op. cit.*, p. 171.

30. Schodrok, *op. cit.*, p. 14, and Rose, *op. cit.*, p. 172.

31. On the second Polish rising, see Wambaugh, *Plebiscites*, Vol. I, pp. 235-38, and Germany, Auswärtiges Amt, *Der Aufstand im oberschlesischen Industriegebiet, August und September 1920*, pp. 10-12.

32. Schodrok, *op. cit.*, pp. 14-16.

33. For the official results, see Wambaugh, *Plebiscites*, Vol. II, pp. 240-50, reproducing the original documents.

34. *Ibid.*, pp. 241ff.

35. Schumacher, *op. cit.*, p. 49.

36. On the foundry workers, see Wambaugh, *Plebiscites*, Vol. I, p. 247.

37. *Ibid.*, pp. 261ff. Cf. Poland, Ministère des affaires étrangères, *Notes sur le plébiscite en Haute Silèsie, Mars 1921,* pp. 7-43.

38. Wambaugh, *Plebiscites,* Vol. I, pp. 254-56; Hahn, *op. cit.,* pp. 63-83; and Germany, Auswärtiges Amt, *Zusammenstellung von Protokollen über den dritten polnischen Aufstand,* Vol. II, pp. 9-88.

39. Wambaugh, *Plebiscites,* Vol. I, p. 63.

40. *Ibid.*, pp. 65ff.

41. The decisions of October 20, 1921, are reproduced in Kaeckenbeeck, *op. cit.,* pp. 558-823.

42. Text of the Geneva Convention and the rules of procedure of the Arbitrary Tribunal and the Mixed Commission as given in *ibid.,* pp. 823-44.

43. Census figures of 1925 as quoted by Robert Machray, *The Problem of Upper Silesia,* pp. 74-76, 373, and 503. Bilingual persons: 373,503; Poles, 154,743 and Germans, 711,807. The 1933 census showed 266,375 bilingual persons and 90,193 Poles in the province. See also O. Ewwers, *Die polnische Minderheit in Oberschlesien,* pp. 12-18.

44. Kaeckenbeeck, *op. cit.,* pp. 43-119 and 298-351.

45. Hutchison, *op. cit.,* pp. 63-67, reproducing the original text of Korfanty's attack on Grazynski.

46. *Concise Statistical Yearbook of Poland, 1930.* Yet in the same year, Grazynski himself admitted the presence of 130,000 Germans in Śląsk. "Neuf années de travail polonais en Silèsie," in Smorgorzewski, *La Silèsie polonaise,* pp. 241ff.

47. Josef F. Winiewicz, *The Polish-German Frontier,* pp. 32-33.

48. Rose, *op. cit.,* pp. 10-26; Robert Machray, *East Prussia: Menace to Poland and Peace,* pp. 11-15 and 90-100.

49. Cf. Wilson's statement about siding with the Poles against the Germans, Mermeix, *op. cit.,* p. 233f. See also President Roosevelt and Prime Minister Churchill at Yalta, *infra,* pp. 116-18.

50. *Erbe und Aufgabe des Deutschen Ostens: Reden und Aufsätze Dr. Ottomar Schreibers,* ed. by F. Gause (München, Gräfe und Unzer, 1955), pp. 33-43; 94-96. For a detailed analysis of *Junkers* and peasants, see Walter Görlitz, *Die Junker: Adel und Bauer im deutschen Osten,* pp. 251-321.

51. Rauschning, *op. cit.,* pp. 340-41.

52. Rhode, *op. cit.,* pp. 102-17, especially pp. 114-17.

53. Friedrich Heiss (ed.), *Deutschland und der Korridor,* pp. 114-16.

54. Wladyslaw Studnicki, *Irrwege in Polen,* pp. 22-24. See also Kurt Lück, *Deutsche Aufbaukräfte in der Entwicklung Polens,* pp. 127-72, 236-58, and 377-412.

55. Remark of the Italian Foreign Minister, Count Ciano, to this effect in Germany, Auswärtiges Amt, *Documents on German Foreign Policy, 1918–1945,* Series D, Vol. V, *Poland; The Balkans; Latin America; The Smaller Powers, June 1937–March 1939,* p. 149 (Telegram 88 of April 13, 1939).

56. For a racist National Socialist approach to the Poles, see the memorandum of Dr. E. Wetzel and Dr. G. Hecht in *Rassenpolitischer Amt,* reproduced in *Documenta occupationis teutonicae,* Vol. V, *Hitlerowske "Prawo" Okupacyjne w Polsce* (cited hereafter as *Documenta occupationis*), pp. 5-7. For the Polish side, see Kazimierz M. Smogorzewski, *Poland's Access to the Sea,* pp. 81ff., and Henryk Baginski, *Poland and the Baltic,* pp. 49-107.

57. Heiss, *op. cit.,* pp. 119ff., recognizes the Polish character of the largest part of the province.

58. Wiskemann, *op. cit.,* p. 11.

59. For a description of the revolt as seen by the Germans, see Georg Cleinow, *Der Verlust der Ostmark,* pp. 79-93.

60. Rauschning, *op. cit.,* pp. 340-41.

61. On the Commission, see Smogorzewski, *Poland's Access to the Sea*, pp. 63-66. On Chancellor Bülow's policy, see his article, "The Policy of the Eastern Provinces," in *Deutsche Politik* (1916).

62. Waclaw Sobieski, *Der Kampf um die Ostsee von den ältesten Zeiten bis zur Gegenwart*, p. 226. Cf. Ludwig Bernhard, *Das polnische Gemeinwesen im preussischen Staat*, and Erich Keyser *et al.*, *Der Kampf um die Weichsel*, p. 147.

63. Kazimierz M. Smogorzewski, *La Pologne, l'Allemagne et le "Corridor"* (cited hereafter as *Corridor*), p. 26.

64. Heiss, *op. cit.*, pp. 41-42.

65. The 1910 census as reproduced by Rauschning, *op. cit.*, pp. 340-41.

66. Smogorzewski, *Poland's Access to the Sea*, pp. 101-102.

67. For the text, see "A Suggested Settlement of the Peace," in Ray S. Baker, *Woodrow Wilson and World Settlement*, Vol. III, pp. 37-38.

68. *Ibid.*, pp. 42ff.

69. H. N. Brailsford in the *London Daily News*, January 18, 1919: "Germany needs not only Danzig but Posen." For Professor Gooch's view, see Smogorzewski, *Poland's Access to the Sea*, p. 110.

70. For Colonel House's interpretation of the Fourteen Points on October 29, 1918, see Charles Seymour (ed.), *The Intimate Papers of Colonel House*, Vol. IV, pp. 153 and 200.

71. For the Cambon Commission report, see David Hunter Miller, *My Diary at the Conference of Paris*, Vol. VI, pp. 350ff., Report No. 1 of the Commission on Polish Affairs.

72. For Lloyd George's memorandum, see Great Britain, *Parliamentary Papers*, Cmd. 1614, 1922, "Some Considerations for the Peace Conference Before They Finally Draft the Terms," *passim*.

73. For results of the Marienwerder plebiscite, see Paul Hoffman, *op. cit.*, p. 7. Total, 105,004 votes; for Germany, 96,894; for Poland, 7,947 (7.58 per cent).

74. The statistics are based on Rauschning, *op. cit.*, pp. 340-41. Cf. George Königk, *Der Kampf um die deutsche Ostgrenze in Versailles*, pp. 52-58 and 68-86.

75. Rauschning, *op. cit.*, pp. 10-14.

76. Rauschning, *op. cit.*, p. 10.

77. *Ibid.*, pp. 13-14.

78. *Ibid.*, p. 85. Cf. St. Grabski in October, 1919: "The love of our compatriots is different from those of aliens. Their percentage in our country is definitely too high. . . . The alien element will have to see whether it would not be more advantageous for it to live elsewhere. Polish land is exclusively here for Poles." Richard Breyer, *Das Deutsche Reich und Polen, 1932–1937*, p. 51.

79. Rauschning, *op. cit.*, pp. 250-72.

80. *Ibid.*, pp. 132-45.

81. *Ibid.*, p. 16.

82. *Ibid.*, pp. 270-71.

83. *Ibid.*, pp. 304-308. Die allgemeine Bergriffsverwirrung, dass nur der Pole Katholik sein könnte, in Verbindung mit dem einseitig Gefühlsmässigen der polnischen Glaubensart, hatten schon vor dem Kriege dazu geführt, den deutschen Katholiken als den schlimmsten Feind des Katholizismus und des polnischen Volkes zu brandmarken."

84. Rauschning, *op. cit.*, pp. 340-41.

85. Rauschning, *op. cit.*, p. 341. Cf. Heiss, *op. cit.*, pp. 41-42. See also E. Lindow, "Danzig," in Thalheim and Ziegfield, *op. cit.*, pp. 81-98.

86. Jan F. D. Morrow, *The Peace Settlement in the German-Polish Borderlands*, pp. 67-75. For a Polish account, Theodor Bierowki, *La ville libre de Dantzig et la guerre polono-bolchevique de 1920*, pp. 3-30.

87. John B. Mason, *The Danzig Dilemma: A Study in Peace-Making by Compromise*, pp. 192-213. Cf. Smogorzewski, *Poland's Access to the Sea*, pp. 298-303.

88. Morrow, *op. cit.*, pp. 80-90. See also *Entscheidungen des Hohen Kommissar des Völkerbundes in der Freien Stadt Danzig*, Vol. I, pp. 15-21, and Vol. IV, p. 4.

89. For the PCIJ advisory opinion, see PCIJ, *Advisory Opinions*, Series B, No. 1, *Polish Postal Service in Danzig*, pp. 8-17 and 29-41.

90. Morrow, *op. cit.*, pp. 40-44.

91. Smogorzewski, *Poland's Access to the Sea*, pp. 332-51, and Mason, *op. cit.*, pp. 130-39. Cf. *Collections des documents concernant l'adresse du Gouvernement de la Ville libre de Dantzig, soumise pour décision au Haut Commissaire de la Société des Nations à Dantzig sur la question de Dantzig-Gdingen*, pp. 4-39 and 103-68.

92. Theodor Johannsen, *Gdingen*, in Ostland-Institut, *Ostland-Schriften*, Heft 1, pp. 17-23.

93. Morrow, *op. cit.*, pp. 140-52. Cf. Smogorzewski, *Poland's Access to the Sea*, pp. 351-58.

94. Hans L. Leonhardt, *The Nazi Conquest of Danzig*, pp. 55ff.

95. The compromise is described in Morrow, *op. cit.*, pp. 152-59. Cf. Mason, *op. cit.*, pp. 136-38.

96. For the figures, see Morrow, *op. cit.*, pp. 187f.

97. For the zloty question in 1932, see *ibid.*, pp. 119-24, and Leonhardt, *op. cit.*, pp. 25f.

98. Morrow, *op. cit.*, pp. 108-19, and Mason, *op. cit.*, pp. 259-84. Cf. *Sammlung der Dokumente in der Streitsache zwischen der Freien Stadt Danzig und der Republik Polen betreffs Artikel 33 des Danzig-polnischen Vertrages vom 9. November 1920*, pp. 113-213 and 414-26.

99. Morrow, *op. cit.*, pp. 160-72, and Leonhardt, *op. cit.*, pp. 41-80.

100. Leonhardt, *op. cit.*, pp. 42-43.

101. *Ibid.*, pp. 45-48 and 55-61.

102. For Rauschning's foreign policy, see *ibid.*, pp. 62ff. His statement at the visit to Marshal Pilsudski: "I realized that I had seen a personality who is the living symbol of a resuscitated nation called to accomplish great deeds."

103. Breyer, *op. cit.*, pp. 120-21. Beck followed the policy of his political teacher, Marshal Pilsudski, to wit: policy should be based on the military-political power of the state; alliances are only of secondary importance; cordial relations should be maintained with neighbors on the basis of reciprocity.

104. Leonhardt, *op. cit.*, pp. 177-290, and Herbert Maschke, *Die Grundlagen des Internationalen Statuts von Danzig*, pp. 42-52.

105. Results as given in Worgitzki, *op. cit.*, p. 142.

106. "Ausschuss zur Untersuchung der Erzeugungs- und Absatzbedingungen der deutschen Wirtschaft," II. *Unterausschuss*, Vol. VIII, *Die Lage der Landwirtschaft in Ostpreussen*, pp. 5-36.

CHAPTER IV

1. For the text of the treaty, see Poland, *Ministrowo spraw zagranicznych, Die polnisch-deutschen und die polnisch-sowjetrussischen Beziehungen* (cited hereafter as *Polnisches Weissbuch*), pp. 24-26.

2. Germany, Auswärtiges Amt, *Documents on the Events Preceding the Outbreak of the War*, pp. 53-78.

3. Frank L. Benns, *Europe Since 1914*, p. 239.

4. For Pilsudski's concept, see Josef Pilsudski, *Erinnerungen und Dokumente*, Vol. IV, *passim*. For the Rapallo policy, see Wipert von Blücher, *Deutschlands Weg nach Rapallo*, pp. 80-92 and 153ff.

5. See Ribbentrop's insistence on Poland's accession to the Anti-Comintern Pact and Hitler's proposal at the Berchtesgaden Conference in *Documents,* Vol. V, pp. 155-56 and 160-61.

6. *Ibid.,* pp. 152-54, for Hitler; see also Jean Szembek, *Journal, 1933–1939,* p. 384.

7. For Polish distrust toward Germans and Germany, see Kurt Lück, *Der Mythos vom Deutschen in der polnischen Volksüberlieferung und Literatur,* pp. 23-37, 214-29, and 257-66.

8. Karl Hans Fuchs, *Danzig—What Is It All About?* pp. 21-22. Cf. Lord Halifax's statement to League High Commissioner Karl Burckhardt, "Danzig and the Corridor are an absurdity," in *Documents,* Vol. V, p. 48.

9. *Documents,* Vol. V, p. 167.

10. Adolf Hitler, *Mein Kampf,* p. 297 and pp. 735-36: "Halb war die Polenpolitik. Man reizte, ohne jemals ernstlich durchzugreifen. Das Ergebnis war weder ein Sieg des Deutschtums noch eine Versöhnung mit Polen."

11. *Documents,* Vol. V, p. 168.

12. *Polnisches Weissbuch,* p. 32.

13. Szembek, *op. cit.,* p. 414.

14. *Documents,* Vol. V, p. 157. Cf. Leon Noel, *L'aggression allemande contre la Pologne,* p. 206. See also *Documents,* Vol. II, pp. 973-74 (Moltke's account). For the documentation of the Polish-Czech negotiations between the Munich Conference and the cession of Teschen, see *ibid.,* pp. 819, 849-50, 861, 915-18, 933-34, 970, 975, 983, and 997, and *Documents,* Vol. V, pp. 78-81.

15. *Documents,* Vol. V, p. 200.

16. *Documents,* Vol. I, pp. 35ff.

17. *Polnisches Weissbuch,* pp. 63-66.

18. *Ibid.,* pp. 65-66.

19. *Documents,* Vol. V, pp. 148-49.

20. *Ibid.,* pp. 124-25, 144-45, and 179-81.

21. *Ibid.,* pp. 128 and 158.

22. Cf. the comment of the semi-official PAT News Agency's communiqué of November 26, 1938, on the Polish-Soviet declaration: "This declaration may also be regarded as a hint to Germany and in the second place to those within and without the country who support certain minority nationalist movements which tend to create an irredentism which menaces the sovereignty of the Polish state."

23. On normalization of relations, see *Documents,* Vol. V, p. 157. On English influence, see *ibid.,* pp. 172 and 183. See also Great Britain, Foreign Office, *Documents on British Foreign Policy,* Third Series, Vol. IV, pp. 434 and 533.

24. *Documents,* Vol. V, p. 154.

25. Szembek, *op. cit.,* p. 384.

26. *Ibid.,* p. 411.

27. *Documents,* Vol. V, pp. 167-68.

28. *Ibid.,* pp. 172-73.

29. *The German White Book,* pp. 165-67 and 168-69.

30. *Documents,* Vol. V, pp. 174-77.

31. Josef Beck, *Dernier rapport . . . Politique Polonaise* (cited hereafter as *Politique Polonaise*), p. 189, and *British Documents,* Vol. IV, p. 434.

32. *Documents,* Vol. VI, p. 70.

33. *Polnisches Weissbuch,* pp. 80-81. Cf. Szembek, *op. cit.,* pp. 434-38.

34. *Documents,* Vol. VI, p. 70.

35. For the speeches of Chamberlain and Halifax on March 17 and 20, 1939, see *The German White Book,* pp. 292-94. For the March 21 and 22 conferences, see *British Documents,* Vol. IV, pp. 423-27 and 457-60.

36. For Sir Kennard's conversations with Beck on March 30, see *British Documents,* Vol. IV, p. 548.

37. *Documents,* Vol. VI, pp. 101 and 110.

38. *Ibid.,* pp. 117-20: "The Führer does not wish to solve the Danzig question by force." Also: "A solution in the near future would have to be based on especially favorable political preconditions. In such a case Poland would have to be beaten down so that, during the next few decades, she need not be taken into account as a political factor. In a solution of this kind the Führer envisaged an advanced frontier, extending from the eastern border of East Prussia to the eastern tip of Silesia."

39. *Ibid.,* p. 122.

40. Beck's proposals as reprinted in *Documents,* Vol. VI, pp. 122-24.

41. *The German White Book,* p. 298.

42. See France, Minister des affaires éstrangères, *The French Yellow Book,* p. 124, for the April 13 declaration. For comment, see Noel, *op. cit.,* p. 102.

43. *Infra,* Chap. IV.

44. *The French Yellow Book,* p. 149.

45. *The German White Book,* pp. 375-425, has a whole list of alleged atrocities and excesses, not all of them fabrications.

46. Polish measures against Danzig as described in *The German White Book,* pp. 425ff. German provocations and excesses have been documented in *Polnisches Weissbuch,* pp. 119-23, 126-27, and 137-41.

47. Cf. *Chamberlain's* letter of August 22, 1939, in *The British Blue Book,* pp. 125-27, and Daladier's personal appeal of August 26 in *The French Yellow Book,* pp. 311-12, both confirming the irrevocable decision of joining the war should Germany attack Poland. As Chamberlain put it, after reminding himself of the charge that in 1914 the British had not made their position completely clear: "If the need should arise, they are resolved, and prepared, to employ without delay all the forces at their command, and it is impossible to foresee the end of hostilities once engaged."

48. *Izvestia,* September 1, 1939, p. 1.

49. Miss Wiskemann denies Bromberg's "Bloody Sunday," but the story of the German Foreign Office book *Die polnischen Greueltaten an den Volksdeutschen in Polen* was for the Bromberg murders accepted by the German Ministry for the Expellees' publication *Die Vertreibung der Deutschen aus Ost-Mitteleuropa* (cited hereafter as *Die Vertreibung*). See Wiskemann, *op. cit.,* pp. 45-47, and *Die Vertreibung,* Vol. I (1), p. 124E. Cf. Rhode, *op. cit.,* p. 118, and Theodor Bierschenck, *Die deutsche Volksgruppe in Polen, 1934–1939,* p. 381.

50. K. M. Pospieszalski, "Hitlerowskie Prawo Okupacyjne Polsce," in *Documenta Occupationis Teutonicae,* p. 48.

51. *Erlass des Führers und Reichskanzlers über die Gliederung und Verwaltung der Ostgebiete vom 8. Oktober 1939,* in *Documenta Occupationis,* pp. 84-86.

52. On the area and population, see Poland, Ministrowo spraw zagranicznych, *German Occupation of Poland,* p. 5.

53. *Die Frage der Behandlung der Bevölkerung der ehemaligen polnischen Gebiete nach rassenpolitischen Gesichtspunkten,* in *Documenta Occupationis,* p. 8.

54. *Ibid.,* pp. 88-95 and 96-97; additional regulations for the reorganization of the annexed provinces.

55. Wiskemann, *op. cit.,* pp. 55-56. The deportations took place between November 26, 1939, and February 10, 1940.

56. *Erwerb der deutschen Staatsangehörigkeit in den in das Deutsche Reich eingegliederten Ostgebieten* and *Verordnung über die deutsche Volksliste und die deutsche Staatsangehörigkeit in den eingegliederten Ostgebieten vom 4. März 1941 in der Fassung der Verordnung vom 31. Januar 1942,* in *Documenta Occupationis,* pp. 108-18 and 119-39.

57. Joseph Bühler (ed.), *Das General-Gouvernement: Seine Verwaltung und seine Wirtschaft*, p. 6.

58. *Documenta Occupationis*, pp. 127-30.

59. Wiskemann, *op. cit.*, p. 27.

60. *The Polish White Book*, p. 41.

61. Benns, *op. cit.*, p. 496.

62. According to Krüger, in Max Freiherr von DuPrel, *Das General-Gouvernement*, p. 52: "Die seelische Veranlagung der Polen, ihr Hass und die vorangegangene Verhetzung liessen kein williges Eingehen auf die Tätigkeit deutscher Behörden erwarten. Um das Land für das Reich zu sichern und bewirtschaften . . . konnte nur einer deutschen Vollverwaltung gelingen, die all massgeblichen öffentlichen Funktionen in deutsche Hände legte und nur die rein technische ausführende oder aber rein lokale Tätigkeit einhemischen Kräften überliess."

63. A well-written story from a human interest and political standpoint of the events is given by Ian Karski, *The Secret State*, pp. 45-106.

64. DuPrel, *op. cit.*, pp. 364-65.

65. Karski, *The Secret State*, p. 89.

66. *Ibid.*, p. 93.

67. *Ibid.*, pp. 211-14 and 221-28.

68. *Documenta Occupationis*, pp. 380-81, gives the text of the German verdict.

69. Wiskemann, *op. cit.*, p. 57.

70. Wladislaw Studnicki, *Irrwege in Polen*, p. 66. My translation.

71. *Ibid.*, p. 64.

72. *Ibid.*, p. 71.

73. *Ibid.*, pp. 70-76.

74. *Ibid.*, pp. 80-85.

75. *Polish-Soviet Relations, 1918–1943: Official Documents*, pp. 107-108.

76. Cf. Studnicki's account of conversations with a German Gestapo jail warder who volunteered to go to the front as a private rather than to commit atrocities (beatings) on women inmates. Studnicki, *op. cit.*, pp. 74-75.

77. *Ibid.*, pp. 91-92.

78. *Supra*, pp. 76-77.

79. Studnicki, *op. cit.*, pp. 92-93 and 101-104.

80. *Infra*, Chap. V.

81. For German regulations on the Polish Jewry, see *Documenta Occupationis*, pp. 246-48: "Verordnung über die Einführung der Vorschriften zur Entjudung der deutschen Wirtschaft in den eingegliederten Ostgebieten." For a long list of death sentences, see *ibid.*, pp. 351-70, "Notatki prasowe o wirokach."

82. See A. Lozovski's statement of July 31, 1941, as quoted in Roman Umiastowski, *Poland, Russia and Great Britain, 1941–1945: A Study of Evidence*, p. 25.

83. The Convention of Alvensleben was signed by von Alvensleben and Prince Gortschakoff in 1863 and promised suppression of the Polish revolt and continuing military co-operation between the two states to this end.

84. *Polnisches Weissbuch*, pp. 210-14.

85. Stanislaw Sopicki, "The Eastern Frontiers of Poland," *Free World Review*, Vol. III (Spring-Summer, 1957), pp. 14-17.

86. See *Polnisches Weissbuch*, pp. 220-25, for the text.

87. *Documents*, Vol. VI, *The Last Months of Peace, March-August, 1939*, pp. 121ff and 129ff.

88. During the French-British-Soviet negotiations in July, 1939, Molotov wanted to define indirect aggression, which would give the U.S.S.R. power to move into Poland as any "internal *coup d'état* or any political change favorable to the aggressors," and Voroshilov requested the Western powers to obtain the consent of Poland and Rumania

for the free passage of Russian troops in case of war. See *Documents on British Foreign Policy*, Third Series, Vol. VII, pp. 32-33 and 572, for the proposal made by Voroshilov. See also George E. Bonnet, *De Washington à Quai d'Orsay*, p. 194, for Molotov's definition and pp. 276-80 for Voroshilov on August 12.

89. The Agreement of Tauroggen was concluded in January, 1814, between Prussian General von York and the Russian commander and provided for the neutrality of the Prussian corps against Russia in contradiction to the instructions of the King, who was pressured by Napoleon to continue fighting.

90. U.S. Department of State, *Nazi-Soviet Relations, 1939–1941: Documents from the Archives of the German Foreign Office* (cited hereafter as *Nazi-Soviet Relations*), pp. 234-47 and 247-55.

91. *Ibid.*, pp. 39-40.

92. *Ibid.*, pp. 78-79.

93. *Nazi-Soviet Relations*, p. 101.

94. *Ibid.*, p. 108.

95. *Ibid.*, pp. 102-103.

96. *Ibid.*, p. 108.

97. Hitler, *Mein Kampf*, p. 757.

98. *Ibid.*, p. 742.

99. *Ibid.*, p. 743.

100. *Nazi-Soviet Relations*, pp. 260-64.

101. *Ibid.*, pp. 280-98; Hitler's explanation to Japanese Foreign Minister Matsuoka.

102. On Operation Barbarossa, see *Nazi-Soviet Relations*, pp. 260-64.

103. For Hitler's speech of June 22, 1941, see Adolph Hitler, *Aufrufe, Tagesbefehle und Reden des Führers im Kriege 1939–1941*, pp. 225-32.

104. See *Official Documents*, pp. 107-108 for the text of the July treaty.

105. For the text of the December declaration, see *ibid.*, pp. 109-10; for a narrative, see Umiastowski, *op. cit.*, pp. 42-44.

106. Umiastowski, *op. cit.*, pp. 44f.

107. Ian Ciechanowski, *Defeat in Victory*, p. 67.

108. Text in *Official Documents*, pp. 165-66.

109. *Official Documents*, p. 57; text of the note of January 16, 1943.

110. *Ibid.*, pp. 170-71.

111. Umiastowski, *op. cit.*, p. 109.

112. See *ibid.*, p. 113, for Korneichuk and *ibid.*, pp. 115-16, for the text of the Tass declaration.

113. *Ibid.*, p. 115.

114. *Ibid.*, pp. 116-18.

115. *Ibid.*, pp. 126-27; text of Molotov's note of April 25, 1943.

116. *Ibid.*, p. 149.

117. *Ibid.*, pp. 150-51.

118. *Ibid.*, p. 152.

119. *Ibid.*, pp. 157-59.

120. For the text, see *W dziesiata rocznice poswtania Polskiej Partii Robotniczej (Materialy i dokumenty)*, pp. 229-37.

121. Bronislaw Kusnierz, *Stalin and the Poles*, pp. 169-72.

122. *Ibid.*, pp. 171-72.

123. *Ibid.*, pp. 173-75. Cf. Umiastowski, *op. cit.*, pp. 250-52.

124. Kusnierz, *op. cit.*, pp. 174-75.

125. On the Warsaw uprising, see Stanislaw Mikolajczyk, *The Pattern of Soviet Domination*, pp. 73-101, and Umiastowski, *op. cit.*, pp. 284-323.

126. Cf. Cordell Hull, *The War Memoirs of Cordell Hull*, Vol. II, pp. 1448-49.

127. Kusnierz, *op. cit.*, p. 179. Concerning the exchange of telegrams between Roosevelt and Stalin, see Arthur Bliss Lane, *I Saw Poland Betrayed*, pp. 73ff.

128. Lane, *op. cit.*, pp. 89-122, 179-213, and 303-17.

CHAPTER V

1. E. von Puttkammer, *Irrtum und Schuld, passim*, brings an eyewitness story of the German Committee on Liberation.

2. Cf. Stalin's remark to the Polish Prime Minister: "Communism to a German is like a saddle on a cow." Mikolajczyk, *op. cit.*, p. 87.

3. See Churchill's account on Stalin's views at the Teheran Conference in Winston S. Churchill, *The Second World War*, Vol. V, *Closing the Ring*, pp. 359-61.

4. *Ibid.*, pp. 361-62.

5. See Sikorski's memorandum of December, 1942, as commented upon by the *London Observer* of April 13, 1947.

6. Wolfgang Wagner, *Die Entstehung der Oder-Neisse Linie in den diplomatischen Verhandlungen des Zweiten Weltkrieges*, p. 17: "Die polnischen Gebietsforderungen waren nie eine isolierte Erscheinung; sie waren ein Teil des Traumes von der polnischen Grossmacht, die allein oder im Bündnis mit anderen slawischen Nationen das Gebiet zwischen den drei Meeren beherrschen sollte."

7. Stanislaw Kudlicki, *Upper Silesia*, pp. 9-14 and 24-30.

8. Gotthold Rhode and Wolfgang Wagner, *Quellen zur Entstehung der Oder-Neisse Linie*, pp. 12-13.

9. *Ibid.*, pp. 14-15, quoting a resolution by the Polish National Council at London.

10. Two excerpts of this unpublished Sikorski memorandum may be found in *Dziennik Polski*, December 9, 1952 (Aleksander Bregman), and in the *London Observer* of April 1, 1947.

11. Bregman in *Dziennik Polski*, December 9, 1952.

12. Mikolajczyk, *op. cit.*, pp. 297-300.

13. K. Pruszynski, "Wobec Rosji," *Wiadomsosci Polski*, October 4, 1942.

14. Wagner, *op. cit.*, p. 53.

15. Wagner, *op. cit.*, pp. 54-56.

16. Churchill, *Closing the Ring*, pp. 361-62.

17. Memorandum of October 8, 1943, by the Polish Ambassador in London to the American Foreign Minister. Herbert Feis, *Roosevelt, Churchill, Stalin: The War They Waged and the Peace They Sought*, p. 194.

18. Wagner, *op. cit.*, pp. 56-57.

19. Churchill, *Closing the Ring*, pp. 362 and 394-96.

20. *Ibid.*, p. 397.

21. Mikolajczyk, *op. cit.*, p. 60.

22. Wagner, *op. cit.*, p. 60. Cf. Feis, *op. cit.*, p. 287.

23. Churchill, *Closing the Ring*, pp. 394-95.

24. Robert E. Sherwood, *Roosevelt and Hopkins: An Intimate History*, p. 748.

25. Kusnierz, *op. cit.*, pp. 172-76.

26. Churchill, *Closing the Ring*, p. 397.

27. *Infra*, Chap. VI.

28. Churchill, *Closing the Ring*, pp. 450-51, and Mikolajczyk, *op. cit.*, pp. 52-53.

29. Mikolajczyk, *op. cit.*, p. 56, recalling the January 20, 1944 discussion with Churchill after the Teheran Conference. Cf. Hull, *op. cit.*, Vol. II, p. 1438.

30. Mikolajczyk, *op. cit.*, pp. 61-62.

31. *Ibid.*

32. (Bor) Thadeus Komorowski, *Armia podzienna*, pp. 195-96.

33. Mikolajczyk, *op. cit.*, pp. 316-20, and Ciechanowski, *op. cit.*, pp. 305-306.

34. Mikolajczyk, *op. cit.*, pp. 69-70.

35. *Ibid.*, pp. 104-106.

36. *Ibid.*, p. 613.

37. *Ibid.*, pp. 74-75.

38. *Ibid.*, p. 86.

39. *Ibid.*, pp. 84-85.

40. *Ibid.*, p. 90. Cf. Edward J. Rozek, *Allied Wartime Diplomacy*, p. 258, reproducing Radio Lublin's version of the Warsaw uprising on October 6, 1944.

41. For the text of the appeal, see Rozek, *op. cit.*, p. 235.

42. Alfons Klafkowski, *Podstawy prawne granicy Odra-Nysa na tle unow: Jaltanskiej i Poczdamskiej*, p. 36.

43. On September 4, 1944, Churchill wrote: "I am afraid that the fall of Warsaw . . . will fatally undermine the position of Mikolajczyk himself." Churchill, *Closing the Ring*, pp. 141-42.

44. *Manchester Guardian*, August 31, 1944.

45. Mikolajczyk, *op. cit.*, pp. 104-106.

46. *Ibid.*, pp. 106-109.

47. As reprinted in Rozek, *op. cit.*, pp. 274-75, from the official Polish minutes of the October 13, 1944 meeting of Mikolajczyk, Stalin, and Churchill.

48. See *ibid.*, pp. 294-95, for the text of Mikolajczyk's reports to the London Polish Cabinet on October 24 and 30, 1944.

49. The questions of the London Polish government as quoted in Mikolajczyk, *op. cit.*, p. 114.

50. Among other places, the text of the Cadogan Letter is reproduced in *ibid.*, pp. 115-16.

51. Churchill told Mikolajczyk on October 26, 1944, of his hope that a fifty-fifty combination, with Mikolajczyk as Premier, would still be possible. Rozek, *op. cit.*, p. 297.

52. *Ibid.*, p. 312.

53. See the conversation between Ambassador Harriman and Mikolajczyk on November 22, 1944, in *ibid.*, p. 313.

54. For a British appraisal, see *The Scotsman*, November 27, 1944.

55. On the Russian winter offensive, see Jürgen Thorwald, *Es begann an der Weichsel*, pp. 33-42 and 63-66, and Kurt von Tippelskirch, *Geschichte des Zweiten Weltkrieges*, pp. 534-51.

56. *Malta and Yalta*, pp. 508-509.

57. *Malta and Yalta*, p. 617. See the Matthews minutes: "I can get the people and Congress to co-operate fully for peace, but not to keep an army in Europe a long time. Two years would be the limit."

58. John L. Snell (ed.), *The Meaning of Yalta*, pp. 110-16.

59. For the conference declaration on Poland, see *Malta and Yalta*, p. 938.

60. *Ibid.*, p. 509.

61. Mikolajczyk, *op. cit.*, pp. 141-48.

62. See Churchill's famous saying at Yalta: "It would be a pity to stuff the Polish goose so full of German food that it got indigestion." *Malta and Yalta*, p. 717.

63. *Ibid.*, pp. 905-906, Churchill on the Polish government and the Oder frontier.

64. Snell, *op. cit.*, pp. 112-18.

65. See Archizewski's interview in connection with the parliamentary debate at London in the *Sunday Times*, December 17, 1944.

66. See the Polish Memorandum of January 22, 1945, in Mikolajczyk, *op. cit.*, pp. 332-33.

67. The Stettinius-Eden agreement as presented to Roosevelt on February 4, 1945. *Malta and Yalta*, p. 568.

68. *New York Times,* February 6, 1945.

69. *The Economist,* February 10, 1945.

70. *Keesing's Contemporary Archives, 1945,* p. 7328.

71. As quoted in Rhode and Wagner, *op. cit.,* p. 219, on the basis of *Keesing's Contemporary Archives, 1945* (German edition), pp. 212-13.

72. *Supra,* pp. 94-96.

73. For the text of the Treaty in Polish, Russian, and German, see Rhode and Wagner, *op. cit.,* pp. 217-19.

74. *Ibid.,* p. 219.

75. For text of the renewed agreement and the negotiations thereto, see Mikolajczyk, *op. cit.,* pp. 159-61, and Rhode and Wagner, *op. cit.,* pp. 271-73.

76. Lane, *op. cit.,* p. 256.

77. Lane, *op. cit.,* p. 256.

78. Unfortunately, neither note (April 8 and May 8, 1945) has been published in full. A narrative can be found in *ibid.,* p. 257.

79. *Ibid.,* p. 258.

80. For the Polish-Russian exchange, see Rozek, *op. cit.,* p. 417, quoting Premier Mikolajczyk's private files. For a superficial treatment, see Eugen M. Kulischer, *Europe on the Move,* pp. 282-92.

81. Even Miss Wiskemann describes the tragedy of Breslau: "It is scarcely necessary to insist that in blinding snowstorms and with frozen roads in a hopelessly slippery condition, intersecting streams of refugees with horse and hand-carts crammed with possessions made wretchedly slow progress. After earlier evacuations and air raids, accommodation was very hard to come by at night. Sometimes a stream of returning refugees who had failed to find refuge made confusion worse confounded. And inevitably Russian tanks would often overtake the people on the roads and cut them off." Wiskemann, *op. cit.,* p. 91.

82. For Guderian's fight with Hitler for the transfer of the Panzer divisions to the east, see Thorwald, *op. cit.,* pp. 27-40, and Theodor Schieder (ed.), *The Expulsion and Flight of the German Population from the Territories East of the Oder-Neisse Line* (cited hereafter as *Expulsion and Flight*), pp. 8-12.

83. Thorwald, *op. cit.,* pp. 43-50 and 83-94.

84. For Amberger's testimony, see the German edition of *Expulsion and Flight, Die Vertreibung der deutschen Bevölkerung aus den Gebieten östlich der Oder und Neisse* (cited hereafter as *Die Vertreibung*), Vol. I (1), p. 7.

85. The text of K. P.'s testimony is in *ibid.,* p. 8.

86. *Ibid.,* p. 8.

87. Miss Wiskemann's theory that these were "primitive excesses" can hardly be accepted in view of the frequency of mass rapings. The author has hardly talked to any woman from the area who escaped them, and *Die Vertreibung* has countless testimonies on raids which could not have been undertaken without the consent of officers and commanders.

88. *Die Vertreibung,* Vol. I (1), pp. 194, 266, 297, and 479.

89. *Ibid.,* Vol. I (1), pp. 298 and 476; Vol. I (2), pp. 302f. and 319.

90. *Ibid.,* Vol. I (1), pp. 196, 223, and 299; Vol. I (2), pp. 190 and 218.

91. *Expulsion and Flight,* pp. E51-52, states that these newspapers are now in the archives of the Federal Ministry for Expellees at Bonn. Cf. Sabik-Wogolow in *W pobejdenoi Germanij,* February, 1947, pp. 9-17.

92. *Expulsion and Flight,* pp. 50-52.

93. *Ibid.,* p. 51.

94. *Ibid.,* p. 208f. Cf. Thorwald, op. cit., pp. 75-79, describing a particularly revolting raping-killing episode led by a Russian sergeant in a German village in western Poland.

95. Thorwald, *op. cit.,* p. 52.

96. See Sabik-Wogolow, *loc. cit.*, p. 17, and Order of the Commissar of Defense of the Soviet Union of December, 1944, on sending packages from Germany to Russia by Red Army men in *Expulsion and Flight*, p. 355.

97. *Expulsion and Flight*, p. 53.

98. *Ibid.*, p. 52. Cf. Wiskemann, *op. cit.*, p. 92.

99. Wiskemann, *op. cit.*, pp. 93-94.

100. *Expulsion and Flight*, pp. 65-68. Number of deported civilians: Silesia, 62,000; western Poland, eastern Brandenburg (western half), and Pomerania (Zhukov group), 57,000; western East Prussia, Pomorze, and eastern half of Pomerania (Rokkosowski group), 55,000; East Prussia (Tcherniakowski), 44,000.

101. Wiskemann, *op. cit.*, p. 87.

102. *Expulsion and Flight*, pp. 54ff.

103. *Expulsion and Flight*, p. 57.

104. *Ibid.*, p. 61.

105. *Ibid.*, p. 122.

106. Miss Wiskemann's figuring can be only partially accepted. Whether one should assume that the figure 958,000 was 200,000 higher than the actual number of Germans in Poland in 1939 remains questionable because if her contention were correct, the losses of the German minority during the Second World War and the expulsion would have been only 17,000. Yet the death sentences and the victims of concentration camps alone exceeded this figure several times.

107. *Expulsion and Flight*, pp. 122-23.

CHAPTER VI

1. Hull, *op. cit.*, Vol. II, pp. 1248-52.

2. See Sir Harold Nicolson, *The Congress of Vienna*, pp. 122-23, for an excellent exposition of the British concept of European balance of power in the nineteenth and early twentieth centuries.

3. *Ibid.*, pp. 125-26.

4. Erich Eyck, *Wilhelm II, passim.*

5. Arnold Toynbee (ed.), *Survey of International Affairs, 1939–1946: The World in March, 1939*, pp. 40-44.

6. *New York Times*, November 20, 1939.

7. *Bulletin of International News, XVI* (1939), p. 50.

8. For a treatise with patently pro-Polish bias, see Machray, *East Prussia: Menace to Poland and Peace* and *The Problem of Upper Silesia, passim.*

9. Wagner, *op. cit.*, pp. 30-31, and Boris Meissner, *Russland, die Westmächte und Deutschland*, pp. 11-12.

10. Umiastowski, *op. cit.*, pp. 77-149.

11. *Infra*, pp. 104-105.

12. Winston S. Churchill, *The Grand Alliance*, pp. 390-92, and *The Hinge of Fate*, pp. 332f.

13. *War and Peace Aims of the United Nations*, Vol. I, p. 2.

14. Sir Harold Nicolson, *The Meaning of Prestige*, p. 9.

15. For the text, see *Documents on American Foreign Relations*, Vol. IV, pp. 209-10. For the British evaluation of the Charter as a "publicity handout," see Sherwood, *op. cit.*, p. 362.

16. See Hull, *op. cit.*, Vol. II, p. 1248.

17. For a stinging attack on the pro-Communist elements, see John T. Flynn, *The Roosevelt Myth*, pp. 303-309: "It mattered not what the New Deal touched, it became a

torch for use in his [Roosevelt's] adventures in social engineering, and after June, 1941, when Hitler turned on his partner, Stalin, these bureaus became roosting places for droves of Communist termites who utilized their positions as far as they dared to advance the interests of Soviet Russia and to help 'to dispense with the superficial paraphernalia of capitalism' in this country under cover of the war."

18. Hull, *op. cit.*, Vol. II, p. 1168.

19. *Ibid.*, p. 1169.

20. *Ibid.*, p. 1169.

21. *Ibid.*, p. 1172.

22. *Ibid.*, p. 1468.

23. *Ibid.*, p. 1247.

24. *Ibid.*, p. 1465.

25. *Ibid.*, p. 1465.

26. *Ibid.*, pp. 1465-66.

27. For American military opinion on Russian participation in the Far East War, see Feis, *op. cit., passim.*

28. Churchill, *The Hinge of Fate*, pp. 648-59.

29. Churchill, *Closing the Ring*, pp. 375-87.

30. Sherwood, *op. cit.*, pp. 784f.

31. Forrest Davis, "Roosevelt's World Blueprint," *Saturday Evening Post*, (March 20, 1943).

32. Hull, *op. cit.*, Vol. II, p. 1465.

33. Joseph E. Davies, *Mission to Moscow, passim.*

34. Flynn, *op. cit.*, pp. 340-42.

35. Hull, *op. cit.*, Vol. II, pp. 1265-72.

36. Feis, *op. cit.*, pp. 192ff., quoting Roosevelt as of March, 1943, favoring Polish claims to that province.

37. Joseph Mackiewycz, *The Katyn Wood Murders, passim;* Churchill, *The Hinge of Fate*, pp. 757-61; Hull, *op. cit.*, Vol. II, pp. 1265-73; U.S. House of Representatives, *Hearings Before the Select Committee to Conduct an Investigation of the Facts, Evidence and Circumstances of the Katyn Forest Massacre*, 82nd Congress, 1st Session, *passim.*

38. Umiastowski, *op. cit.*, pp. 159-70 ("Propaganda Attack in England"). The BBC used the expression "old Polish frontier" for the 1939 Polish-Russian frontier as early as January, 1943.

39. Flynn, *op. cit.*, pp. 343-45.

40. *Ibid.*, pp. 344-45.

41. Feis, *op. cit.*, p. 283, quoting the Polish memorandum of November, 1943, to Roosevelt.

42. Cf. the text of the memorandum of the Polish exile government to Secretary Hull dated October 6, 1943: "Even though the Soviet government should, in compensation, support Polish claims to some German territories in the West, these new frontiers would make Poland dependent on its eastern neighbor and enable the Soviet Union to use her as a springboard for extending its domination over Central Europe and Germany in particular." Feis, *op. cit.*, p. 194.

43. Umiastowski, *op. cit.*, pp. 159-70.

44. Hull, *op. cit.*, Vol. II, pp. 1305-1306, and Flynn, *op. cit.*, pp. 344-46.

45. Feis, *op. cit.*, p. 196.

46. Churchill, *Closing the Ring*, pp. 395-97.

47. Feis, *op. cit.*, pp. 286-89.

48. Churchill, *Closing the Ring*, pp. 373-74.

49. The best published sources are *ibid.*, pp. 342-407; Sherwood, *op. cit.*, pp. 776-92; and Admiral William D. Leahy, *I Was There*, pp. 203-13.

50. Churchill, *Closing the Ring*, pp. 396-97.

51. Sherwood, *op. cit.*, p. 782.

52. The decision for Overlord was made at the First Quebec Conference, and though he was still in favor of creating a "side theater" in the Balkans, Churchill regarded the cross-Channel invasion after August, 1943, as the "keystone of the arch of Anglo-American co-operation." See Churchill to Field Marshall Smuts on September 11, 1943, in Churchill, *Closing the Ring*, p. 131. For Churchill's quest for an Adriatic front, cf. *ibid.*, pp. 33, 253-54, 350-58, and 366-73; Sherwood, *op. cit.*, pp. 746-47; and Hanson W. Baldwin, *Great Mistakes of the War*, pp. 25-44.

53. Winston S. Churchill, *Triumph and Tragedy*, pp. 74-79.

54. Churchill, *Closing the Ring*, p. 451.

55. Churchill omits in his memoirs his negotiations with Mikolajczyk. The program is reproduced by Mikolajczyk, *op. cit.*, pp. 56-57.

56. The two notes of the Polish exile government were literally reproduced in *ibid.*, pp. 309-15.

57. See *ibid.*, p. 58, for an extract of the British reply.

58. See *ibid.*, pp. 321-24, for a literal reproduction of the document.

59. *Ibid.*, pp. 315-16.

60. Leahy, *op. cit.*, p. 232.

61. *Ibid.*, p. 233.

62. *Ibid.*, p. 231.

63. See Mikolajczyk, *op. cit.*, pp. 65-68.

64. See *Malta and Yalta*, p. 988.

65. *Supra*, Chap. VI.

66. Lane, *op. cit.*, pp. 58ff. For the reception of the leaders of the Polish American Congress on October 11, 1944, see James T. Shotwell, *Poland and Russia, 1919–1945*, pp. 73-74.

67. Hull, *op. cit.*, Vol. II, pp. 1141-42.

68. Mikolajczyk, *op. cit.*, pp. 64-65.

69. *Ibid.*, p. 66.

70. *Ibid.*, p. 66.

71. See *Malta and Yalta*, pp. 202-203, for Harriman's report on the Churchill-Stalin agreement on the Oder Line in October, 1944.

72. See the Cadogan Letter as reproduced in English in Rhode and Wagner, *op cit.*, pp. 115-16.

73. See *Malta and Yalta*, p. 505, for the Eden-Stettinius discussions, and on Eden's report to Churchill, see *ibid.*, p. 509. The report excludes both Breslau and Stettin from the Oder Line.

74. Anders, *op. cit.*, p. 210.

75. Letter from Mikolajczyk to Roosevelt on March 19, 1944, in Mikolajczyk, *op. cit.*, pp. 316-20.

76. See *ibid.*, pp. 328-30, for the "New Plan" of the London Poles, August 30, 1944.

77. *Poland, Germany and European Peace*, pp. 707-708.

78. On Mikolajczyk's resignation, see Mikolajczyk, *op. cit.*, pp. 117-18.

79. Message to Harriman, *Malta and Yalta*, p. 214.

80. Churchill's December 15 speech, in Great Britain, *Parliamentary Debates, 1939–1947*, pp. 1480-90.

81. *Malta and Yalta*, p. 215.

82. *Ibid.*, pp. 219-21.

83. For the first message, see *ibid.*, pp. 217-18.

84. For Stalin's answer and the message of December 30, 1944, see *ibid.*, pp. 220-25.

85. *Ibid.*, pp. 225-26.

86. *Life* (September 6, 1948).

87. Flynn, *op. cit.*, p. 394.

88. *Supra,* Chap. V.

89. Churchill, *Triumph and Tragedy,* p. 351.

90. Edward R. Stettinius, Jr., *Roosevelt and the Russians,* pp. 99-100.

91. Snell, *op. cit.*, pp. 38f.

92. Lord Robert Vansittart, *Bones of Contention,* pp. 46-69.

93. Donald F. Lach, "What They Would Do About Germany," *Journal of Modern History,* Vol. XVII (September, 1945), pp. 227-43, and H. D. Willcock, "Public Opinion: Attitudes to the German People," *Political Quarterly* (London), Vol. XIX (April-June, 1948), pp. 160-66.

94. *Malta and Yalta,* p. 625.

95. *Ibid.,* pp. 717-18.

96. *Ibid.,* pp. 716-17.

97. *Ibid.,* pp. 792-93.

98. *Ibid.,* pp. 505 and 509.

99. *Ibid.,* p. 509.

100. *Ibid.,* pp. 660-71, 716-17, 774-81, 846-50, and 897-901.

101. Samuel I. Rosenman (ed.), *The Public Papers and Addresses of Franklin D. Roosevelt, 1944–1945,* pp. 581ff.

102. Yalta Declaration, *Malta and Yalta,* p. 973.

103. *Ibid.*

104. *Ibid.,* p. 850 (Bohlen Minutes).

105. *Ibid.,* p. 793 (American proposal of February 8, 1945).

106. Yalta Declaration, *ibid.,* p. 973.

107. *Ibid.,* p. 852.

108. *Ibid.,* p. 854.

109. *Ibid.,* pp. 970-71; for discussion, see *ibid.,* pp. 709-11.

110. *Ibid.,* pp. 867-68.

111. Stettinius, *op. cit.,* pp. 315-16.

112. Cf. Churchill, *Triumph and Tragedy,* pp. 453-54 and 482, quoting Stalin's message to him: "In President Roosevelt the Soviet people saw a . . . rigid champion of close co-operation between the three States."

113. *Supra,* Chap. V.

114. Nicholson, *The Meaning of Prestige,* p. 51: ". . . the jealousies, rivalries and suspicions which in any protracted war arise between partners to an Alliance generate poisons which war-wearied arteries are inelastic to eliminate."

115. Churchill, *Triumph and Tragedy,* pp. 400ff.

116. *Supra,* p. 91.

117. See Churchill, *Triumph and Tragedy,* pp. 487-97, for the text of the message.

118. Churchill, *ibid.,* pp. 599ff.

119. *Ibid.,* p. 599.

120. Harry S. Truman, *Memoirs,* Vol. I, pp. 366-69.

121. *Ibid.,* p. 388.

122. *Ibid.,* p. 353, and Leahy, *op. cit.,* p. 466.

123. Truman, *op. cit.,* Vol. I, pp. 368-69.

124. *Ibid.,* p. 368.

125. *Ibid.,* p. 369. He believed "that the Russians had killed the German population or had chased them into our zones."

126. Churchill, *Triumph and Tragedy,* pp. 672ff.

127. *Ibid.,* pp. 670-75.

128. Truman, *op. cit.,* Vol. I, p. 405.

GERMANY'S EASTERN FRONTIERS

129. *Ibid.*, p. 389, reproduces the American plan.

130. James F. Byrnes, *Speaking Frankly*, pp. 80-82.

131. Truman, *op. cit.*, Vol. I, pp. 403-408.

132. *Ibid.*, pp. 406ff.

133. *Ibid.*, p. 405. Cf. Byrnes, *Speaking Frankly*, p. 81: "To remove an excuse for Poland or the Soviet Union to claim that the line had been established or that there was any promise to support a particular line, the Potsdam Protocal declared: The three heads of government reaffirmed their opinion that the final delimitation of the western frontiers of Poland should await a peace settlement. In the light of this history, it is difficult to credit with good faith any person who asserts that Poland's western boundary was fixed by the Conferees."

134. Churchill, *Triumph and Tragedy*, pp. 661-67ff.

135. *Ibid.*, pp. 651-54.

136. Rhode and Wagner, *op. cit.*, pp. 257-58.

137. Truman, *op. cit.*, Vol. I, pp. 406ff.

138. Wiskemann, *op. cit.*, pp. 106-11.

CHAPTER VII

1. Louis de Jong, *The German Fifth Column in the Second World War*, pp. 34-36.

2. *Ibid.*, pp. 43ff., also relates the suffering of the *Volksdeutsche* during the German-Polish campaign.

3. *Supra,* Chap. IV.

4. De Jong, *op. cit.*, pp. 47ff.

5. Ciechanowski, *op. cit.*, p. 185, quoting Ian Karski to President Roosevelt: "I would be rather frank with you, Mr. President. Nothing on earth will stop the Poles from taking some kind of a revenge on the Germans after the Nazi collapse. There will be some terrorism, probably short-lived, but it will be unavoidable."

6. *Infra*, pp. 135f.

7. Countless cases are reproduced in *Die Vertreibung*, Vol. I (2), pp. 41ff., 258f., 345, 353, 377, 385ff., 396ff., 412, and 423ff.

8. See *Dziennik Ustaw*, Pos. 57/45, for the decree establishing the voivodship Gdańsk.

9. *Die Vertreibung*, Vol. I (2), p. 46.

10. *Ibid.*, Vol. I (1), p. 108E.

11. *Ibid.*, Note 3.

12. *Ibid.*, Vol. I (2), p. 653-55.

13. *Ibid.*, pp. 653 and 659-60.

14. *Ibid.*, p. 655.

15. *Ibid.*, p. 464.

16. *Ibid.*, pp. 665-701.

17. *Ibid.*, pp. 670-81.

18. *Ibid.*, pp. 687-89, 695, and 698-99.

19. Byrnes, *Speaking Frankly*, p. 113.

20. *Die Vertreibung*, Vol. I (2), pp. 666, 682, and 782.

21. Rhode and Wagner, *op. cit.*, pp. 256-58, reproduce the text of the Potsdam Declaration; the text of the Control Council plan is reprinted in *Europa-Archiv*, Vol. II (August, 1947), p. 823.

22. *Die Vertreibung*, Vol. I (2), pp. 707-709.

23. *Ibid.*, pp. 707-708 and 786.

24. *Ibid.*, pp. 722-24 and 729f.

25. *Ibid.*, pp. 726-28 and 729-31.

26. *Ibid.,* pp. 741 and 753.

27. *Ibid.,* Vol. I (1), p. 147E.

28. *Ibid.,* p. 155E.

29. A heart-rending description of the conditions prevailing among them can be found in *Documents on Expulsion,* Vol. I, pp. 94-103, richly documented in *ibid.,* pp. 254-317.

30. *Die Vertreibung,* Vol. I (2), pp. 204-206, reproduces the request of the *starost* of Nidziza (Neidenburg); see also p. 726.

31. Reproduced in *Europa-Archiv,* Vol. II (August, 1947), p. 823.

32. See *Die Vertreibung,* Vol. I (2), pp. 759-834, for details.

33. *Ibid.,* pp. 762ff.

34. *Ibid.,* Vol. I (1), p. 148E.

35. *Ibid.,* pp. 148-49E.

36. *Das deutsche Flüchtlingsproblem* (*Sonderheft der Zeitschrift für Raumforschung*), pp. 4ff.

37. For details, see *Die Vertreibung,* Vol. I (2), pp. 783-85 and 846f.

38. *Ibid.,* pp. 150-51E, and Vol. I (2), pp. 832-54.

39. *Ibid.,* Vol. I (1), p. 150E.

40. *Ibid.,* p. 151E.

41. *Ibid.,* pp. 877-96.

42. Cf. *Dziennik Polski* (London), January 2, 1958, about Liegnitz.

43. For a detailed and professional treatment of the epidemics in East Prussia, see Wilhelm Starlinger, *Grenzen der Sowjetmacht.*

44. On conditions under Russian occupation, see *Die Vertreibung,* Vol. I (2), pp. 119, 142, 151, and 160.

45. Hugo Linck, *Königsberg, 1945–1948,* pp. 107ff., 136ff., and 146ff.

46. *Documents on Expulsion,* p. 117.

47. Andrzej Wydrzynski, "Terra incognita," *Po Prostu,* (January 6, 1957). Cf. *Slowo Polskie* (May 4, 1957).

48. For decrees of extraordinary criminal courts, see *Dziennik Ustaw* Pos. 21/44 (September 12, 1944), and *ibid.,* Pos. 354-46. Cf. *Documents on Expulsion,* pp. 247-54.

49. On transfer of wealth, see *Dziennik Ustaw,* Pos. 97/45 and 179/45 and finally *ibid.,* Pos. 182/46.

50. For the establishment of the Ministry of Recovered Territories, see *ibid.,* Pos. 295/45 (November 13, 1945).

51. *Infra,* Chap. VII.

52. Edmund S. Kerstein, *Red Star over Poland,* pp. 83ff.

53. Praca Zbiorowa (ed.), *Odbudowa Ziem Odzyskanych (1945–1955)* (cited hereafter as *Odbudowa*), p. 20, gives the following figures: Nysa (Neisse), 55 per cent; Opole (Oppeln), 35 per cent; Rybnik, 60 per cent.

54. *Ibid.,* p. 95.

55. *Ibid.,* p. 142.

56. *Ibid.,* p. 297.

57. *Ibid.,* p. 355.

58. *Ibid.,* pp. 340-41. For the cities, see also *Warmia i Masury,* Vol. II, p. 208. A less depressive report, expressing doubts on the correctness of war damage calculations, is given by Joseph Nieroda, *Miasta Pomorze Wachodniego,* p. 13.

59. *Poland: Recovered Territories,* p. 24.

60. *Supra,* Chap. V.

61. *Statistical Yearbook of Poland 1947,* pp. 28-29, gives the figures on resettlement.

62. Wiskemann, *op. cit.,* pp. 213ff.

63. "The Polish Three-Year Plan," *The World Today* (March, 1947), p. 107.

64. Decree of the Transfer of German Property as of March 2, 1945, in *Dziennik Ustaw*, Pos. 45/1945, and with final amendment, *ibid.*, 87/1946 (March 8, 1946).

65. *Die Vertreibung*, Vol. I (1), pp. 115-17E.

66. Kerstein, *op. cit.*, pp. 87-113.

67. *Statistical Yearbook of Poland 1947*, pp. 20-21.

68. Kerstein, *op. cit.*, p. 111.

69. *Statistical Yearbook of Poland 1947*, p. 20, recognizes only 289,000 Germans, yet in 1947 alone, 450,000 Germans were expelled by Poland according to *Documents on Expulsion*, p. 155E.

70. *Statistical Yearbook of Poland 1947*, p. 42.

71. *Ibid.*, pp. 40-42.

72. Z. Szoga, "Sprawy zien Zachodnych," *Zycie gospodarcze* (January 12, 1957), brings the extent of wasteland and uncultivated land as one million hectares in 1956.

73. Wiskemann, *op. cit.*, pp. 213ff.

74. *Zycie gospodarcze* (March 31, 1957), brings an indictment of Communist agricultural practices and gives average acreage yields for 1947-48 in eastern Pomerania as 12 to 15 dz and in south East Prussia as the same, which averages fell by 1956-57 to 4 to 6 dz in Pomerania and 8 to 9 dz in East Prussia.

75. Jean Malera and Lucienne Rey, *La Pologne d'une occupation à l'autre (1944–1952)*, pp. 91-145.

76. *Statistical Yearbook of Poland 1947*, pp. 47-52.

77. Lane, *op. cit.*, p. 262.

78. For the Brynes speech, see *infra*, pp. 155-56.

79. Lane, *op. cit.*, p. 262.

80. *Infra*, pp. 155-57.

81. As quoted in *Osthandbuch*, Heft XIX, p. 24.

82. *Dziennik Ustaw*, Pos. 295/45 (November 13, 1945).

83. For a short background on Gomulka, see *Who's Who of the Regime in Poland*, pp. 25-27.

84. On the relocation of the territories, see *Europa-Archiv*, Vol. II, (1946-47), pp. 593-95.

85. For the redistribution, see maps in *Odbudowa, passim*, and Rhode, *op. cit.*, p. 147.

86. See geographic descriptions of Szczecin and Koszalin in *Odbudowa*, pp. 200-205 and 294-96.

87. On Upper Silesia, see *ibid.*, pp. 21-30.

88. Repatriation figures, 1955-57, are given in "Niezalatwione zagadnienia na Ziemiach Zachodnich," *Narodowiec* (January 10, 1958): 1955, 8,000; 1956, 32,000; 1957, 82,000. Of the sixteen repatriation centers, thirteen are in the Oder-Neisse region.

89. Rudolf Neumann (ed.), *Ostpreussen unter polnischer und sowjetischer Verwaltung* (Vol. I of *Ostdeutschland unter fremder Verwaltung, 1945–1955*), pp. 19-23, shows that by the end of 1953, some 33 per cent of the population lived in towns, while the rural population was 29 per cent lower than in 1939; 14 out of 44 towns have become villages, while eight towns exceed their 1939 population.

90. Peter Heinz Seraphim, *Industriekombinat Oberschlesien*, pp. 71-76.

91. "The Western Territories in Figures," *Poland and Germany* (Summer, 1957), pp. 32ff., gives 6,913,000. *Narodowiec* (January 10, 1958) gives 7,200,000.

92. On the unwillingness of the repatriates, see *Trybuna Ludu* (August 17, 1957).

93. "64,000 Aussiedler aus den Ostgebieten," *Pressedienst der Heimatvertriebenen* (30), 1957, p. 7. Cf. also *Po prostu* (April 15, 1957) on East Prussia, *Glos Koszalinski* (October 4, 1956) on Pomerania, *Gazeta Zielonogorska* (February 22, 1957) on eastern Brandenburg, and *Trybuna Ludu* (August 22, 1956) on Silesia.

94. Bodo Jaxtheimer, "Schlesien unter sowjetpolnischer Verwaltung," *Ost-Kurier*, Vol. I (1), 1958, pp. 1-4. For a different description, see B. Z. "Okruchy z jednego Miasteczka,"

Slowo Polskie (May 4, 1957), reporting on assault and battery on German minors in Silesia by Poles.

95. Wydrzynski, "Terra incognita," *Po prostu,* (January 6, 1957). Wiskemann also recognizes the friction. Wiskemann, *op. cit.,* pp. 217-19.

96. *Odbudowa,* pp. 34-35, 100-101, 149ff., 224, 300ff., 364f., and 440ff.

97. New data on acreage yields, see Note 74 of this chapter. See also the article in *Nowe rolnictwo* (November 11, 1956), pp. 820-23, on East Prussia. For eastern Pomerania and Brandenburg, see *Glos Olsztynski* (October 7, 1957) and *Gazeta Zielonogorska* (November 11, 1957).

98. "Sprawy ziem Zachodnich," *Zycie gospodarcze,* Nos. 4-6 (1957).

99. Peter H. Seraphim, *Wirtschaft Ostdeutschlands,* p. 82.

100. *Trybuna Ludu* (July 17, 1954).

101. *Poland and Germany* (Summer, 1957), p. 33.

102. On the neglect of the areas by the government and population fluctuation, see Barbara Kalamaczka, "Prszeszkadza zawsze to samo," *Glos Szczecinski* (April 14, 1957), Zybmunt Dmochowski, "Szczecin od macochy?" *Glos Szczecinski* (May 22, 1957), and the article in *Wyboje* (Poznań) (May 3, 1957).

103. *Washington Evening Star,* February 2, 1958.

104. Wiskemann, *op. cit.,* p. 227, quoting S. Jedrychowski, *Nowe Drogi* (November, 1953).

105. *Zyczie gospodarcze* (May 26, 1957).

106. About the "feeling of provisionality," see *ibid.* (February 10, 1957) scolding the second period of stagnation; see also *Gromada—Rolnik polski* (August 12, 1957) condemning those opposing the purchase of land in the provinces as an illegal measure of the People's Republic (i.e., done in violation of international law).

107. Wiskemann, *op. cit.,* pp. 263-64, and Peter H. Seraphim, *Wirtschaft Ostdeutschlands,* pp. 84-94.

108. Production figures for 1945 were: 20.2 million tons of hard coal; 1948 figures: 38.4 million tons. *Statistical Yearbook of Poland 1947,* p. 86, and *Odbudowa,* pp. 46-47.

109. *Odbudowa,* pp. 44-46, and Wiskemann, *op. cit.,* p. 245.

110. United Nations, Economic Commission for Europe, *Economic Survey of Europe, 1956,* p. A-44.

111. See Gomulka's speech at the beginning of December, 1956, about the situation of Polish economy as reproduced in *Pressedienst der Heimatvertriebenen,* 50 (1956), p. 3, and the insistence of the Polish negotiators on mining equipment during the spring, 1957 negotiations at Washington. Cf. the February, 1958 loan agreement, between Poland and the United States, providing for $25,000,000 credit to Poland. *Washington Sunday Star,* February 16, 1958.

112. *Dziennik Zachodni* (February, 1957) reports the loss of 38,000 miners in the last quarter of 1956 alone. They were replaced by newly recruited miners who did not know their profession. In some mines, the percentage of unskilled employees is as high as 42 per cent.

113. Peter H. Seraphim, *Wirtschaft Ostdeutschlands,* pp. 83-91.

114. Wiskemann, *op. cit.,* pp. 264-66.

115. Peter H. Seraphim, *Wirtschaft Ostdeutschlands,* pp. 91-98.

116. See Gomulka's speech on Polish economy in November, 1956, as reproduced in *Pressedienst der Heimatvertriebenen* 50 (1956).

117. The effect of the reduction of Nordic trade on the use of the Oder as a waterway was admitted even in the times of Bierut in *Gospodarka Planowa* (1) 1953, p. 35.

118. Wiskemann, *op. cit.,* pp. 264-65.

119. For coal export statistics, see *ibid.,* p. 246, giving 69.5 million metric tons out of 91.6 million metric tons as home consumption, 15.5 million metric tons for exports within

the Soviet Russian bloc, and only 6.3 million metric tons for other parts of the world.

120. *Economic Survey of Europe, 1956*, p. A-44.

121. *Ibid.*

122. Figures for 1946-53 show a similar proportion of production in the area and in Poland proper. No figures for 1956 are available in *ibid.*

123. Peter H. Seraphim, *Industriekombinat*, pp. 62-63.

124. Production in 1938 was 1,856,000 metric tons, and 1955 production was 2,378,000 metric tons, according to *Gwiazda Polarna* (January 4, 1958).

125. Peter H. Seraphim, *Industriekombinat*, p. 64, quoting *Trybuna Ludu* (February 9, 1952).

126. *Zycie gospodarcze* (December 16 and 31, 1951); see also Peter H. Seraphim, *Industriekombinat*, p. 65.

127. Peter Heinz Seraphim, *Deutschlands verlorene Montanwirtschaft, passim.*

128. *Dziennik Polski* (London), August 9, 1952, and Peter H. Seraphim, *Industriekombinat*, p. 65.

129. Wiskemann, *op. cit.*, p. 247.

130. Figures for 1956: 4.04 million metric tons of cement in Poland. *Economic Survey of Europe, 1956*, p. A-44.

131. Rhode, *op. cit.*, p. 191.

132. *Przeglad Techniczny* (May, 1957).

133. *Wirtschaftsdienst* (May, 1954), p. 22.

134. *Przeglad Techniczny* (May, 1957).

135. *Economic Survey of Europe, 1956*, p. A-44.

136. Rhode, *op. cit.*, pp. 223-24.

137. *Ibid.*, p. 224.

138. *Ibid.*

139. *Ibid.*, p. 225.

140. "Ziemie Zachodnie Polski," *Czas* (Canada), December 11, 1957, quoting Polish statistics.

141. Rhode, *op. cit.*, p. 223.

142. Jaxtheimer, "Schlesien unter sowjetpolnischer Verwaltung," *Ost-Kurier*, Vol. I (1), 1958, p. 3.

143. Rhode, *op. cit.*, p. 225.

144. *Odbudowa*, pp. 244-45. For 1957 figures, see *Glos Koszalinski* (January 16, 1958). For a detailed exposé, see Jan Kwiatowski, "Szczecin miasto portowe," *Glos Szczecinski* (January 25-26, 1958), decrying the decay of the city and the silly division of the port and town.

145. *Przekroj* (May, 1957) interview with Dr. Stanislaw Darski, Minister of Marine Affairs.

146. *Economic Survey of Europe, 1956*, p. A-44. For 1957, see Wladyslaw Swirski, "Po Roku—Na *Ziemiach Zachodnich*," *Glos Polski-Gazeta Polska* (Toronto), January 2, 1958.

147. *Pressedienst der Heimatvertriebenen* (46) 1957, p. 3, quoting Polish sources. For Wrocław (Breslau), see "Inisjabywa Wrocława Wsprawach Mieszkaniowych," *Glos Polski-Gazeta Polska* (Toronto), January 2, 1958, remarking that two-thirds of the undestroyed residences of the city need substantial reparations, and in the next five years, funds are available to repair only one-third of them.

148. In the first five months of 1957, repatriate new settlers amounted to only 5,000 families. *Pressedienst der Heimatvertriebenen* (27) 1957, p. 5.

149. Jaxtheimer, "Schlesien unter sowjetpolnischer Verwaltung," *Ost-Kurier*, Vol. I (1), 1958, pp. 2-3, and "Preussentum tut uns not," *Pommersche Zeitung* (May 17, 1958), quoting Polish newspaper sources.

150. *Die deutschen Ostgebiete jenseits von Oder und Neisse im Spiegel der polnischen*

Presse, ed. by Göttinger Arbeitskreis (Würzburg, Holzner, 1958), pp. 58-99 brings dozens of Polish accounts reaffirming the shady side of life in the provinces.

151. *Odbudowa* is one of the publications of the Instytut, but many other publications deal with the fate of Silesia in the German Reich.

152. Report as reproduced in *Pressedienst der Heimatvertriebenen* (31) 1957.

153. Thaddeus Machrowitz, *On Polish Provinces East of the Oder-Neisse Line and Economic, Historical, Legal and Political Aspects Involved,* pp. 3-4.

154. *Ibid.,* p. 16.

155. Stephan Arski, *The New Polish-German Border: Safeguard of Peace,* p. 6.

156. *Ibid.,* p. 11.

157. *Ibid.*

158. *Ibid.,* pp. 14-18.

159. Jaxtheimer, "Schlesien unter sowjetpolnischer Verwaltung," *Ost-Kurier,* Vol. I (1), 1958, p. 3, to quote a fairly objective German source.

160. Witold Nowosad, "Pochodnia Nadzici," *Syrena* (Paris), January 31, 1958.

161. Machrowitz, *op. cit.,* p. 4.

162. As quoted in *Glos Koszalinski* (January 3, 1958).

163. "Niezalatwione zagadnienia na Ziemiach Zachodnich," *Narodowiec* (January 10, 1957), gives 27.2 per thousand births in the provinces compared to 19.4 per thousand in Poland proper.

164. On population fluctuation, see *Zycie gospodarcze* (February 3, 1957); *Po prostu* (April 14, 1957); *Glos Koszalinski* (October 4, 1956); *Gazeta Zielonogorska* (February 22, 1957); *Miasto* (Warsaw), September, 1956. Cf. *Pressedienst der Heimatvertriebenen* (3) 1958, pp. 2-3; *ibid.* (6) 1958, pp. 5-6, quoting *Nowa Kultura; ibid.* (8) 1958, p. 2, quoting *Odra* (Wrocław); *ibid.* (16) 1958, p. 5, quoting *Kurier Szczecinski.* Cf. "What was, at first, a trickling beeline leading back to Poland proper is gradually taking the proportion of a rising tide." Carroll Reece, *On German Provinces East of the Oder-Neisse Line, and Economic, Historical, Legal and Political Aspects Involved,* p. 7.

165. On the death of small towns, see Neumann, *op. cit.,* pp. 23-25. Cf. *Rada Narodo* (June 8, 1957); *Slowo Polskie* (January 6-7, 1957); *Gazeta Zielonogorska* (November 5, 1957); *Zycie gospodarcze* (August 11, 1957); *Glos Koszalinski* (March 26, 1957); and *Gazeta handlowa* (December 14, 1957).

166. Reece uses the figure 6.7 million, Lipsius 6.5 million in *Pressedienst der Heimatvertriebenen,* 27 (1957), while a Polish broadcast last summer spoke of 7.3 million, and *Narodowiec* (January 10, 1958) uses the figure 7.2 million. About 7 million seems to be correct.

167. *Gazeta Zielonogorska* (December 12, 1957).

168. Arski, *op. cit.,* p. 7.

169. *Ibid.,* p. 36.

170. Wiskemann, *op. cit.,* pp. 5-14.

171. Radio Warsaw, May 31, 1957, as quoted in *Pressedienst der Heimatvertriebenen* (23), 1957, p. 3.

172. Wiskemann, *op. cit.,* p. 209.

173. Alojzy Szoga, "Tej szansy nie marnować," *Zycie gospodarcze* (May 26, 1957).

174. Machrowitz, *op. cit.,* p. 6, and Wiskemann, *op. cit.,* pp. 2-12, to quote only two.

175. As quoted in *Pressedienst der Heimatvertriebenen* (23), 1957, monitoring May 31, 1957, broadcast.

176. In *Bulletin of the Institute for Urban Development* (Warsaw), as quoted in *ibid.* (4), 1958, pp. 4-5.

177. Lipsius, *op. cit.,* p. 3, gives 6.5 million and Reece, *op. cit.,* 6.7 million persons.

178. Not less than twenty-seven Polish reports dealing with the province are reproduced in *Die deutschen Ostgebiete im Spiegel der polnischen Presse,* pp. 53-68, and there

were numerous sources in the years of 1956-58 which are not included in that collection.

179. Radio Warsaw, May 28, 1957, quoting the Polish News Agency (PAP).

180. Machrowitz, *op. cit.*, p. 6.

181. See Larry Rue in the *Chicago Daily Tribune*, May 12, 1957.

182. For the brick processes of Wrocław (Breslau), see *Slowo Polskie* (February 3-4, 1957) and *Glos Szczecinski* (March 9-10, 1957) for the Szczecin (Stettin) wreckings and dismantlings.

183. B. Z., "Okruchy z jednego Miasteczka," *Slowo Polskie* (May 4, 1957). Cf. *Nowa Cultura* about the reappearance of the German language in Upper Silesia, as quoted in *Pressedienst der Heimatvertriebenen* (8) 1957, p. 4. For German commentaries on the "autochthons" and their life, see "Die Wahrheit über die Autochthonen," *Pressedienst der Heimatvertriebenen* (19) 1957, p. 4; Eduard Jennicke, "Autonomie für Autochthonen," *ibid.* (21) 1957, pp. 1-2; "Nicht 65,000, sondern 1.1 Millionen," *ibid.* (34) 1957, pp. 2-3; Eduard Jennicke, "Aus dem polnischen Wörterbuch," *ibid.* (8-12) 1958; "Autochthone," *ibid.* (16) 1957.

CHAPTER VIII

1. Byrnes, *Speaking Frankly*, pp. 80-86.

2. *Parliamentary Debates*, Vol. CDXIII, p. 293.

3. *Ibid.*, pp. 83-84.

4. *Documents on American Foreign Relations*, Vol. VIII, pp. 216-17.

5. Department of State *Bulletin* (April 20, 1947), pp. 693-94.

6. *Ibid.*, p. 693.

7. *Ibid.*, p. 694.

8. *Ibid.*

9. *Ibid.*

10. *Ibid.*

11. *Documents on American Foreign Relations*, Vol. IX, p. 45.

12. Department of State *Bulletin* (April 20, 1947), p. 694.

13. *Ibid.*

14. *Documents on American Foreign Relations*, Vol. IX, p. 45.

15. *Die Neue Zeitung*, June 8, 1950.

16. Herbert Kraus (ed.), *Germany's Eastern Territories*, quoting the *New York Times*, March 26, 1952.

17. *Four Power Conference in Berlin, 1954: Speeches and Documents* (cited hereafter as *Four Power Conference*), p. 60.

18. *New York Times*, September 29, 1955.

19. "Granica na Odrze i Nisie nie moze byc zmieniona," *Narodowiec* (January 22, 1958), quoting editor Matuszewski, Secretary of Polish Socialists in France.

20. *Washington Sunday Star*, February 16, 1958.

21. Ambassador Conant's statement is in *Frankfurter Rundschau* (February 14, 1953).

22. *Survey of International Affairs, 1947–48*, pp. 234-35.

23. *Parliamentary Debates*, Vol. CDXLV, pp. 1876-82. He was backed by Premier Attlee on January 23, 1948, as quoted in Kraus, *Germany's Eastern Territories*, p. 106.

24. *Die Neue Zeitung*, June 8 and 9, 1950.

25. As quoted in Kraus, *Germany's Eastern Territories*, p. 108.

26. *Hannoversche Allgemeine Zeitung*, September 18-19, 1955.

27. *New York Times*, September 29, 1955.

28. Bidault's statement at the Moscow Conference on March 15, 1947, in *Documentation Française*, 593 (April 5, 1947), pp. 1-2.

29. Bidault's speech before the Foreign Affairs Committee of the Assembly on December 20, 1947: "Les modifications intervenues sur la frontière orientale, même si juridiquement elles ne sont pas définitives, nous sont toujours apparues comme malaisement réversibles. Mais la décision définitive ne peut être prise que par un traité de paix qui resolve la problème dans son ensemble." *Documentation Française,* 789 (December 27, 1947), pp. 1-4.

30. *Documents on International Affairs, 1947–48,* pp. 422-44.

31. As quoted in Kraus, *Germany's Eastern Territories,* p. 108.

32. *Pravda,* March 4, 1946.

33. *New York Times,* March 6, 1946.

34. Kraus, *Germany's Eastern Territories,* p. 10.

35. *Documents on International Affairs, 1947–48,* pp. 444ff.

36. Kraus, *Germany's Eastern Territories,* p. 103.

37. *Ibid.,* pp. 103-104.

38. *Ibid.,* pp. 104-105.

39. *Ibid.,* p. 106.

40. *Pressedienst der Heimatvertriebenen,* 46 (1956).

41. *New York Times,* November 27, 1947.

42. *Four Power Conference,* pp. 98-99.

43. *New York Times,* July 27, 1956.

44. *Statistical Pocketbook on Expellees,* pp. 3-4. By 1958, the number of expellees increased to 9,100,000. *Pressedienst der Heimatvertriebenen,* 22 (1958), p. 7.

45. *Statistical Pocketbook on Expellees,* p. 3.

46. *Ibid.,* p. 24.

47. Calculations of the author on the basis of *ibid.,* p. 3.

48. *Deutschlands Ostproblem,* p. 179.

49. *Statistical Pocketbook on Expellees,* p. 5.

50. *Ibid.,* pp. 5-8.

51. *Das deutsche Flüchtlingsproblem,* p. 82.

52. *Ibid.*

53. *Ibid.,* pp. 52-53.

54. *Deutschlands Ostproblem,* p. 181.

55. Eugen Lemberg, *Die Ausweisung als Schicksal und Aufgabe,* pp. 18-23.

56. Wiskemann, *op. cit.,* pp. 192ff.

57. Lemberg, *op. cit.,* pp. 20-22.

58. *Ibid.,* pp. 22f.

59. The Charter is reproduced in *The European Significance of the Oder-Neisse Provinces,* p. 17.

60. At the vote on the Bonn Conventions and the EDC (and also on the Paris Agreements and Germany's accession to NATO), the BHE voted with the government in accepting them.

61. *Deutschlands Ostproblem,* pp. 182-84.

62. *Ibid.,* p. 198. The following paragraphs are based on the past reading of the author of the subject for several years, and it is only for statistical references that *Deutschlands Ostproblem* is used in the footnotes.

63. *Ibid.,* p. 199.

64. *Ibid.*

65. *Ibid.*

66. *Ibid.,* p. 200.

67. *Pressedienst der Heimatvertriebenen,* 22 (1958), p. 8, quoting Federal Republic statistics as of 1957.

68. Cf. Wiskemann, *op. cit.,* pp. 240-46.

69. *Deutschlands Ostproblem,* p. 201.

70. *Ibid.*

71. *Ibid.,* p. 202. Federal Republic, 428 per cent of 1946 level; U.S.S.R., 305 per cent of 1946 level in 1952; Federal Republic, 608 per cent of 1946 level; U.S.S.R., 440 per cent of 1946 level in 1955.

72. Eduard Jennicke, "Die geborgte Prosperität Westdeutschlands," *Pressedienst der Heimatvertriebenen,* 32 (1957), pp. 1-2.

73. *Deutschlands Ostproblem,* p. 204.

74. Wiskemann, *op. cit.,* p. 204. The 1953 figures: 55 per cent positive; 17 per cent perhaps; 20 per cent no; 8 per cent uncertain on return.

75. See *Deutschlands Ostproblem,* pp. 204-205, for the figures.

76. For the 1939 figures, see *supra,* Chap. I.

77. *Deutschlands Ostproblem,* p. 205.

78. Wiskemann, *op. cit.,* pp. 193 and 196.

79. Even Miss Wiskemann recognizes the fact that Professor Oberländer showed moderation as a minister. *Ibid.,* p. 196. For an attack on his personnel policies, see *Süddeutsche Zeitung,* May 21, 1954.

80. Wiskemann, *op. cit.,* p. 193.

81. This record is based on personal conversations of the author with several friends of Professor Oberländer and upon the description of Miss Wiskemann.

82. Wiskemann, *op. cit.,* pp. 192-93.

83. *Frankfurter Allgemeine Zeitung,* July 13, 1953.

84. *Deutschlands Ostproblem,* p. 185.

85. *London Times,* December 20, 1950.

86. U.S. High Commissioner in Germany (ed.), *Elections in Germany, 1945–1952, passim.*

87. For the results of the 1953 elections, see the *Bulletin* of the Press and Information Bureau of the Federal Government (September 17, 1957).

88. A description of the dissensions can be found in both *Deutschlands Ostproblem,* p. 185, and Wiskemann, *op. cit.,* pp. 194-95.

89. *Frankfurter Allgemeine Zeitung,* September 16, 1957.

90. *Deutschlands Ostproblem,* pp. 184-86.

91. *Die Pommersche Zeitung,* January 4, 1958, p. 2.

92. *Ibid.*

93. *Ibid.*

94. For a description of the *Zentralverband,* see *Deutschlands Ostproblem,* pp. 182-83, and Wiskemann, *op. cit.,* pp. 180-84.

95. *Wesen und Bedeutung des landsmannschaftlichen Gendankens, passim,* and Wiskemann, *op. cit.,* pp. 180-84.

96. For a description of the 1958 Kassel Whitsunday meeting of the Pomeranians with 80,000 participants, see *Die Pommersche Zeitung,* May 31, 1958.

97. The *Göttinger Arbeitskreis* alone published more than one hundred books, sixty booklets, and a dozen works in French and English besides its weekly press digest.

98. The best exposition of the German legal argument was given by Professor Herbert Kraus in *Deutschlands Ostproblem,* pp. 11-40, which exposé will be used as basic reference.

99. *Supra,* Chap. VIII.

100. Günter Decker, *Das Selbstbestimmungsrecht der Nationen, passim.*

101. Professor Kraus uses the German term *internationale Ordnungsgrundsatze. Deutschlands Ostproblem,* p. 11.

102. For the Declaration; see U.S. Senate, *A Decade of American Foreign Policy,* 81st Congress, 1st Session, p. 507.

103. *Supra,* Chap. VI.

104. *Parliamentary Debates,* Vol. CCXCVII (1944), pp. 698-99.

105. *Deutschlands Ostproblem,* p. 14.

106. Churchill, *The Grand Alliance,* p. 695.

107. *Deutschlands Ostproblem,* p. 16.

108. *Ibid.,* p. 18.

109. "First: That the principle of conquest shall not, during the continuance of the treaty of arbitration, be recognized as admissible under American Public Law. Second, That all cessions of territory made under the continuance of the treaty of arbitration shall be void if made under threats of war in presence of an armed force." International American Conference, Washington, 1889-90, *Reports,* Vol. II, 1147ff.

110. Pitman B. Potter, *An Introduction to the Study of International Organization,* *passim.*

111. *Deutschlands Ostproblem,* pp. 24-28.

112. *Ibid.,* pp. 27-28.

113. *Ibid.,* p. 29, Note 33, quoting literally the Russian text in German translation.

114. Sarah Wambaugh, *A Monograph on Plebiscites,* p. 950.

115. *United Nations Bulletin XII* (September 1, 1952), p. 253.

116. *Annuaire d'Institut de Droit International,* Vol. XV, p. 271.

117. As quoted in *Deutschlands Ostproblem,* p. 36, Note 21.

118. *Ibid.,* pp. 34-36.

119. *The Trials of Major War Criminals,* Vol. I, p. 256.

120. *Annuaire d'Institut de Droit International* (1952), p. 148 (translation from the French by the author).

121. *Malta and Yalta,* p. 911.

122. *Supra,* Chap. I.

123. To quote just a few: *Pressedienst der Heimatvertriebenen,* 7 (1958), citing articles from *Zycie gospodarcze, Odra,* and *Glos Olsztynski* on these subjects of neglect and lack of resources.

124. Peter H. Seraphim, *Deutschlands verlorene Montanwirtschaft, passim.*

125. *Bulletin* of the Press and Information Bureau of the Federal Government (July 31, 1953).

126. *Tagesspiegel* (Berlin), October 23, 1953.

127. *Government Statement, 20 October 1953,* p. 32.

128. *New York Herald Tribune,* October 4, 1956.

129. For Blücher, see *Verhandlungen des Deutschen Bundestages* (cited hereafter as *Verhandlungen*), XV, 2501C-D. For Kaiser, see *Bulletin* of the Press and Information Bureau of the Federal Government (April 14, 1955), p. 570. For Hallstein, see *Verhandlungen* (February 17, 1955), 3381D and 3382A.

130. "The establishment of diplomatic relations between the government of the Federal Republic of Germany and the government of the U.S.S.R. does not constitute recognition of the present territorial ownership on either side. The final delimitation of Germany's frontiers shall await the Peace Treaty." *Bulletin* of the Press and Information Bureau of the Federal Government (September 15, 1955).

131. *Die Welt* (Hamburg), May 3, 1956.

132. *Bulletin* of the Press and Information Bureau of the Federal Government (May 4, 1956).

133. *Ibid.*

134. *Ibid.*

135. For the letters of Dr. Kather and Baron von Manteuffel-Szoege, see Kraus *Germany's Eastern Territories,* pp. 127-28.

136. *VdL Information* (May 21, 1956).

137. *Hannoversche Allgemeine Zeitung,* May 30, 1956.

138. *New York Times*, September 23, 1957.

139. Wiskemann, *op. cit.*, pp. 12-21.

140. *Ibid.*, Introduction.

141. For the detailed German proposals, see *Deutschlands Ostproblem*, pp. 206ff.

142. *Ibid.*, pp. 210-14.

143. *Ibid.*, p. 209.

144. Cf. Jaxtheimer, "Schlesien unter sowjetpolnisher Verwaltung," *Ost-Kurier*, Vol. I(1), pp. 2-3.

145. *Deutschlands Ostproblem*, p. 214.

146. *Ibid.*, pp. 214ff.

BIBLIOGRAPHY

Documents, Government Publications, and Memoirs

Byrnes, James F. *Restatement of United States Policy in Germany: Address by the Secretary of State Delivered in Stuttgart, Germany, September 6, 1946.* Publications of the Department of State, No. 2616. Washington, Government Printing Office, 1946.

———. *Speaking Frankly.* New York, Harper & Brothers, 1947.

Churchill, Winston S. *Broadcast by the Prime Minister, Mr. Winston Churchill, to the Polish People, May 3, 1941.* New York, British Library of Information, 1941.

———. *The Second World War.* Boston, Houghton Mifflin Company, 1948-53. Six vols. Vol. III, *The Grand Alliance.* Vol. IV, *The Hinge of Fate* Vol. V, *Closing the Ring.* Vol. VI, *Triumph and Tragedy.*

———. *The Sinews of Peace: Post-War Speeches.* Boston, Houghton Mifflin Company, 1949.

———. *War Speeches.* Boston, Houghton Mifflin Company, 1953. Three vols.

Collections des documents concernant l'adresse du Gouvernement de la Ville Libre de Dantzig, soumise pour décision au Haut Commissaire de la Société des Nations à Dantzig sur la question de Dantzig-Gdingen. Danzig, Bäcker, 1930.

Concise Statistical Yearbook of Poland. Warsaw, 1930.

Danzig, Senate. *Amtliche Urkunden zum Vertrage zwischen der Freien Stadt Danzig und der Republik Polen vom 9. November 1920.* Danzig, 1920.

———. *Danzig vor dem Völkerbund.* Danzig, 1922-38. Eight vols.

Deutsches Büro für Friedensfragen. *Osthandbuch.* Stuttgart, 1949. Eighteen vols.

Documenta occupationis teutonicae. Poznań, Instytut Zachodni, 1952. Vol. V, *Hitlerowskie "Prawo" Okupacyjne w Polsce,* ed. by Karol Marian Pospieszalski.

Documents on American Foreign Relations. Ed. by R. Dennett and R. K. Turner. New York, Harper & Brothers, 1946-51. Vols. VIII-XII.

Documents on International Affairs, 1939–1946. New York, Oxford University Press, 1954. Vol. II, *Hitler's Europe.*

Documents on International Affairs, 1947–48. New York, Oxford University Press, 1952.

France, Ministère des affaires étrangères. *The French Yellow Book.* New York, Reynal and Hitchcock, 1940.

Entscheidungen des Hohen Kommissars des Völkerbundes in der Freien Stadt Danzig. Danzig, Kafemann, 1926. Vol. III.

Germany, Auswärtiges Amt. *Amtliches Material zum Massenmord von Katyn, im Auftrage des Auswärtigen Amtes auf Grund urkundlichen Beweismaterials zusammengestellt, bearbeitet und herausgegeben von der Deutschen Informationsstelle.* Berlin, Deutscher Verlag, 1943.

————. *Der Aufstand im oberschlesischen Industriegebiet, August und September 1920.* Berlin, Reichsdruckerei, 1920.

————. *Dokumente polnischer Grausamkeit.* Berlin, Volk und Reich, 1940.

————. *Dokumente zur Vorgeschichte des Krieges.* Basel, Birkhauser, 1940.

————. *Documents and Materials Relating to the Eve of the Second World War.* Moscow, Foreign Languages Publishing House, 1948. Vol. II.

————. *Documents Concerning the Last Phase of the German-Polish Crisis.* Berlin, Reichsdruckerei, 1939.

————. *Documents on German Foreign Policy, 1918–1945.* Washington, Government Printing Office, 1949—. Series D. Vol. II, *Germany and Czechoslovakia, 1937–1938.* Vol. IV, *The Aftermath of Munich, October 1938–March 1939.* Vol. V, *Poland; The Balkans; Latin America; The Smaller Powers, June 1937–March 1939.* Vol. VII, *The Last Days of Peace, August 9–September 3, 1940.* Vol. X, *The War Years, June 23–August 31, 1940.*

————. *Polish Documents Relative to the Origin of the War: First Series.* Berlin, Deutscher Verlag, 1940. Vol. I.

————. *Zusammenstellung von Protokollen über den dritten polnischen Aufstand.* Berlin, 1921. Six vols.

Germany, Statistisches Bundesamt. *Statistical Pocketbook on Expellees in the Federal Republic of Germany and West Berlin.* Wiesbaden, 1953.

Germany, Statistisches Reichsamt. *Statistisches Jahrbuch für das*

Deutsche Reich. Berlin, Verlag für Sozialpolitik, Wirtschaft und Statistik, 1936.

Germany, Press and Information Bureau of the Federal Government. *Four Power Conference in Berlin, 1954: Speeches and Documents.* Berlin, 1954.

———. *Government Statement, 20 October 1953.* Bonn, Bundesverlag, 1953.

Göttinger Arbeitskreis. *Dokumente europäischer Leistung in den Heimatgebieten der deutschen Vertriebenen (European Achievements in the Homelands of the German Expellees).* Kitzingen, Holzner, 1954.

Great Britain, Foreign Office. *Documents on British Foreign Policy, 1919–1939.* London, His Majesty's Stationery Office, 1946—. Vols. III and IV.

Great Britain, House of Commons. *Parliamentary Debates, 1939–1947.* London, His Majesty's Stationery Office, 1940-47.

Hull, Cordell. *The Memoirs of Cordell Hull.* New York, Macmillan, 1948. Two vols.

Marshall, George Catlett. *The Problems of European Survival and German and Austrian Peace Settlements: Address by the Secretary of State.* Publications of the Department of State, No. 2990. Washington, Government Printing Office, 1947.

Poland, Central Statistical Office. *Statistical Yearbook of Poland 1947.* Warsaw, 1948.

Poland, Centrum informacji i dokumentarcji. *German Propaganda of Slander Against Poland.* Angers, 1940.

———. *The Polish Territory Occupied by the Germans.* Angers, 1940.

———. *The Polish Territory Occupied by the Soviets.* Angers, 1940.

Poland, Ministerstwo informacji. *The Black Book of Poland.* New York, G. P. Putnam's Sons, 1942.

Poland, Ministrowo spraw zagranicznych. *Documents on the Hostile Policy of the United States Government Toward People's Poland.* Warsaw, Institute of International Affairs, 1953.

———. *German Occupation of Poland.* New York, Graystone Press, 1942.

———. *Notes sur le plébiscite en Haute Silèsie, Mars 1921.* N.p., 1921.

———. *Official Documents Concerning Polish-German and Polish-Soviet Relations, 1933–39.* London, Hutchinson, 1940.

Poland: Recovered Territories. Poznań, Zachodnia Agenji Prasowa, 1947.

Polish-Soviet Relations, 1918–1943: Official Documents. Washington, Polish Embassy, 1943.

Programm des Blocks der Heimvertriebenen und Entrechteten. Bonn, 1951.

Rosenman, Samuel I. (ed.). *The Public Papers and Addresses of Franklin D. Roosevelt.* New York, Random House, 1938-50. Vols. IX-XIII.

Sammlung der Dokumente in der Streitsache zwischen der Freien Stadt Danzig und der Republik Polen betreffs Artikel 33 des Danzig-polnischen Vertrages vom 9. November 1920. Danzig, Bäcker, 1931.

Schieder, Theodor (ed.). *Dokumentation der Vertreibung der Deutschen aus Ost-Mitteleuropa.* Vols. I (1) and I (2), *Die Vertreibung der deutschen Bevölkerung aus den Gebieten östlich der Oder und Neisse.* Bonn, Bundesministerium für Vertriebene, Flüchtlinge und Kriegsbeschädigte, 1955-56.

Seidl, Alfred (ed.). *Die Beziehungen zwischen Deutschland und der Sowjetunion, 1939—1941: Dokumente des Auswärtigen Amtes.* Tübingen, H. Lampp, 1949.

Societé des Nations, Journal Officiel. *Constitution de la Ville Libre de Dantzig.* Supplement Special, 1922.

Soviet-Polish Relations: A Collection of Official Documents and Press Extracts, 1944–1946. London, "Soviet News," 1946.

Stettinius, Edward R., Jr. *Roosevelt and the Russians: The Yalta Conference.* Garden City, Doubleday, 1949.

Truman, Harry S. *Memoirs.* Garden City, Doubleday, 1955-56. Two vols.

Übereinkommen zwischen der Freien Stadt Danzig und der Republik Polen betreffs die Ausnutzung des Danziger Hafens und die Behandlung polnischer Staatsangehöriger und anderer Personen polnischer Herkunft oder Sprache auf dem Gebiete der Freien Stadt Danzig, vom 5. August 1933 bzw. 18. September 1933. Danzig, 1933.

United States Congress, House of Representatives, Committee on Foreign Affairs. *Terminating the State of War Between the United States and the Government of Germany: Report to Accompany House Joint Resolution 289.* Eighty-second Congress, 1st Session. Washington, Government Printing Office, 1951.

United States Congress, House of Representatives, Select Committee to Conduct an Investigation of the Facts, Evidence and Circumstances of the Katyn Forest Massacre. *Hearings.* Eighty-second

Congress, 1st Session. Washington, Government Printing Office, 1952.

United States Congress, Senate, Committee on Foreign Relations. *A Decade of American Foreign Policy.* Eighty-first Congress, 1st Session. Washington, Government Printing Office, 1950.

United States Department of State. *Foreign Relations of the United States: Diplomatic Papers, 1939.* Vol. I, *General.* Vol. II, *General, British Commonwealth, Europe.*

————. *Foreign Relations of the United States: Diplomatic Papers, 1940.* Vol. II, *General and Europe.*

————. *Foreign Relations of the United States: Diplomatic Papers, The Conferences of Malta and Yalta, 1945.*

————. *The Moscow Meeting of the Council of Foreign Ministers, March 10–April 24, 1947: Address by the Secretary of State.* Publications of the Department of State, No. 2822. Washington, Government Printing Office, 1947.

————. *Nazi-Soviet Relations, 1939–1941: Documents from the Archives of the German Foreign Office.* Washington, Government Printing Office, 1948.

United States Department of State, Office of Coordinator of Information, Research and Analysis Branch, Central European Section. *German-Occupied Poland.* Washington, Government Printing Office, 1942.

United States High Commissioner in Germany. *Elections in Germany, 1945–1952.* Bad Godesberg, 1953.

Die Verhandlungen des Deutschen Bundestages, 1949—1957. Bonn, Bundesverlag, 1949-58.

W dziesiata rocznice poswatania Polskiej Partii Robotniczej (Materialy i dokumenty). Warsaw, 1952.

BIBLIOGRAPHIES

Göttinger Arbeitskreis. *Mein Ostdeutsches Buch.* Würzburg, Holzner, 1955.

————. *Ostdeutsche Bibliographie.* Göttingen, 1954-58. Vols. I-IV.

Hannover, Stadtbibliothek. *Deutscher Osten: Ein Verzeichnis von Büchern und Aufsätzen.* Hannover, 1955. Second ed.

Marzian, Herbert G. *Ostdeutsche Bibliographie.* Kitzingen, Holzner, 1953.

Perlick, Alfons. *Ostdeutsche Bibliographie.* Troisdorf, Der Weg-weiser, 1953.

Rister, Herbert. *Schrifttum über den deutschen Osten, 1945–1951.* Marburg, N. G. Elwert, 1953.

BOOKS, TREATISES, AND MONOGRAPHS

Apenszlak, Jakob. *The Black Book of the Polish Jewry.* New York, The American Federation for Polish Jews, 1943.

Arlt, Fritz. *Siedlung und Landwirtschaft in den eingegliederten Gebieten Oberschlesiens.* Berlin, Sohnrey und Cie., 1942.

————. *Übersicht über die Bevölkerungsverhältnisse im General-gouvernement.* Krakkau, Burgverlag, 1940.

Arski, Stephan. *The New Polish-German Border: Safeguard of Peace.* Washington, Polish Embassy, 1947.

Askezany, F. *Danzig und Polen.* Warsaw, Nakl. Towarzystawa kesow pomorskich, 1919.

Aubin, Hermann. *Der deutsche Osten und das Abendland.* Munich, Volk und Heimat, 1953.

Baer, Max, *Der Adel und der adelige Grundbesitz in Polnischen-Preussen zur Zeit der preussischen Besitzergreifung.* Leipzig, Hir-sel, 1911.

Baginski, Henryk. *Poland and the Baltic: The Problem of Poland's Access to the Sea.* London, Oliver and Boyd, 1942.

Bahr, Ernst. *Ostpommern unter polnischer Verwaltung.* Frankfurt am Main, Metzner, 1957.

Baker, Ray S. *Woodrow Wilson and World Settlement.* Garden City, Doubleday, Page and Company, 1922. Three vols.

Baldwin, Hanson W. *Great Mistakes of the War.* New York, Harper & Brothers, 1950.

Bartlett, Vernon. *East of the Iron Curtain.* New York, McBride, 1950.

Beck, Josef. *Beiträge zur europäischen Politik.* Essen, Essener Verlags-anstalt, 1939.

————. *Dernier rapport . . . Politique Polonaise, 1926–1939.* Neu-chatel, Editiones de la Baconièrre, 1952.

Bernhard, Ludwig. *Die Polenfrage: Der Nationalitätenkampf der Polen in Preussen.* Leipzig, Hirsel, 1930. Third ed.

Bierowki, Theodor. *La Ville libre de Dantzig et la guerre polono-bolchevique de 1920.* Danzig, 1920.

Bierschenk, Theodor. *Die deutsche Volksgruppe in Polen, 1934–1939.* Würzburg, Holzner, 1954. Beiheft X zum *Jahrbuch der Albertus-Universität Königsberg/Preussen.*

Bismarck, Otto Fürst von. *Gedanken und Errinerungen: Reden und Briefe.* Berlin, Safari, 1951.

Blücher, Wipert von. *Deutschlands Weg nach Rapallo: Errinerungen eines Mannes aus dem zweiten Gliede.* Wiesbaden, Limes, 1951.

Bocherau, Abel. *Le Statut de Dantzig.* Poitiers, Poitou, 1924.

Böhmer, Karl. *Deutschland jenseits der Oder-Neisse Linie.* Essen, Tellus, 1956.

Bonnet, Georges Etienne. *Défense de la paix.* Geneva, Editions du Cheval, 1946. Vol. I, *De Washington à Quai d'Orsay.*

Brackmann, Albert (ed.). *Germany and Poland in Their Historical Relations.* Munich, Oldenbourg, 1934.

Breslau, Osteuropa-Institut. *Oberschlesien und der Genfer Schiedsspruch.* Berlin, H. Sack, 1925.

Breyer, Richard. *Das Deutsche Reich und Polen, 1932–1937: Aussenpolitik und Volksgruppenfragen.* Würzburg, Holzner, 1956.

Budish, Jakob. *Warsaw Ghetto Uprising.* New York, United Committee to Commemorate the Tenth Anniversary of the Warsaw Ghetto, 1953.

Bühler, Joseph (ed.). *Das General-Gouvernement: Seine Verwaltung und seine Wirtschaft.* Krakkau, Burgverlag, 1943.

Buzek, Josef. *Historya politiki narod owosciowej rzadu pruskiego wobeci Polskow or traktatow wiedenskich do ustaw wyjatkowych z.r. 1908.* Lwów, Nakl. H. Altenberga, 1909.

Ciechanowski, Ian. *Defeat in Victory.* Garden City, Doubleday, 1947.

Cleinow, Georg. *Der Verlust der Ostmark.* Berlin, Volk und Reich, 1934.

Daniel, Rudolf, and Christoph von dem Ropp. *Pommerland ist abgebrannt.* Hamburg, Christoph von dem Ropp, 1956.

The Dark Side of the Moon. London Faber & Faber, 1946.

Davies, Joseph E. *Mission to Moscow.* Garden City, Doubleday, 1943.

Decker, Günter. *Das Selbstbestimmungsrecht der Nationen.* Göttingen, Schwartz, 1955.

De Jong, Louis. *The German Fifth Column in the Second World War.* Chicago, University of Chicago Press, 1956.

Deresiewicz, Janusz. *Okupacja niemiecka na ziemach polskich wlaczonych do Rzeszy, 1939–1945: Studium hystoryczno-gospodarcze.* Poznań, Instytut Zachodni, 1950.

Dettmann, Fran. *Danzig zwischen Deutschland und Polen.* Berlin, Juncker und Dünnhaupt, 1939.

Das deutsche Flüchtlingsproblem (Sonderheft der Zeitschrift für Raumforschung). Bielefeld, F. Eilers, 1951.

Der deutsche Osten: Referate des ersten Ostseminars der Hochschule für politische Wissenschaften. Munich, Isar, 1956.

Deutsche aus Polen heimatverwiesen. Würzburg, Holzner, 1952.

Deutschlands Ostproblem: Eine Untersuchung der Beziehungen des deutschen Volkes zu seine östlichen Nachbarn. Würzburg, Holzner, 1957.

D'Harcourt, Robert, *et al. Frontière polono-allemande.* Paris, Colombe, 1946.

DuPrel, Max Freiherr von. *Das General-Gouvernement.* Würzburg, K. Triltsch, 1942.

Eggert, Oskar. *Geschichte Pommerns.* Kitzingen, Holzner, 1951.

Erfurt, Werner. *Die sowjetrussische Deutschlandspolitik, 1945–1955.* Esslingen, Bechtle, 1956.

Eyck, Erich. *Bismarck.* Erlenbach-Zürich, Eugen Rentsch Verlag, 1941-44. Three vols.

———. *Das persönliche Regiment Wilhelm II.* Erlenbach-Zürich, Eugen Rentsch Verlag, 1948.

Feis, Herbert. *Roosevelt, Churchill, Stalin: The War They Waged and the Peace They Sought.* Princeton, Princeton University Press, 1957.

Fischer, Peter. *Das Recht und der Schutz der polnischen Minderheit in Oberschlesien.* Berlin, Hobbing, 1931.

Flynn, John T. *The Roosevelt Myth.* New York, Devin-Adair, 1956.

Forster, Albert. *Das nationalsozialistische Gewissen in Danzig.* Danzig, Kafemann, 1936.

Fuchs, Karl Hans. *Danzig—What Is It All About?* 1939.

Fürst, Johann. *The Nonsense of the Corridor.* N.p., 1926.

Gafencu, Grigore. *Vorspiel zum Krieg im Osten.* Zürich, Amstutt, Herdegg, 1944.

Gainborough Commission. *Report of the Gainborough Commission on Life and Labour in Germany.* London, Simpkin, Marshall, Hamilton and Kent Company, 1907.

Gause, Fritz. *Deutsch-slawische Schicksalgemeinschaft, Abriss einer Geschichte Ostdeutschlands und seiner Nachbarländer.* Kitzingen, Holzner, 1952.

Geisler, Walter (ed.). *Zur Wirtschaftsgeographie des deutschen Ostens.*

Vol. III, *Die polnische Minderheit in Oberschlesien,* by Otto Ewers (Breslau, Marcus, 1933). Vol. VIII, *Das niederschlesische Industriegebiet,* by George Keil (Berlin, Volk und Reich, 1935). Vol. XV, *Das östliche Mitteleuropa als Verkehrsraum,* by Walter Geisler (Berlin, Volk und Reich, 1938). Vol. XVIII, *Strukturwandel Schlesiens,* by Emil von Lucadou (Berlin, Volk und Reich, 1943).

Gingerich, William Freiherr. *The German Administration of the General Government of Poland, 1939–1941.* Washington, Georgetown University Thesis, 1949.

Gleitze, Bruno. *Ostdeutsche Wirtschaft: Industrielle Standorte und volkswirtschaftliche Kapazitäten des ungeteilen Deutschlands.* Berlin, Duncker und Humboldt, 1956.

Goguel, Rudi. *Oder-Neisse: Eine Dokumentation.* Berlin, Kongress, 1955.

Görlitz, Walter. *Die Junker: Adel und Bauer im deutschen Osten.* Glücksburg, C. A. Starke, 1956.

Göttinger Arbeitskreis. *Polen und Ostdeutschland.* Kitzingen, Holzner, 1948.

Grimm, Friedrich. *Frankreich und der Korridor.* Hamburg, Hanseatische Verlagsanstalt, 1939.

Hahn, Günter H. *Die deutsche Publizistik im Kampf um Oberschlesien.* Berlin, Inaugural Dissertation, 1940.

Hausdorff, Karl (ed.). *Unser Schlesien.* Stuttgart, K. Mayer, 1954.

Heiss, Friedrich (ed.). *Deutschland und der Korridor.* Berlin, Volk und Reich, 1939.

Hitler, Adolf. *Aufrufe, Tagesbefehle und Reden des Führers im Kriege, 1939–1941.* Karlsruhe, 1941. Ed. by the Chef der Zivilverwaltung im Elsass.

———. *Mein Kampf.* Munich, F. Eher Nachfolger, 1943.

Hoffman, Friedrich. *Die Oder-Neisse Linie, politische Entwicklung und völkerrechtliche Lage.* Frankfurt am Main, J. Heinrich, 1941.

Hoffman, Paul. *Die Volksabstimmung in Westpreussen am 11. Juni 1920.* Danzig, Dauer, 1920.

Hupka, Herbert. *Die Oder.* Munich, Gräfe und Unzer, 1957.

Hutchison, Graham Seton. *Silesia Revisited 1929.* London, Simpkin, Marshall, Hamilton and Kent Company, 1930.

Instytut Zachodni (Poznań). *Dolny Śląsk.* Wrocław, 1949.

———. *Odbudowa ziem Odzyskanych 1945–1955.* Poznań, 1957.

———. *Pomorze Zachodnie.* Poznań, 1947.

———. *Warmia i Masury.* Poznań, 1947.

————. *Ziemia Lubuska.* Poznań, 1947.

Janowicz, Zbigniew. *Ustroj administracyjny ziem polskich wcielonych do Rzeszy Niemieckiej, 1939–1945.* Poznań, Instytut Zachodni, 1951.

Jaworski, Tadeusz, *et al. Zur heutigen Lage der deutschen Ostgebiete unter polnischer Verwaltung.* Marburg, J. G. Herder-Institut, 1957.

Jedlicki, Marjan Zigmunt. *Germany and Poland Through the Ages.* Cambridge, Galloway and Porter, 1942.

Jedrychowski, Stefan. *The Recovered Territories, An Integral Part of Poland.* Warsaw, Ksiazka i Wiedza, 1952.

Jordan, Zigmunt (ed.). *The Oder-Neisse Line: A Study of the Political, Economic and European Significance of Poland's Western Frontier.* London, Polish Freedom Movement, 1952.

Kaeckenbeeck, Georges S. F. C. *The International Experiment of Upper Silesia.* London, Oxford University Press, 1942.

Kampers, Friedrich, *et al. Schlesische Landeskunde.* Leipzig, 1913.

Kapitza, Theodor. *Oberschlesien als bevölkerungspolitisches Problem.* Langelsheim-Harz, Oberschlesische Aktion, 1952.

Kaps, Johannes (ed.). *The Tragedy of Silesia, 1945–1946: A Documentary Account with a Special Survey of the Archdiocese of Breslau.* Munich, "Christ Unterwegs," 1952-53.

Karski, Ian. *The Secret State.* Boston, Houghton Mifflin, 1945.

Kauder, Viktor (ed.). *Das Deutschtum in Polen.* Leipzig, Hirsel, 1939.

Kaufmann, Joseph. *The Relation Between Germans, Cashubians and Poles in West Prussia and Danzig.* Danzig, Kafemann, 1919.

Keesing's Contemporary Archives, 1945. London, Keesing's Ltd., 1945.

Kerstein, Edmund S. *Red Star over Poland: A Report from Behind the Iron Curtain.* Appleton, C. C. Nelson, 1947.

Keyser, Erich. *Danzigs Geschichte.* Danzig, Kafemann, 1928. Second ed.

————. *Geschichte der Stadt Danzig.* Kitzingen, Holzner, 1951.

———— *et al. Der Kampf um die Weichsel: Untersuchungen zur Geschichte des polnischen Korridors.* Stuttgart, Deutsche Verlags-Anstalt, 1926.

Klafkowski, Alfons. *Ocupacja niemiecka w Polsce w swietle prava narodow.* Poznań, Instytut Zachodni, 1946.

————. *Podstawy prawne granicy Odra-Nysa na tle unow: Jaltanskiej i Poczdamskiej.* Poznań, Instytut Zachodni, 1947.

Koenigswald, Heinrich von. *Das dritte Problem.* Troisdorf, Wegweiser, 1957.

———. *Land ohne Frieden*. Darmstadt, Buchner, 1955.

Komorowski, (Bor) Thadeus. *Armia podzienna*. London, Nakl. Katolickiego Osrodka Widawniczego Veritas, 1951.

Königk, George. *Der Kampf um die deutsche Ostgrenze in Versailles*. Berlin, Juncker und Dünnhaupt, 1940.

Krakowski, Edouard. *Pologne et Russie*. Paris, R. Laffont, 1946.

Kraus, Herbert. *Die Oder-Neisse Linie: Eine völkerrechtliche Studie*. Köln-Braunsfeld, R. Müller, 1954.

——— (ed.). *Germany's Eastern Territories*. Würzburg, Holzner, 1957.

Krzezinsky, Andrew J. *Poland's Rights to Justice*. New York, Devin-Adair, 1946.

Krzyzanowski, Stanislaw. *O polskosci Śląska Niemieckiego*. Lwów, 1936.

Kudlicki, Stanislaw. *Upper Silesia*. London, Polish Research Center, 1945. Second ed.

Kuhn, Walter. *Geschichte der deutschen Ostsiedlung der Neuzeit*. Köln, Bohlau, 1955-57. Two vols.

———. *Siedlungsgeschichte Oberschlesiens*. Würzburg, Oberschlesischer Heimatverlag, 1954.

Kulischer, Eugen Michel. *Europe on the Move: War and Population Changes, 1917–1946*. New York, Columbia University Press, 1948.

Kusnierz, Bronislaw. *Stalin and the Poles*. London, Hollis & Carter, 1949.

Küster, Rudolf. *Die polnische Irredenta in Westoberschlesien*. Berlin, Hallig, 1931.

Kutrzeba, Stanislaw. *Gdańsk, przeczlosc i tera zniejszosc, prace zbiorewa*. Lwów, Wydawn, 1928.

Lane, Arthur Bliss. *I Saw Poland Betrayed*. Indianapolis, Bobbs-Merrill, 1948.

Laroche, Jules. *La Pologne de Pilsudski: Souvenirs d'une Ambassade, 1926–1935*. Paris, Flammarion, 1953.

Laun, Rudolf. *Das Recht auf die Heimat*. Hannover, Schroedel, 1951.

Leahy, Admiral William D. *I Was There*. New York, McGraw-Hill, 1950.

Lednicki, Waclaw. *Russian-Polish Relations: Their Historical, Cultural and Political Background*. Chicago, National Polish Alliance, 1944.

Lemberg, Eugen. *Die Ausweisung als Schicksal und Aufgabe*. Munich, Gräfe und Unzer, 1950.

Leonhardt, Hans L. *The Nazi Conquest of Danzig*. Chicago, University of Chicago Press, 1942.

Linck, Hugo. *Königsberg, 1945–1948*. Leer, Rautenberg & Mockel, 1952.

Lohmeyer, Karl. *Geschichte von Ost- und Westpreussen*. Gotha, F. A. Perthes, 1881.

Lowenstein, Hubertus Prinz zu, and Volckmar von Auhlsdorff. *Deutschlands Schicksal, 1945—1957*. Bonn, Athenäum, 1957.

Lück, Kurt. *Deutsche Aufbaukräfte in der Entwicklung Polens: Forschungen zur deutsch-polnischen Nachbarschaft im ostmitteleuropäischen Raum*. Plauen, G. Wolff, 1934.

Luczak, Czeslaw. *Przyczynski do gospodarki niemieckiej w latach 1939–1945*. Poznań, Instytut Zachodni, 1949.

Ludat, Herbert. *Der europäische Osten in abendländischer und sowjetischer Sicht*. Köln-Braunsfeld, R. Müller, 1954.

———. *Vorstufen und Entstehung des Städtewesens in Osteuropa*. Köln-Braunsfeld, R. Müller, 1955.

Machray, Robert. *East Prussia: Menace to Poland and Peace*. London, Allen and Unwin, 1943.

———. *The Polish-German Problem*. London, Allen and Unwin, 1941.

———. *The Problem of Upper Silesia*. London, Allen and Unwin, 1945.

Machrowitz, Thaddeus. *On Polish Provinces East of the Oder-Neisse Line and Economic, Historical, Legal and Political Aspects Involved*. Washington, Government Printing Office, 1957.

Mackiewycz, Joseph. *The Katyn Wood Murders*. London, Hollis & Carter, 1951.

Maleczynski, E., *et al. Dolny Śląsk*. Wrocław, Ksiaznica-Atlas, 1948.

Malera, Jean, and Lucienne Rey. *La Pologne d'une occupation à l'autre (1944–1952)*. Paris, Editions des Fuseau, 1952.

Maschke, Herbert. *Die Grundlagen des Internationalen Statuts von Danzig*. Berlin, Stilke, 1936.

Mason, John Brown. *The Danzig Dilemma: A Study in Peace-Making by Compromise*. Stanford, Stanford University Press, 1946.

Mauldin, W. Parker, *et al. The Population of Poland*. Washington, Government Printing Office, 1954.

Meissner, Boris. *Russland, die Westmächte und Deutschland*. Hamburg, H. H. Nolke, 1953.

Mermeix (pseud. of Gabriel Terrail). *Le Combat de Trois: Notes et*

Documents sur la Conférence de la Paix. Paris, Ollendorf, 1922. Fourth ed.

Mikolajczyk, Stanislaw. *The Pattern of Soviet Domination.* London, Sampson, Low, 1948.

Miller, David Hunter. *My Diary at the Conference of Paris.* New York, Appeal, 1924. Twenty-one vols.

Montfort, Henri de. *Dantzig: Port de Pologne dans le passé et dans le présent.* Paris, Bibliothèque Polonaise, 1939.

Morrow, Jan F. D. *The Peace Settlement in the German-Polish Borderlands.* London, Oxford University Press, 1936.

Neumann, Rudolf (ed.). *Ostpreussen unter polnischer und sowjetischer Verwaltung.* Frankfurt am Main, A. Metzner, 1955. Vol. I of *Ostdeutschland unter fremder Verwaltung, 1945–1955.*

Newmann, Bernard. *The Three Germanies.* London, R. Hale, 1957.

Nicolson, Sir Harold. *The Congress of Vienna.* New York, Harcourt, Brace and Company, 1946.

———. *Diplomacy.* London, Oxford University Press, 1950. Second ed.

Nieroda, Josef. *Miasta Pomorze Wachodniego.* Danzig, Instytut Balticki, 1947.

Noel, Léon. *L'aggression allemande contre la Pologne.* Paris, Flammarion, 1946.

Normann, Käthe von. *Ein Tagebuch aus Pommern, 1945–1946.* Bonn, Bundesministerium für Vertriebene, Flüchtlinge und Kriegsgeschädigte, 1955.

Osborne, Sidney. *The Upper Silesian Question and Germany's Coal Problem.* London, Allen and Unwin, 1920.

Ostdeutschland: Ein Hand- und Nachschlagebuch für die Gebiete ostwärts von Oder und Neisse. Kitzingen, Holzner, 1953. Third ed.

Ostland-Schriften, Vol. I, *Gdingen,* by Theodor Johannsen (pseud.) (Danzig, Bureau, 1928). Vol. III, *Polens Zugang zum Meere,* by Walter Recke (Danzig, Bureau, 1930). Vol. IV, *Ostpreussen im polnischen Schrifttum,* by Rudolf Neumann (Danzig, Bureau, 1931). Vol. VI, *Der Abfall Posens 1918–19 im polnischen Schrifttum,* by A. Loessner (Danzig, Danziger Verlagsanstalt, 1933).

Pagel, Karl (ed.). *The German East.* Berlin, K. Lemmer, 1954.

Pardex, Walter. *Das grössere Schlesien.* Breslau, Korn, n.d.

Peuckert, Willi Erich. *Schlesien: Biographie der Landschaft.* Hamburg, Classen, 1950.

Pilsudski, Josef. *Errinerungen und Dokumente.* Essen, Essener Verlagsanstalt, 1935-36. Four vols.

Plutynski, Antony. *Śląsk i Pomorze.* Warsaw, Military Institute for Culture and Education, 1937.

La Pologne et ses terres récouvrées. Paris, Bureau d'information polonaises, 1947.

Potter, Pitman B. *An Introduction to the Study of International Organization.* New York, Appleton-Century-Crofts, 1948.

Puleston, William Dilworth. *The Influence of Force in Foreign Relations.* New York, Van Nostrand, 1955.

Quante, Peter. *Die Bilanz des deutschen Ostens: Zur Frage der Ostodergebiete als Wirtschaftsstandort und Bevölkerungsraum.* Kitzingen, Holzner, 1953.

La question de Dantzig. Paris, Bulletin de Centre Europèen de la Donation Carnegie, 1933.

Rauschning, Hermann. *Die Entdeutschung Westpreussens und Posens.* Berlin, Hobbing, 1930.

Reece, Carroll. *On German Provinces East of the Oder-Neisse Line and Economic, Legal and Political Aspects Involved.* Washington, Government Printing Office, 1957.

Rhode, Gotthold (ed.). *Die Ostgebiete des Deutschen Reiches.* Würzburg, Holzner, 1956.

Rochlin, R. P. *Die Wirtschaft Polens von 1945 bis 1952.* Berlin, Duncker und Humboldt, 1953.

Rose, William John. *The Dream of Upper Silesia.* Brattleboro, S. Daye, 1935.

Rothfels, Hans. *Bismarck-Briefe.* Göttingen, Vandenhoecks & Rupprecht, 1955.

———. *Deutscher Osten und slawischer Westen.* Tübingen, Mohr, 1955.

Rozek, Edward J. *Allied Wartime Diplomacy: A Pattern in Poland.* New York, John Wiley and Sons, 1958.

Sandow, Erich. *Die polnisch-pomerellische Grenze 1309–1454.* Würzburg, Holzner, 1953. Beiheft VI zum *Jahrbuch der Albertus-Universität Königsberg/Preussen.*

Sasse, Hans Günther. *Die ostdeutsche Frage auf den Konferenzen von Teheran bis Potsdam.* Tübingen, M. Niemeyer, 1954.

Schalaster, Herbert. *Der deutsche Osten in seiner geschichtlichen Entwicklung.* Köln-Braunsfeld, R. Müller, 1956.

Schechtmann, Joseph B. *European Population Transfers, 1939–1945.* New York, Oxford University Press, 1946.

Schieder, Theodor. *Die Probleme des Rapallo-Vertrages: Eine Studie über die deutsch-russischen Beziehungen 1922 bis 1926.* Köln, Westdeutscher Verlag, 1956.

Schlenger, Herbert (ed.). *Handbuch der deutschen Ostgebiete.* Stuttgart, Brentano, 1952-56. Three vols. Vol. I, *Die Wirtschaft Ostdeutschlands vor und nach dem Zweiten Weltkriege,* by Peter Heinz Seraphim. Vol. II, *Die Entstehung der Oder-Neisse Linie in den diplomatischen Verhandlungen während des Zweiten Weltkrieges,* by Wolfgang Wagner. Vol. III, *Quellen zur Entstehung der Oder-Neisse Linie in den diplomatischen Verhandlungen während des Zweiten Weltkrieges,* by Gotthold Rhode and Wolfgang Wagner.

Schodrok, Karl (ed.). *Das Erlebnis der oberschlesischen Volksabstimmung.* Neumarkt, Kulturstelle Schlesien, 1951.

Schohl, Eugen. *Die Polenfrage in Oberschlesien.* Mainz, Alldeutsche Verlag, 1911.

Scholtis, August. *Ostwind: Roman der oberschlesischen Katastrophe.* Berlin, S. Fischer, 1932.

Schreiber, Ottomar. *Erbe und Aufgabe des deutschen Ostens.* Munich, Gräfe und Unzer, 1955.

Schumacher, Bruno. *Geschichte Ost- und Westpreussens.* Würzburg, Holzner, 1956.

Seabury, Paul. *The Wilhelmstrasse: A Study of German Diplomacy under the Nazi Regime.* Berkeley, University of California Press, 1946.

Segal, Simon. *Nazi Rule in Poland.* London, Robert Hale, 1943.

Selle, Götz von. *German Thought in East Prussia.* Munich, Gräfe und Unzer, 1948.

―――. *Ostdeutsche Biographien.* Würzburg, Holzner, 1955.

Seraphim, Heinz G. *Die deutsch-russischen Beziehungen 1939–1941.* Hamburg, H. H. Nolke, 1956.

Seraphim, Peter Heinz. *Deutschlands verlorene Montanwirtschaft, die Eisen- und Stahlindustrie Oberschlesiens.* Stuttgart, W. Kohlhammer, 1955.

―――. *Industriekombinat Oberschlesien: Das Ruhrgebiet des Ostens unter sowjetischer Führung.* Köln-Braunsfeld, R. Müller, 1953.

―――. *Ostdeutschland und das heutige Polen.* Braunschweig, G. Westermann, 1953.

————. *Die Ostseehäfen und Ostseeverkehr*. Berlin, Volk und Reich, 1937.

————. *Ostwärts der Oder und Neisse*. Hannover, Wissenschaftlicher Verlagsanstalt, 1949.

Seton-Watson, Hugh. *The East European Revolution*. London, Meuthen, 1956.

Seyda, Marian. *Poland and Germany*. London, Polish Information Center, 1942.

Seymour, Charles (ed.). *The Intimate Papers of Colonel House Arranged as a Narrative*. Boston, Houghton, Mifflin, 1930. Four vols.

Sherwood, Robert E. *Roosevelt and Hopkins: An Intimate History*. New York, Harper & Brothers, 1950.

Shotwell, James T. *Poland and Russia, 1919–1945*. New York, King's Crown Press, 1945.

La Silèsie polonaise. Paris, Gebethner & Wolff, 1932.

Smogorzewski, Kazimierz M. *East Prussia Must Disappear*. London, Free Europe, 1944.

————. *Poland's Access to the Sea*. London, Allen and Unwin, 1934.

————. *La Pologne, l'Allemagne et le "Corridor."* Paris, Gebethner & Wolff, 1929.

————. *La Pomeranie polonaise*. Paris, Gebethner & Wolff, 1932.

————. *Sprawa Śląska na konferencji pokojowej 1919 roku*. Katowice, 1919.

Snell, John L. (ed.). *The Meaning of Yalta*. Baton Rouge, Louisiana State University Press, 1956.

Sobieski, Waclaw. *Der Kampf um die Ostsee von den ältesten Zeiten bis zur Gegenwart*. Leipzig, Marckert und Peters, 1933.

————. *Walka o Pomorze*. Poznań, Nakl. Sw. Wojciecha, 1928.

Sommerfeld, Wilhelm von. *Geschichte der Germanisierung des Herzogthums Pommern*. Leipzig, Duncker und Humboldt, 1896.

Sonntag, Ernst. *Adalbert (Wojciech) Korfanty: Ein Beitrag zur Geschichte der polnischen Ansprüche auf Oberschlesien*. Kitzingen, Holzner, 1953. Beiheft VII zum *Jahrbuch der Albertus-Universität Königsberg/Preussen*.

Starlinger, Wilhelm. *Grenzen der Sowjetmacht*. Würzburg, Holzner, 1955. Beiheft IX zum *Jahrbuch der Albertus-Universität Königsberg/Preussen*.

Studnicki, Wladyslaw. *Irrwege in Polen.* Göttinger Arbeitskreis, 1951.

Survey of International Affairs, 1939–1946. Ed. by Arnold Toynbee. Vol. I, *The World in March 1919* (London, Oxford University Press, 1952). Vol. II, *Hitler's Europe* (London, Oxford University Press, 1954). Vol. III, *Four Power Control in Germany and Austria* (London, Oxford University Press, 1956).

Survey of International Affairs, 1947–1948. Ed. by Peter Calvoressi. London, Oxford University Press, 1952.

Szembek, Jean. *Journal, 1933–1939.* Paris, Plon, 1952.

Szende, Stefan. *The Promise Hitler Kept.* New York, Roy, 1945.

Teichmann, Ulrich. *Die Politik der Agrarpreisunterstützung: Marktbeeinflussung als Agrarinterventionismus in Deutschland.* Köln-Deutz, Bundesverlag, 1955.

Thalheim, Karl Christian, and A. Hillen Ziegfield (eds.). *Der deutsche Osten: Seine Geschichte, sein Wesen und seine Aufgabe.* Berlin, Propyläen Verlag, 1936.

Thorwald, Jürgen. *Es begann an der Weichsel.* Stuttgart, Steingruben, 1950.

———. *The Flight in the Winter.* London, Hutchinson, 1953.

Tippelskirch, Kurt von. *Geschichte des Zweiten Weltkrieges.* Bonn, Athenäum, 1956. Second ed.

Tymieniecki, Kazimierz. *History of Polish Pomerania.* Poznań, Society of the Lovers of History, 1929.

Umiastowski, Roman. *Poland, Russia and Great Britain, 1941–1945: A Study of Evidence.* London, Hollis & Carter, 1946.

Vansittart, Lord Robert Gilbert. *Bones of Contention.* New York, Knopf, 1945.

Violations de Traité de Paix par les Allemands en Haute-Silèsie. Paris, Laure, 1920.

Volz, Wilhelm. *Die ostdeutsche Wirtschaft: Eine wirtschaftsgeographische Untersuchung uber die natürlichen Grundlagen des deutschen Ostens und seine Stellung in der gesamtdeutschen Wirtschaft.* Langensalza, J. Beltz, 1930.

Wambaugh, Sarah. *A Monograph on Plebiscites.* Washington, Carnegie Endowment for International Peace, 1920.

———. *Plebiscites Since the World War with a Collection of Official Documents.* Washington, Carnegie Endowment for International Peace, 1933. Two vols.

Wandel, Paul. *Die junkerlich-imperialistische Politik des "Dranges nach Osten"—ein Unglück für das deutsche und polnische Volk.* Berlin, Verlag Volk und Wissen, 1952.

Warriner, Doreen. *Revolution in Eastern Europe.* London, Turnstille, 1950.

Wasilewski, Stanislaw. *Na Śląska Opolskim.* Katowice, Instytut Śląsky, 1937.

Wassermann, Charles. *Unter polnischer Verwaltung: Tagebuch 1957.* Hamburg, Blüchert, 1957.

Wehberg, Hans. *Krieg und Eroberung im Wandel des Völkerrechts.* Frankfurt am Main, A. Metzner, 1953.

Wende, Gerhard. *Die Auswirkungen der Grenzziehung auf die oberschlesische Montanindustrie.* Stuttgart, Deutsche Verlags-Anstalt, 1932.

Wesen und Bedeutung des landmannschaftlichen Gedankens. Munich, "Christ Unterwegs," 1952.

Who's Who of the Regime in Poland. Edinburgh, Scottish League for European Freedom, 1947.

Wilder, Jan Antoni. *The Polish Regained Provinces.* London, W. Hodge, 1948.

Winiewicz, Josef F. *Aims and Failures of the German New Order.* London, Polish Research Center, 1943.

———. *The Polish-German Frontier.* London, W. Hodge, 1945.

Wiskemann, Elizabeth. *Germany's Eastern Neighbors.* London, Oxford University Press, 1956.

Worgitski, M. *Geschichte der Abstimmung in Ostpreussen.* Leipzig, Hirsel, 1921.

Zachodnia Agencja Prasowa. *Jezyk Polski na Śląsku Opolskim w latach 1910–1939: Swiadectwa Niemieckie.* Poznań, 1957.

Zaleska, Maria. *Odra-Nysa, najlepsza granica Polski.* Poznań, Instytut Zachodni, 1946. Second ed.

Zawidzki, Marian (ed.). *Prusy Wschodine: Przeszlosci teraźniejszość.* Poznań, Instytut Zachodni, 1932.

Zehn Jahre nach der Vertreibung: Äusserungen des In- und Auslandes und eine Zeittafel. Bonn, Bundesministerium fur Vertriebene, Flüchtlinge und Kriegsgeschädigte, 1956.

Zielinski, Henryk. *Population Changes in Poland, 1939–1950.* New York, Mid-European Studies Center, 1954.

Zink, Harold. *The United States in Germany, 1944–1955.* New York, Van Nostrand, 1956.

ARTICLES

"Die Antwort auf die Cyriankiewycz-Aktion," *Pressedienst der Heimatvertriebenen* (16), 1957.

"Die Berliner Erklärung und die Oder-Neisse Frage," *Pressedienst der Heimatvertriebenen* (31), 1957.

Brailsford, H. M. "Germany Needs Not Only Danzig But Posen," *London Daily News,* January 18, 1919.

Brehm, Bruno. "Polens Schicksal als Beispiel," *Der europäische Osten* (December, 1957), pp. 742-45.

Brzezinski, Zbigniew. "Die grosse Wandlung in Polen," *Der europäische Osten* (January, 1958), pp. 37-40.

Buczak, Edward. "Polska Ostenda, Optymizm Kolobrzegu," *Dziennik Balticki,* January 23, 1958.

"Bywa i tak," *Trybuna Ludu,* February 1, 1958.

B. Z. "Okruchy z jednego Miasteczka," *Slowo Polskie* (May 4, 1957).

Celovsky, Boris. "Pilsudskis Präventivkrieg gegen das nationalsozialistische Deutschland," *Die Welt als Geschichte* (1954), pp. 53-70.

"Die Cyrankiewicz-Aktion," *Pressedienst der Heimatvertriebenen* (42), 1957.

Dabrowa, Marek, *et al.* "Sprawy Ziem Zachodnich," *Zycie gospodarcze,* February 3, 10, and 17, 1957.

Decker, Günther. "Die Rechtspflicht zur Wiedervereinigung," *Pressedienst der Heimatvertriebenen* (39), 1957.

"Deutsche Welle-Ost," *Pressedienst der Heimatvertriebenen* (3), 1957.

Dmochowski, Zygmunt. "Szczecin od macochy?" *Glos Szczecinski,* May 22, 1957.

"Do czego zmierza reżymowa akcja łacznosci z Krajem?" *Narodowiec,* January 11, 1958.

Dolinski, A. "Ekologia spoleczna Ołsztyna," *Warmia i Masury,* January 12, 1958.

"Engerer Kontakt mit Warschau?" *Pressedienst der Heimatvertriebenen* (48), 1956.

"Zur Entwicklung des deutschsprachigen Schulwesens in den polnisch besetzten Gebieten," *Pressedienst der Heimatvertriebenen* (3), 1957.

"Die geborgte Prosperität Westdeutschlands," *Pressedienst der Heimatvertriebenen* (32), 1957.

Gierczynski, J. "Dwunasty alarm," *Glos Koszalinski,* March 25, 1957.

Gleitze, Bruno. "Deutschlands Verflechtung mit dem Osten," *Der europäische Osten* (August, 1957), pp. 465-71.

"Gomulka und Tito," *Pressedienst der Heimatvertriebenen* (37), 1957.

Gordon, Edmund von. "Die deutsch-polnische Annäherung," *Der europäische Osten* (August, 1957), pp. 449-50.

————. "Gemeinsame deutsch-polnische Ostpolitik," *Der europäische Osten* (January, 1958), pp. 1-2.

Görlitz, Walter. "Preussens Polenpolitik," *Der europäische Osten* (March, 1958), pp. 162-67.

"Granica na Odrze i Nisie nie mose byc zmieniona," *Narodowiec,* January 22, 1958.

Groba, Kurt. "Wirtschaftswende im schlesischen Raum," *Schlesisches Jahrbuch* (1940), pp. 61ff.

"Die Hamburger Polenspekulation," *Pressedienst der Heimatvertriebenen* (6), 1957.

"Die Hintergründe der Gordon-Erklärung," *Pressedienst der Heimatvertriebenen* (7), 1957.

Izydorczyk, Jan. "W obliczu powaznych zadan," *Trybuna Ludu,* May 26, 1957.

Jaksch, Wenzel. "Westeuropa-Ostdeutschland-Gesamteuropa," *Aussenpolitik* (August, 1957), pp. 487-502.

Jaxtheimer, Bodo. "Das Leben in Schlesien heute," *Der europäische Osten* (February, 1958), pp. 104-10.

————. "Schlesien unter sowjetpolnischer Verwaltung," *Ost-Kurier,* I (1), 1958, pp. 1-4.

Jennicke, Eduard. "Aus dem polnischem Wörterbuch," *Pressedienst der Heimatvertriebenen* (8-12), 1958.

————. "Autonomie für die Autochthonen," *Pressedienst der Heimatvertriebenen* (21), 1957.

————. "Die Folgen der Austreibung," *Pressedienst der Heimatvertriebenen* (39), 1956.

————. "Gründe und Hintergründe der Spätaussiedlung," *Pressedienst der Heimatvertriebenen* (10), 1957.

————. "Die 'Monroe-Doktrin' der Ostvertriebenen," *Pressedienst der Heimatvertriebenen* (28), 1956.

————. "Moskau und die Oder-Neisse Frage," *Pressedienst der Heimatvertriebenen* (48), 1957.

————. "Um eine realistische Ostpolitik," *Pressedienst der Heimatvertriebenen* (40), 1957.

————. "Ungerecht Gut gedeiht nicht," *Pressedienst der Heimatvertriebenen* (50), 1956.

————. "Zur Entstehungsgeschichte des ethnischen Nationalismus," *Pressedienst der Heimatvertriebenen* (2), 1957.

Jerzykiewicz, F. E. O. "Zur deutsch-polnischen Frage," *Der europäische Osten* (October, 1956), pp. 595ff.

Kalamaczka, Barbara. "Prszeszkadza zawsze to samo," *Glos Szczecinski,* April 14, 1957.

"Kanal Odra-Dunaj," *Dziennik Polski,* January 23, 1958.

Katelback, Tadeusz. "Was Deutschland und Polen verbindet," *Der europäische Osten* (April, 1958), pp. 215-20.

Kedzior, Jozef. "Nie jestemy tu od wczoraj," *Katolik* (Opole), January 5, 1958.

Klinga, S. "Komunizm i polska gospodarka," *Orzel Bialy,* April 20 and 27, 1957.

Kolarczyk, Reinhold. "Niemandsland Schlesien," *Der europäische Osten* (May, 1957), pp. 292-96.

"Kontakte mit der polnischen Bevölkerung," *Pressedienst der Heimatvertriebenen* (29), 1957.

Kraus, Herbert. "Das deutsche Rechtsanspruch auf die Gebiete ostwärts der Oder und Neisse," *Pressedienst der Heimatvertriebenen* (5), 1957.

————. "Die Kampf um das Recht," *Pressedienst der Heimatvertriebenen* (16), 1957.

————. "Um einen gerechten Frieden," *Pressedienst der Heimatvertriebenen* (27), 1956.

————. "Verteidigung des Unrechts," *Pressedienst der Heimatvertriebenen* (33), 1956.

Kuh, Frederick. "Polen heute," *Aussenpolitik* (February, 1958), pp. 89-99.

Kwiatowski, Jan. "Szczecin miasto portowe," *Glos Szczecinski,* January 25 and 26, 1958.

Lach, Donald F. "What They Would Do About Germany," *Journal of Modern History,* Vol. XVII (September, 1945), pp. 222-43.

Lauen, Herbert. "Ist eine deutsch-polnische Verständigung möglich?" *Der europäische Osten* (March, 1957), pp. 145-53.

Legut, Jan. "Wiecej uwagi dla Ziem Zachodnich," *Glos Szczecinski,* June 6, 1957.

Lin, Wincenty. "Serdecznie gratuljeny budownictwu śląskiemu," *Dziennik Zachodni,* January 11, 1958.

Lipsius, Oskar L. "Analyse der Ostpolitik," *Pressedienst der Heimatvertriebenen* (50), 1956.

————. "Die Bulganin-Botschaft," *Pressedienst der Heimatvertriebenen* (7), 1957.

————. "Gemeinsame Ostpolitik," *Pressedienst der Heimatvertriebenen* (50), 1957.

————. "Die heimatpolitische Bedeutung des Lastenausgleichs," *Pressedienst der Heimatvertriebenen* (1), 1957.

————. "Die Hintergründe der Oder-Neisse Politik Warschaus," *Pressedienst der Heimatvertriebenen* (9), 1957.

————. "Polnische Orientierung der deutschen Ostpolitik?" *Pressedienst der Heimatvertriebenen* (8), 1957.

————. "Die 'Potsdamer Erklärung' der drei Satelliten," *Pressedienst der Heimatvertriebenen* (20), 1957.

————. "Der 'Revisionismus' und 'sowjetische Hegemonie,' " *Pressedienst der Heimatvertriebenen* (25), 1957.

————. "Die vierte Parole," *Pressedienst der Heimatvertriebenen* (27), 1957.

————. "Zweigleisige Oder-Neisse Politik Moskaus," *Pressedienst der Heimatvertriebenen* (46), 1956.

Mieroszewski, Juliusz. "Das Provisorium in Polen," *Der europäische Osten* (November, 1957), pp. 669-74.

Mortensen, Hans. "Zur Geschichte der deutschen Ostsiedlung," *Zeitschrift für Ostforschung*, V (2), 1956, pp. 263-67.

Müller, K. V. "Der Heimkehrwille der Vertriebenen," *Pressedienst der Heimatvertriebenen* (30), 1957.

"The negative freedom . . . in Mr. Gomulka's Poland," *Tablet*, May 25, 1957.

"Nicht 65,000, sondern 1.1 Millionen," *Pressedienst der Heimatvertriebenen* (34), 1957.

"Niezalatwione zagadnienia na Ziemiach Zachodnich," *Narodowiec*, January 10, 1958.

Niwinski, Zygmunt. "Co przyniosą nam najbliższe lata," *Gazeta Zielonogorska*, December 31, 1957.

Nowosad, Witold, "Pochodnia Nadzici," *Syrena* (Paris), January 11, 1958.

"Olsztyńskie w liczbach," *Warmia i Masury*, February 2, 1958.

"Die Parolen zur Verteidigung der Oder-Neisse Grenze," *Pressedienst der Heimatvertriebenen* (23), 1957.

"Die 'Pekinger Deklaration' und die Oder-Neisse Frage," *Pressedienst der Heimatvertriebenen* (19), 1957.

"Perspektywa świetnej przyszłości Szczecina," *Glos Szczecinski*, January 18 and 19, 1958.

"Podsluchane," *Dziennik Polski*, January 2, 1958.

"The Polish Three-Year Plan," *The World Today* (March, 1947), pp. 107ff.

"Die polnische Kriegsschäden-Aufstellung," *Pressedienst der Heimatvertriebenen* (30), 1957.

"Die polnische Wissenschaft im Dienste der polnischen Propaganda," *Pressedienst der Heimatvertriebenen* (20), 1957.

"Polnischer Sonderbericht über das südliche Ostpreussen," *Pressedienst der Heimatvertriebenen* (44), 1956.

"Population of Poland," *Polish Affairs* (April, 1956), pp. 15-16.

Pruszynski, K. "Wobec Rosji," *Wiadomsosci Polski*, October 4, 1942.

"Ein Querschnitt durch die Situation des Verkehrswesens jenseits der Oder-Neisse," *Pressedienst der Heimatvertriebenen* (35), 1956.

Quintus, Julius. "Die Aussenministerkonferenzen in Moskau und London," *Pressedienst der Heimatvertriebenen* (33), 1957.

————. "Gefahrvolle Wege," *Pressedienst der Heimatvertriebenen* (51), 1957.

Rabl, Kurt. "Rechtsgrundlagen der deutschen Ostpolitik," *Der europäische Osten* (January, 1958), pp. 9-17.

"Die Raubwirtschaft in den Wäldern der Oder-Neisse Gebiete," *Pressedienst der Heimatvertriebenen* (23), 1957.

Rhode, Gotthold. "Aussenminister Josef Beck und Staatssekretär Graf Szembek," *Vierteljahresheft für Zeitgeschichte* (1954), pp. 86-94.

Richthofen, Bolko Freiherr von. "The Oder-Neisse Frontier," *Free World Review*, II (2), 1956.

"Rolle der Ostgebiete in der Wirtschaft Deutschlands," *Arbeiterstimme*, January 4 and 5, 1958.

"Der rote Springer," *Pressedienst der Heimatvertriebenen* (26), 1957.

Rudzki, Adam. "The Western Frontiers of Poland," *Free World Review*, II (2), 1956.

"Schlesien unter polnischer Regie," *Aussenpolitik* (September, 1952), pp. 595-601.

Schwucht, Herbert. "Das Dilemma der deutsch-polnischen Gespräche," *Der europäische Osten* (January, 1956), pp. 9ff.

"Die Sejmwahlen in der Wojewodschaft Kattowitz," *Pressedienst der Heimatvertriebenen* (5), 1957.

Seraphim, Peter Heinz. "Sowjetisches Normensystem in Oberschlesien," *Der europäische Osten* (November, 1956), pp. 643ff.

Sopicki, Stanislaw. "Probleme der Nachbarschaft," *Der europäische Osten* (July, 1956), pp. 389ff.

———. "The Eastern Frontiers of Poland," *Free World Review*, III (1-2), 1952, pp. 14-17.

———. "Zum deutsch-polnischen Problem," *Der europäische Osten* (February, 1956), pp. 137ff.

Staniewicz, Jan. "Prawda o rozwoju przemplu na ziemiach Zachodnich," *Gwiazda Polarna*, January 4, 1958.

Stasiewski, Bernhard. "Schlesien im Rahmen der Dokumentation über die Vertreibung der Deutschen," *Zeitschrift für Ostforschung*, V (2), pp. 267-72.

Stefanski, Piotr. "Historyczne Zadania," *Tygodnik Demokratczny* (Warsaw), June 11, 1957.

Sternfeld, Nikolaus. "Für die Danziger Freiheit," *Pressedienst der Heimatvertriebenen* (26), 1957.

Swirski, Wladyslaw. "Inicjatywa Wrocławaia w sprawach mieszkaniowych," *Glos Polski-Gazeta Polska*, January 2, 1958.

———. "Po Roku—Na *Ziemiach Zachodnich*," *Glos Polski-Gazeta Polska*, January 2, 1958.

Szoga, Alojzy. "Czy is tot nie rzekoma . . ." *Zycie gospodarcze*, March 31, 1957.

———. "Tej szansy nie marnować," *Zycie gospodarcze*, May 26, 1957.

"Terroraktionen gegen Ostdeutsche am laufenden Bande," *Pressedienst der Heimatvertriebenen* (34), 1957.

"Tschous Oder-Neisse Erklärung," *Pressedienst der Heimatvertriebenen* (4), 1957.

Tymieniecki, Kazimierz. "Kolonizacja a germanizacja Śląska w wiekach srednich," *Polski Śląsk* (No. 27), 1937, pp. 1-38.

"Die Wahrheit über die Autochthonen," *Pressedienst der Heimatvertriebenen* (19), 1957.

"Was von der polnischen Pressefreiheit übrig blieb," *Pressedienst der Heimatvertriebenen* (45), 1957.

"Der Westen, das Nationalkommunismus, und die Oder-Neisse Frage," *Pressedienst der Heimatvertriebenen* (46), 1956.

"Die Westhilfe für Polen und die Oder-Neisse Frage," *Pressedienst der Heimatvertriebenen* (13), 1957.

"Weterany Polsky w Kanadzie w Obronoie Granizy Odra-Nysa," *Czas*, January 15, 1958.

"Wieder Austreibungen," *Pressedienst der Heimatvertriebenen* (50), 1957.

Willcock, H. D. "Public Opinion: Attitudes to the German People," *Political Quarterly* (April-June, 1948), pp. 160-66.

"Die wirtschaftliche Bedeutung der ostdeutschen Gebiete für Polen," *Aussenpolitik* (May, 1956).

"Wspolne oswiasczenie parlamentow Polski, NRD i Czechoslowacji," *Trybuna Ludu,* May 12, 1957.

Wydrzynski, Andrzej. "Terra incognita," *Po prostu,* January 6, 1957.

Zajaczkowski, Waclaw. "Apel o jednolity front," *Gwiazda Polarna,* December 28, 1957.

"Zakonczono budowa pierwszego stopnia wodnego na Odrze," *Glos Olsztynski,* January 28, 1958.

"Zespolic wysilki nad Odbudowa ziem Zachodnich," *Glos Szczecinski,* January 22, 1958.

"Zielonogorska Sprawy," *Trybuna Ludu,* February 8, 1958.

"Der 'Ziemer' Plan," *Pressedienst der Heimatvertriebenen* (49), 1957.

"Ziemie Zachodnie Polski," *Czas* (Canada), December 11, 1957.

Zipfel, Friedrich. "Vernichtung und Austreibung der Deutschen aus den Gebieten östlich der Oder-Neisse Linie," *Jahrbuch für die Geschichte Mittel- und Ostdeutschlands* (1954), pp. 145-89.

"Der Zusammenschluss der Vertriebenenverbände," *Pressedienst der Heimatvertriebenen* (44), 1957.

INDEX